THE PLAIN (FATTY) TRUTH

Americans eat too much fat—over 40 percent of our total daily calorie intake consists of fat.

Doctors now recommend that we reduce this amount to less than 30 percent in order to combat the risks of cardiovascular disease and breast and colon cancers. But to avoid fat-laden foods, you have to know the facts about fat—how many grams are in that 4-ounce serving of fresh salmon (15) or in just 3 Oreo cookies (6)?

The Fat Counter gives the latest information on the amount of fat in hundreds of food items and uses everyday portions so that you can keep track of your daily fat intake.

And, *The 22-Gram Solution* spells out the optimal way to combine a low-fat diet with a delicious weight-loss program that lets you trim inches away while boosting your climb to health.

Also by Corinne T. Netzer

THE BRAND-NAME CARBOHYDRATE GRAM COUNTER
THE LOW-SALT DIET COUNTER
THE DIETER'S CARBOHYDRATE GRAM COUNTER
THE DIETER'S CALORIE COUNTER
THE FIBER COUNTER
THE BRAND-NAME CALORIE COUNTER

THE FAT COUNTER AND THE 22-GRAM SOLUTION

Corinne T. Netzer

A DELL BOOK

Published by
Dell Publishing
a division of
The Bantam Doubleday Dell Publishing Group, Inc.
666 Fifth Avenue
New York, New York 10103

The trademark Dell® is registered in the U.S. Patent
and Trademark Office.

ISBN: 0-440-12488-3

Printed in the United States of America

May 1987

10 9 8 7 6 5 4 3 2

KRI

The Fat Counter
and
The 22-Gram Solution

(CTN's Low-Fat Weight-Loss Diet)

Fat is not funny—not eating it and not being it. The "jolly" fat man is one big lie: he's laughing in order to keep from crying.

I am not a scientist, but a concerned dieter. In this book I'm going to tell you, in the simplest and most direct way I know, why you should cut down on your fat intake and how you can lose weight by doing it.

WHAT IS FAT?

The National Academy of Science's Committee on Diet, Nutrition and Cancer recommends that the consumption of both saturated and unsaturated fats be reduced in the average American diet.

How do these fats differ? There is a chemical distinction in the structure of each fat molecule; specifically, in the number of hydrogen atoms. When the fat is carrying as many hydrogen atoms as it can hold it is considered *saturated* with hydrogen. When the fat contains room for more hydrogen it is called *unsaturated*. Unsaturated fats are further divided into *mono*unsaturated and *poly*unsaturated.

Although there are exceptions, animal fats are generally more saturated than vegetable fats. Another general rule is that saturated fats are usually solid at room temperature while unsaturated fats are usually liquid at room temperature. Fats can be made more solid by adding hydrogen. That's the difference between soft and stick margarines: the hard stick has had hydrogen added. This is a process called *hydrogenation* and, although there are exceptions, the more hydrogen added to a fat or oil, the more saturated and firm it becomes.

THE TROUBLE WITH FAT

I doubt if there is a dieter in the United States who isn't aware of the fact that studies indicate saturated fats contribute to cardiovascular disease, particularly heart attacks and stroke. We have been bombarded with the idea that polyunsaturates are "heart-healthy" and saturates (especially animal fats which contain cholesterol) are unhealthy. Consequently there has been a distinct decline in our consumption of red meats and eggs, and an increase in the use of polyunsaturated oils. This is fine as far as it goes—but it doesn't go far enough.

Heart disease is not the only problem to be concerned about when you're eating fat. High-fat diets of *both* saturated and unsaturated fats have been tied to cancer. Studies have linked "fatty" eating to colon/rectal cancers. President Reagan's doctors advised him to change his diet to one lower in fat and higher in fiber to reduce his risk of developing a second colon cancer. And there is mounting evidence from international studies that too much fat in the diet leads to increased risk of breast and prostate cancers.

No one knows for certain if fat starts cancer or if it accelerates already existing cancer, but the fact is that there is a definite link.

Contrary to the studies on heart disease, which point a finger at saturated fats, research indicates that unsaturated fats seems to increase cancer risk even more than saturated fats. (Fish oils may be the rare exception to the rule. Preliminary work indicates a possibility that fish oil may be helpful in lowering the risk of cardiovascular disease and cancer. But these studies are in an early stage and are by no means conclusive.)

Since high-fat diets of both kinds of fat have been linked to disease, most heart and cancer experts agree that it's best to reduce the amount of *all* fat in the diet.

FAT AND DIETING

Ounce for ounce, spoon for spoon, fat contains more calories than carbohydrates or protein. A gram of fat contains nine calories, while a gram of protein or carbohydrate has only four. Do you think a tablespoon of sugar is fattening? Just compare it to a tablespoon of butter or margarine. The sugar has about 40 calories, the fat a whopping 100! Consider this: an ounce of *any* fat is more fattening than an ounce of pasta or potato—or anything!

So, not only is fat unhealthy, fat is fattening!

The government suggests that since we now eat too much fat (over 40 percent of our diet) we reduce our fat to 30 percent of intake. This means that no more than 30 percent of our calories should come from fat. Such diet gurus as the late Nathan Pritikin suggest a 5- to 10-percent intake. I have found that you can lose weight, feel good, and still not feel denied with an intake of 20 percent fat in relation to total calories.

How do you know how much fat you are having? Simple. This book is a fat-gram counter and everything you eat will be listed with its gram count. Total the grams and you know how many you have each day. Multiply this amount by nine (the number of calories in a fat gram) and you know how many calories of fat you've had.

THE 22-GRAM SOLUTION
(CTN's Low-Fat Weight-Loss Diet)

This diet is designed for you to lose weight while lowering your fat intake. The 22-Gram Solution works for me and it works for all of my friends who've tried it—and it should work for you. The principles are easy to remember and, with a little willpower, very easy to follow. Remember, not only will you be thinner—you'll be eating healthier.

This plan is based on a daily intake of 1000 calories which, for most people, allows maximum weight loss without sacrificing nutrition.

You may have 1000 calories per day. If you don't already own a calorie counter, I suggest you buy one so that you can plan your meals in advance and know, without question, how many calories you're consuming.

Limit yourself to no more than 22.2 fat grams per day. Use this book to look up each and every thing you eat and drink. You may go below 22.2 grams—in fact that is to be encouraged—but *never* more than that amount. You may choose your own foods as long as you stay within the limit.

Have at least 1 serving of fruit and 1 serving of vegetables every day. One of the main points of low-fat dieting is to encourage intake of food with complex carbohydrates and fiber. Actually, you'll find yourself willingly adding more fruit and vegetables to your diet because they're low in fat and help you stay within your gram goal. You'll find you're *automatically* eating more nutritionally as well as losing those pounds because you'll be limiting fatty foods.

One of the reasons this diet works so well is the hunger factor. Remember, fat has nine calories a gram—carbohydrates and protein only four, so when you cut down on fats you can actually eat more food, be more "filled," and not have that diet hungry feeling.

Vary the kinds of food you eat. It is not healthy to eat the same exact thing every day. The body needs different kinds of nutrients that can only be gotten from different kinds of foods.

If you don't vary your diet you won't stay on it because it will become tiresome. My friend Joy, who had never, *ever,* been able to stick to a diet regimen, was successful with The 22-Gram Solution. She was able to choose from a multitude of foods and she didn't get bored eating the same cottage-cheese-and-carrot-sticks every day. She made a game out of making up her menus —and it worked!

I have found that if you don't vary your choices the body eventually becomes accustomed to a sameness of input and after a while, no matter how strict you are, the body "plateaus" (it's happened to all of us on diets) and adjusts to the input and you stop losing weight.

The beauty of this diet is that the options are yours as long as you stick to the 1000 calories, 22.2 fat grams per day.

Walk half an hour every day (unless you're on a doctor-regulated exercise program). If you already walk, good. If you don't, start. A half hour a day is not a lot to devote to fitness, and walking is not so strenuous that you can find an excuse not to do it. Walk briskly and continuously. Walk to work, walk around the block, walk to lunch, walk around the house if it's raining—but walk. It's good for your diet and it's "heart healthy." And if you're so busy a person that you can't find a half an hour in the day, then take two brisk 15-minute tours. Try it, you'll feel better.

The 22-Gram Solution Diet Tips:
• Cut *all* visible fat off meat and poultry.
• Fry nothing (it uses too much oil or fat). Bake, broil or boil foods, or use non-stick pans.
• Poach fish. Fish has few calories and contains those oils that may be good for you.
• On salads use lemon with herbs and spices added—it may

not taste as good as oil but you will get used to it and it's good for you.

• Steam vegetables and use herbs and spices instead of butter or margarine to "spike" them. Experiment—go to the store and buy some spices you've never tried before and use them to top your veggies.

• When eating in a restaurant, inquire how things are prepared before you order. If a sauce is included tell the waiter to leave it off or put it on the side. Restaurants are accustomed to dieters and no longer get upset at such requests.

• Limit your alcohol intake. No, there's no fat here, but it's highly caloric without being nutritious. The same is true of most sweets.

• Finally, consult your doctor before going on this or any other diet.

HOW TO USE THIS BOOK

This book is alphabetized so there's no index. Simply look up the food you are interested in and you will find its fat gram content.

Look up everything you eat in a day and you will get your total. Again, plan your menus in advance so that the total won't come as some sort of awful surprise after the fact.

If you are following The 22-Gram Solution you will not go over 22.2 fat grams per day. However, if losing weight is not your goal or if you do not want to go below the government-recommended 30 percent of fat in your diet, there is a simple formula for figuring out how many fat grams you should have. Take 30 percent of the calories you consume per day and divide by nine (the number of calories in a fat gram). For instance, if you have 1500 calories per day, 30 percent of 1500 is 450, and 450 divided by nine is 50—and that should be your maximum fat-gram intake.

If your goal is 20 percent fat in your diet, take 20 percent of your caloric intake and divide by nine. If your caloric intake is 1500, 20 percent is 300, which divided by nine is 33.3.

No matter what your desired fat percentage is the equation remains the same—percentage of calories divided by nine. That is how you find your maximum intake permitted and that is the number you should not go over. And when you use this counter you won't.

SOURCES OF DATA

The information contained in this book is based on data obtained from the United States Department of Agriculture and the various producers and processors of brand-name foods.

It contains the most complete and up-to-date fat gram material ever compiled in book form. It is, I feel, easy to use because you will find all the information you need listed in sensible, common household measures.

As we go to press this book has the most accurate data available. However, food companies do change their recipes with time. If need be, these changes will be dealt with in future editions. In the interim, should a food you're particularly fond of suddenly sport a label reading "new" or "improved," you may wish to write directly to the manufacturer to see if there has been a change in fat content.

Good luck and good dieting!

C.T.N.

ABBREVIATIONS IN THIS BOOK

fl. . . . . fluid
" . . . . inch
lb. . . . . pound
oz. . . . . ounce
pkg. . . . . package
tbsp. . . . . tablespoon
tsp. . . . . teaspoon
< . . . . less than

$$\boxed{A}$$

	fat grams
Abalone, raw, meat only, 4 oz.	.6
Acapulco dip:	
with American cheese *(Ortega),* 1 oz.	4.6
with Cheddar *(Ortega),* 1 oz.	4.9
with Monterey Jack *(Ortega),* 1 oz.	4.5
without cheese *(Ortega),* 1 oz.	.1
Acerola, fresh:	
raw, whole, 1 lb.	1.1
raw, 10 cherries	.1
juice, raw, 1 cup	.7

A la king sauce, mix *(Durkee)*, 1.1-oz. pkg. 8.0
Albacore, raw, meat only, 4 oz. 8.6
Ale, see "Beer, ale and malt liquor"
Alewife, raw, meat only, 4 oz. 5.6
Alfalfa seeds, sprouted, raw, 1 cup 2
Allspice, ground (all brands), 1 tsp. 2
Almond:
  blanched, natural *(Planters)*, 1 oz. 15.0
  dried, shelled, 4 oz. 59.3
  dried, shelled, 1 cup 74.1
  dried, chopped, 1/2 cup 33.9
  dried, slivered, 1/2 cup 24.5
  dry-roasted, 1 oz. 14.7
  oil-roasted, 1 oz. 16.4
  smoked *(Planters)*, 1 oz. 15.0
Almond butter:
  raw, blanched *(Hain)*, 1 tbsp. 9.0
  toasted, blanched *(Hain)*, 1 tbsp. 9.5
Almond meal, partially defatted, 1 oz. 5.2
Almond paste, 1 oz. 7.7
Amaranth, fresh:
  raw, 1 cup 1
  boiled, drained, 1 cup 2
Anchovy, canned, fillets *(Granadaisa Brand)*, 2 oz. 5.0
Anise seed (all brands), 1 tsp. 3
Apple:
  fresh, with skin, 1 apple, 2 3/4" diam. 5
  fresh, pared, 1 apple, 2 3/4" diam. 4
  canned, sliced (all brands), 4 oz. . . . . . . < .1
  dehydrated (sulfured), uncooked, 1 cup 4
  dried (sulfured), uncooked, 1 cup 3
  dried or dehydrated (sulfured), cooked, 1 cup 2
  frozen, dried, sliced, unsweetened, 1 cup 6
Apple, escalloped, frozen *(Stouffer's)*, 4 oz. 3.0
Apple butter, 1 oz. 2
Apple criss-cross pastry, frozen *(Pepperidge Farm)*, 2
  oz. 9.0
Apple croissant, frozen *(Sara Lee Le Pastrie)*, 3.3 oz. 11.0
Apple danish:
  (Hostess), 1 piece 20.0

Apple danish, continued
frozen *(Sara Lee)*, 1.3 oz.	6.0
refrigerated *(Pillsbury Best)*, 1 piece	11.0

Apple drink or juice, plain or with blended juices,
canned, frozen* or mix* (all brands), 6 fl. oz.	< .1

Apple dumpling, frozen *(Pepperidge Farm)*, 3 oz. 14.0
Apple fritter, frozen *(Mrs. Paul's)*, 2 fritters 15.0
Apple fruit square, frozen *(Pepperidge Farm)*, 1 piece 12.0
Apple sticks, frozen:
breaded, fried *(Chill Ripe/Gold King Fries)*, 4 oz.	6.2
breaded, fried *(Farm Rich)*, 4 oz.	8.0

Apple strudel, frozen *(Pepperidge Farm)*, 3 oz. 11.0
Apple turnover:
frozen *(Pepperidge Farm)*, 1 piece	17.0
refrigerated *(Pillsbury)*, 1 piece	8.0

Applesauce, canned (all brands), 1/2 cup .... < .5
Apricot:
fresh, 3 apricots, about 12 per lb.	.4
fresh, pitted, halves, 1 cup	.6
candied, 1 oz.	.1
canned or frozen (all brands), 1/2 cup	< .3
dehydrated, uncooked, 1 cup	.7
dehydrated, cooked, 1 cup	.6
dried, uncooked, 10 halves	.2
dried, cooked, sweetened, halves, 1 cup	.4

Apricot nectar, canned, 1 cup 2
Arby's:
sandwiches, 1 serving:	
bac 'n cheddar deluxe, 8 oz.	34.0
beef 'n cheddar, 6.7 oz.	21.0
chicken breast, 7.4 oz.	27.0
hot ham 'n cheese, 5.7 oz.	13.0
roast beef, regular, 5.2 oz.	15.0
roast beef, junior, 3 oz.	8.0
roast beef, king, 6.7 oz.	19.0
roast beef, super, 8.3 oz.	22.0
turkey deluxe, 7 oz.	17.0
potato, baked, plain, 11-oz. serving	.5

---

* *Prepared according to package directions*

Arby's, continued

potato cakes, 3-oz. serving	14.0
potato, superstuffed, 1 serving:	
broccoli and cheddar, 12 oz.	22.0
deluxe, 11 oz.	38.0
mushroom and cheese, 10.5 oz.	22.0
taco, 15 oz.	27.0
French fries, 2.5-oz. serving	8.0
shakes, 1 serving:	
chocolate, 10.6 oz.	11.0
jamocha, 10.8 oz.	10.0
vanilla, 8.8 oz.	10.0
Arrowhead, fresh, raw or boiled, 1 medium, 2⅝″	
diam.	< .1
Arthur Treacher's:	
chicken, 2 patties or 4.8 oz.	21.6
chicken sandwich, 5.5-oz. piece	19.2
cod, bake 'n broil, 5-oz. serving	14.2
fish, 2 pieces or 5.2 oz.	19.8
fish sandwich, 5.5-oz. piece	24.0
shrimp, 7 pieces or 4 oz.	24.4
chips, 4-oz. serving	13.2
chowder, 6-oz. serving	5.4
cole slaw, 3-oz. serving	8.2
Krunch Pup, 2-oz. piece	14.8
Lemon Luv, 3-oz. piece	13.9
Artichoke, globe or French:	
fresh, raw or boiled, 1 medium, 11.3 oz.	.2
hearts, boiled, canned or frozen, ½ cup	.1
hearts, marinated, canned *(S&W),* 3.5 oz.	26.0
Artichoke, Jerusalem, see "Jerusalem artichoke"	
Asparagus:	
fresh, raw, whole or cut, 1 cup	.3
fresh, boiled, drained, 4 medium spears	.2
fresh, boiled, drained, whole or cut, 1 cup	.6
canned or frozen (all brands), ½ cup	< .1
Asparagus with mornay sauce in pastry, frozen	
(Pepperidge Farm), 1 piece	16.0
Au jus gravy:	
canned *(Franco-American),* 2 oz.	0

Au jus gravy, continued
   mix *(Durkee)*, 1-oz. pkg. 3
   mix *(Durkee Roastin' Bag)*, 1-oz. pkg. 1.0
   mix *(French's)*, 1/4 cup*   0
Avocado, fresh:
   California, fresh, 1 average, 8 oz. 30.0
   California, purée, 1 cup 39.9
   Florida, fresh, whole, 1 average or 1 lb. 27.0
   Florida, purée, 1 cup 20.4
Avocado dip:
   (Kraft Guacamole), 2 tbsp. 4.0
   (Nalley), 1 oz. 12.0

---

* *Prepared according to package directions*

	fat grams
Bacon, cooked:	
4.48 oz. (yield from 1 lb. raw)	62.5
(Armour Star), .3-oz. slice	3.1
(Armour Star), .2-oz. slice	2.4
(Hormel Black Label), 2 slices	5.0
(Hormel Range Brand), 2 slices	9.0
(Hormel Red Label), 3 slices	10.0
(Oscar Mayer), 1/5-oz. slice	3.1
(Oscar Mayer Center Cut), 1/6-oz. slice	1.7
thick sliced *(Oscar Mayer)*, 1/4-oz. slice	1.0

Bacon, Canadian, cooked:

2 slices, 6 per 6-oz. pkg.	3.9
(Armour 1877), 2 oz.	4.0
(Eckrich Calorie Watcher), 1 oz.	1.0
(Hormel), 1 oz.	2.0
(Jones Dairy Farm), 1 oz.	1.4
(Oscar Mayer), 1-oz. slice	1.4

Bacon, substitute, cooked:

beef *(Oscar Mayer* Breakfast Strips), 2/5-oz. strip	3.8
beef *(Sizzlean/Firebrand)*, 2 strips	4.0
pork *(Oscar Mayer* Breakfast Strips), 2/5-oz. strip	4.5
pork *(Sizzlean)*, 2 strips	6.0

Bacon bits:

(Bac*Os), 1 tbsp.	1.0
(Durkee), 1 tbsp.	.4
real bacon *(Hormel)*, 1 tbsp.	2.0
real bacon *(Oscar Mayer)*, 1/4 oz.	1.0

Bacon chips *(Durkee)*, 1 tbsp.	2.0

Bacon and horseradish dip:

(Kraft), 2 tbsp.	5.0
(Kraft Premium), 1 oz.	4.0

Bacon and onion dip *(Nalley)*, 1 oz.	11.8
Bacon-onion seasoning *(Lawry's)*, 1 tsp.	.2

Bagels, frozen:

all varieties *(Lender's)*, 2-oz. bagel	1.0
plain or onion *(Lender's* Bagelettes), .9-oz. bagel	< 1.0
plain, onion or poppy seed *(Sara Lee)*, 3-oz. bagel	1.0
egg or cinnamon-raisin *(Sara Lee)*, 3-oz. bagel . . .	2.0

Baking powder, all types, 1 tsp.	< .1

Balsam pear, fresh:

leafy tips, raw, 1 cup	.3
leafy tips, boiled, drained, 1 cup	.1
pods, raw, 1 pod, 9½" × 1½"	.2
pods, raw or boiled, ½" pieces, 1 cup	.2

Bamboo shoots:

fresh, raw, cuts, 1 cup	.5
fresh, boiled, drained, pieces, 1 cup	.3
canned, drained *(Chun King)*, 8.5 oz.	.7
canned, drained *(La Choy)*, 1/4 cup	< 1.0

Banana:
fresh, 1 banana, 8¾" long 6
fresh, mashed, 1 cup 1.1
dehydrated, 1 cup 1.8
Banana, baking, see "Plantain"
Banana, red, fresh, whole, 1 lb. 6
Banana chips, freeze-dried *(Mountain House),* ¼ cup 19.0
Banquet loaf, beef *(Eckrich Smorgas Pac),* 1 slice . . . 4.0
Barbados cherry, see "Acerola"
Barbecue dip *(Nalley),* 1 oz. 11.8
Barbecue loaf:
(Armour), 1 oz. 3.0
(Eckrich Calorie Watcher), 1 oz. 2.0
(Oscar Mayer Bar-B-Q), 1-oz. slice 2.5
Barbecue sauce, in jars (all brands), 2 tbsp. . . . . . . < 1.0
Barley, pearled:
light, uncooked, 8 oz. 2.3
pot or scotch, uncooked, 8 oz. 2.5
medium or quick *(Quaker* Scotch) ¼ cup 5
Barracuda, Pacific, raw, meat only, 4 oz. 2.9
Basil leaves, ground (all brands), 1 tsp. 1
Baskin-Robbins:
ice, daiquiri, 1 junior scoop 0
ice, pineapple, 1 junior scoop . . . . < .1
ice cream, 1 junior scoop:
butter pecan 10.2
chocolate 7.9
chocolate fudge 9.1
chocolate mint 9.2
chocolate mousse royale 8.5
jamoca 8.0
pralines'n cream 8.2
rocky road 7.0
strawberry 6.0
vanilla 8.2
vanilla, French 11.8
ice cream cone, cake, 1 cone, without ice cream . .3
ice cream cone, sugar, 1 cone, without ice cream 1.0
sherbet, orange, 1 junior scoop 1.5
sherbet, raspberry sorbet, 1 junior scoop 0

Bass, Black Sea, raw, meat only, 4 oz. 1.4
Bass, smallmouth and largemouth, raw, meat only, 4
oz. 2.9
Bass, striped, raw, meat only, 4 oz. 3.1
Bay leaves, crumbled (all brands), 1 tsp. 1
Bean curd, see "Soybean curd"
Bean dip:
  hot *(Hain),* 4 tbsp. 5.0
  jalapeño bean, see "Jalapeño dip"
  onion *(Hain),* 4 tbsp. 6.0
Bean flour, lima, 1 oz. 4
Bean salad, canned:
  four-bean *(Joan of Arc),* 1/2 cup . . . . < 1.0
  green bean, German *(Joan of Arc),* 1/2 cup 2.0
  marinated *(S&W),* 1/2 cup 1.0
  three-bean *(Green Giant/Joan of Arc),* 1/2 cup . . . < 1.0
Bean sprouts:
  kidney, mature seeds, raw, 1 cup 9
  mung, raw, 1 cup 2
  navy, mature seeds, raw, 1 cup 7
  pinto, mature seeds, raw, 4 oz. 1.0
  soy, raw, 1 cup 4.7
  soy, steamed, 1 cup 4.2
  canned, drained *(Chun King),* 28-oz. can 1.6
  canned, drained *(La Choy),* 2/3 cup 0
Beans and franks dinner, frozen *(Banquet American
Favorites),* 101/4 oz. 19.0
Beans, baked, canned:
  (Campbell's Home Style), 8 oz. 4.0
  (Campbell's Old Fashioned), 8 oz. 3.0
  (Grandma Brown's Home Baked), 8 oz. 1.7
  (S&W Brick Oven), 1/2 cup 2.0
  and bacon *(Hormel* Short Order), 71/2 oz. 12.0
  barbecue style *(B&M),* 8 oz. 6.0
  brown sugar *(Van Camp's),* 1 cup 5.1
  and franks *(Campbell's),* 77/8 oz. 14.0
  and franks *(Heinz),* 73/4 oz. 15.0
  and franks *(Nalley),* 31/2 oz. 5.0
  and franks *(Van Camp's Beanee Weenee),* 1 cup . . . 15.4
  and ham *(Hormel* Short Order), 71/2 oz. 18.0

Beans, baked, continued

maple sugar *(S&W)*, 1/2 cup	1.0
pea, small *(B&M)*, 8 oz.	8.0
and pork *(Campbell's)*, 8 oz.	3.0
and pork *(Hunt-Wesson)*, 4 oz.	1.0
and pork *(Joan of Arc)*, 1/2 cup	< 1.0
and pork *(S&W)*, 1/2 cup	2.0
and pork *(Van Camp's)*, 1 cup	1.9
red kidney or yelloweye *(B&M)*, 8 oz.	7.0
smoked *(S&W Smokey Ranch)*, 1/2 cup	2.0
vegetarian *(B&M)*, 8 oz.	2.0
vegetarian *(Heinz)*, 8 oz.	1.0
vegetarian *(Van Camp's)*, 1 cup	.6
western style *(Van Camp's)*, 1 cup	3.8
and wieners *(Hormel Short Order)*, 7 1/2 oz.	14.0

Beans, barbecue, canned:

(Campbell's Barbecue), 7 7/8 oz.	4.0
and beef *(Nalley)*, 3 1/2 oz.	4.0
in sauce *(S&W Texas Style)*, 1/2 cup	1.0

Beans, black turtle, canned *(Progresso)*, 8 oz. — 1.0

Beans, blackeye, see "Blackeye peas"

Beans, broad, see "Broad beans"

Beans, burrito filling mix, canned *(Del Monte)*, 1/2 cup — 1.0

Beans, butter, see "Butterbeans"

Beans, cannellini, see "Beans, kidney, white"

Beans, chili, canned:

(Hunt's), 4 oz.	1.0
(Joan of Arc), 1/2 cup	1.0
(Van Camp's Mexican Style), 1 cup	2.4
in sauce *(Hormel)*, 5 oz.	3.0
in sauce *(S&W)*, 1/2 cup	1.0

Beans, fava, canned *(Progresso)*, 8 oz. — 1.0

Beans, great northern:

dry, uncooked, 8 oz.	3.6
dry, cooked, 8 oz.	1.4
canned *(Joan of Arc)*, 1/2 cup	< 1.0

Beans, green:

fresh, raw, 1 lb.	.5
fresh, raw, 1 cup	.1

Beans, green, continued
fresh, boiled, drained, 1 cup 4
canned or frozen, plain (all brands), 1/2 cup . . . . .   < .1
frozen, in butter sauce *(Green Giant)*, 1/2 cup 1.0
frozen and spaetzle, Bavarian *(Birds Eye)*, 3.3 oz.   6.0
frozen, with toasted almonds *(Birds Eye)*, 3 oz.   2.0
Beans, green, mushroom casserole *(Stouffer's)*, 4 3/4 oz.   12.0
Beans, green, with mushroom sauce, in pastry, frozen
(Pepperidge Farm), 1 piece 17.0
Beans, kidney:
red, dried, uncooked, 8 oz. 3.4
red, cooked, 8 oz.   1.1
red, canned (all brands), 1/2 cup . . . .   < 1.0
white, canned *(Progresso* cannellini), 8 oz. 1.0
Beans, lima:
raw, shelled, 1 cup 1.3
boiled, drained, 1 cup 5
canned or frozen (all brands), 1/2 cup . . . .   < 1.0
frozen, baby, in butter sauce *(Green Giant)*, 1/2 cup   2.0
Beans, lima, and ham, canned, *(Nalley)*, 3 1/2 oz. . . .   3.0
Beans, mung, dry, uncooked, 8 oz. 2.9
Beans, pea or navy:
dry, uncooked, 8 oz. 3.6
dry, cooked, 8 oz.   1.4
canned *(Joan of Arc)*, 1/2 cup . . . .   < 1.0
Beans, pinto, canned:
(Joan of Arc), 1/2 cup . . . .   < 1.0
(Progresso), 8 oz.   1.0
Beans, red, canned:
(Van Camp's), 1 cup 6
small *(Joan of Arc)*, 1/2 cup . . . .   < 1.0
Beans, refried:
canned *(Del Monte)*, 1/2 cup 2.0
all varieties, canned *(Rosarita)*, 4 oz. 2.0
spicy, canned *(Del Monte)*, 1/2 cup 2.0
frozen *(Patio* Boil-in-Bag), 4 oz. 7.0
Beans, Roman, canned *(Progresso)*, 8 oz. 1.0
Beans, shellie, canned *(Stokely's Finest)*, 1/2 cup . . .   0
Beans, yellow or wax:
fresh, raw, 1 cup 1

Beans, yellow or wax, continued

fresh, boiled, drained, 1 cup	.4
canned or frozen (all brands), ½ cup	< .1
Beans, white, dry, uncooked, 8 oz.	3.6
Béarnaise sauce, dehydrated, .9-oz. packet	2.2
Beaver, roasted, 8 oz.	15.5
Beechnuts, shelled, 4 oz.	56.8

Beef, choice grade, retail trim, meat only:

chuck, arm, roast or steak:	
lean with fat, braised, drained, 4 oz.	21.8
lean (fat trimmed), braised, drained, 4 oz.	7.9
chuck, rib roast or steak:	
lean with fat, braised, drained, 4 oz.	41.6
lean (fat trimmed), braised, drained, 4 oz.	11.6
chuck, stewing:	
lean with fat, stewed, drained, 4 oz.	27.1
lean (fat trimmed), stewed, drained, 4 oz.	10.8
club steak, lean with fat, broiled, 4 oz.	46.0
flank steak, boneless, lean, braised, drained, 4 oz.	8.3
ground, regular cooked, 4 oz.	23.0
ground, lean, cooked, 4 oz.	12.8
plate, lean with fat, simmered, drained, 4 oz.	48.5
plate, lean (fat trimmed), simmered, drained, 4 oz.	11.9
porterhouse steak, lean with fat, broiled, 4 oz. . . .	47.9
porterhouse steak, lean (fat trimmed), broiled, 4 oz.	11.9
rib roast, lean with fat, roasted, 4 oz.	44.7
rib roast, lean (fat trimmed), roasted, 4 oz.	15.2
round steak, lean with fat, braised or broiled, 4 oz.	17.5
round steak, lean (fat trimmed), braised or broiled,	
4 oz.	6.9
rump roast, lean with fat, roasted, 4 oz.	31.0
rump roast, lean (fat trimmed), roasted, 4 oz. . . .	10.5
sirloin steak:	
double bone, lean with fat, broiled, 4 oz.	39.3
double bone, lean (fat trimmed), broiled, 4 oz.	10.8
hipbone, lean with fat, broiled, 4 oz.	50.9
hipbone, lean (fat trimmed), broiled, 4 oz.	14.2
round bone, lean with fat, broiled, 4 oz.	36.3
round bone, lean (fat trimmed), broiled, 4 oz.	8.7
T-bone steak, lean with fat, broiled, 4 oz.	49.0

Beef, continued
T-bone steak, lean (fat trimmed), broiled, 4 oz. . . .   11.7
Beef, corned:
    cooked, medium fat, 4 oz. 34.5
    canned, medium fat, 4 oz. 16.1
    (Carl Buddig), 1 oz. 2.0
    (Dinty Moore), 2 oz. 8.0
    (Eckrich Calorie Watcher Slender Sliced), 1-oz. slice   2.0
    (Oscar Mayer), 3/4-oz. slice 4
Beef, corned, hash, canned:
    (Mary Kitchen), 7½ oz. 24.0
    (Mary Kitchen, 25-oz. can), 8⅓ oz. 27.0
    (Nalley), 3½ oz.   11.0
Beef, corned, spread *(Hormel)*, ½ oz. 3.0
Beef, dried (chipped):
    uncooked, 5-oz. jar 8.9
    sliced *(Hormel)*, 1 oz. 1.0
Beef, freeze-dried, steak, rib eye *(Mountain House)*, 1
    steak 9.0
Beef, frozen:
    rib eye *(Snow King)*, 2 oz. 40.0
    steak, chip *(Snow King)*, 2 oz. 2.0
    steak, flake *(Snow King)*, 2 oz. 14.0
Beef, Italian style *(Oscar Mayer)*, 3/4-oz. slice 6
Beef dinner, frozen:
    (Banquet American Favorites), 10 oz. 19.0
    (Banquet Extra Helpings), 16 oz. 46.0
    (Morton), 11 oz.   5.5
    (Swanson), 11½ oz. 8.0
    Burgundy *(Dinner Classics)*, 10½ oz. 14.0
    chopped *(Banquet American Favorites)*, 11 oz. . . .   30.0
    chopped *(Banquet Extra Helpings)*, 18 oz. 67.0
    chopped sirloin *(Le Menu)*, 12¼ oz. 23.0
    chopped sirloin *(Swanson)*, 11½ oz. 17.0
    chopped steak *(Swanson Hungry-Man)*, 17¼ oz. . .   29.0
    Oriental *(Lean Cuisine)*, 8⅝ oz. 8.0
    pepper Oriental *(La Choy)*, 12 oz. 3.0
    pepper steak *(Classic Lite)*, 10 oz. 7.0
    pepper steak *(Le Menu)*, 11½ oz. 14.0
    Salisbury steak, see "Salisbury steak dinner"

Beef dinner, frozen, continued

short ribs, boneless *(Dinner Classics)*, 10½ oz. . . .	25.0
sirloin tips *(Dinner Classics)*, 11 oz.	17.0
sirloin tips *(Le Menu)*, 11½ oz.	18.0
sliced *(Morton Lite)*, 11 oz.	7.0
sliced *(Swanson Hungry-Man)*, 16 oz.	12.0
sliced, and broccoli *(Classic Lite)*, 10¼ oz.	7.0
steak Diane mignonettes *(Classic Lite)*, 10 oz. . . .	9.0
steak teriyaki *(Dinner Classics)*, 10 oz.	16.0
Stroganoff *(Dinner Classics)*, 11¼ oz.	17.0
Stroganoff *(Le Menu)*, 9¼ oz.	24.0
Swiss steak *(Swanson)*, 10 oz.	14.0
Szechuan *(Classic Lite)*, 10 oz.	9.0
Yankee pot roast, see "Pot roast"	

Beef dinner mix, pepper steak *(La Choy)*, ⅕ pkg.   0
Beef enchilada, see "Enchilada"
Beef entrée, canned:

chow mein *(Chun King Stir-Fry)*, 6 oz. with beef	19.4
chow mein *(La Choy)*, ¾ cup	1.0
chow mein, drained *(Chun King Divider Pak—2 servings)*, 8.11 oz.	1.7
chow mein, drained *(Chun King Divider Pak—4 servings)*, 7.14 oz.	1.5
chow mein pepper Oriental, drained *(Chun King Divider Pak)*, 7.05 oz.	4.2
goulash *(Heinz)*, 7½ oz.	11.0
goulash *(Hormel Short Order)*, 7½ oz.	12.0
pepper Oriental *(La Choy)*, ¾ cup	2.0
pepper steak *(Chun King Stir-Fry)*, 6 oz.*	16.6
stew *(Dinty Moore)*, 7½-oz. can	9.0
stew *(Dinty Moore, 24 oz.)*, 8 oz.	12.0
stew *(Dinty Moore, 40 oz.)*, 8 oz.	11.0
stew *(Heinz)*, 7½ oz.	9.0
stew *(Nalley)*, 3½ oz.	6.0
stew *(Wolf)*, 7½ oz.	7.5
stew, chunky *(Nalley Big Chunk)*, 3½ oz.	3.0

Beef entrée, freeze-dried:

Almondine *(Mountain House)*, 1 cup	8.0

---

* *Prepared according to package directions*

Beef entrée, freeze-dried, continued

and rice, with onions *(Mountain House)*, 1 cup . . .	12.0
stew *(Mountain House)*, 1 cup	9.0
Stroganoff *(Mountain House)*, 1 cup	13.0

Beef entrée, frozen:

barbecue sauce and *(Banquet Cookin' Bag)*, 4 oz.	5.0
Burgundy *(Freezer Queen Single Serve)*, 9.5 oz.	8.0
Burgundy *(Light & Elegant)*, 9 oz.	4.0
chipped, creamed *(Banquet Cookin' Bag)*, 4 oz.	5.0
chipped, creamed *(Freezer Queen Cook-in-Pouch)*, 5 oz.	4.0
chipped, creamed *(Stouffer's)*, 5½ oz.	17.0
chop suey *(Stouffer's)*, 12 oz.	12.0
chop mein Mandarin *(Van de Kamp's Chinese Classics)*, 11 oz.	10.0
gravy and *(Banquet Family Entrees)*, 8 oz.	13.0
gravy with *(Banquet Cookin' Bag)*, 4 oz.	9.0
julienne *(Light & Elegant)*, 8½ oz.	7.0
mushroom gravy and charcoal patties:	
(Banquet Family Entrees), 5⅓ oz.	13.0
(Freezer Queen, 2 lb.), 10.67 oz.	28.0
(Freezer Queen Cook-in-Pouch), 5 oz.	9.0
onion gravy and patties *(Freezer Queen, 2 lb.)*, 8 oz.	24.0
Oriental *(The Budget Gourmet)*, 10 oz.	9.0
Oriental, and broccoli *(Benihana)*, 1 serving	6.0
pepper Oriental *(Chun King Boil-in-Bag)*, 10 oz.	8.8
pepper Oriental *(La Choy)*, ⅔ cup	1.0
pepper steak *(Stouffer's)*, 10½ oz.	11.0
pepper steak, Oriental *(Benihana)*, 1 serving	6.0
pepper steak, Oriental, with rice *(Dining Lite)*, 9.3 oz.	6.4
pepper steak, with rice *(The Budget Gourmet)*, 1 serving	9.0
and peppers *(Freezer Queen Single Serve)*, 9.5 oz.	3.0
pizza patties *(Banquet Entree Express)*, 3 oz.	20.0
roast, hash *(Stouffer's)*, 5¾ oz.	15.0
short ribs *(Stouffer's)*, 5¾ oz.	20.0
sirloin, in herb sauce *(The Budget Gourmet)*, 10 oz.	12.0
sirloin tips *(The Budget Gourmet)*, 1 serving	18.0
sliced *(Swanson Hungry-Man)*, 12¼ oz.	8.0

Beef entrée, frozen, continued

sliced, gravy and *(Freezer Queen,* 2 lb.), 8 oz.	5.0
sliced, gravy and *(Freezer Queen* Cook-in-Pouch), 5 oz.	2.0
sliced, gravy and *(Morton* Lite), 8 oz.	9.0
sliced, gravy and *(Swanson),* 8 oz.	6.0
sliced, and vegetables *(Benihana),* 1 serving	10.0
steak, breaded *(Hormel),* 4 oz.	30.0
stew *(Banquet Family Entrees),* 8 oz.	13.0
stew *(Freezer Queen,* 2 lb.), 8 oz.	2.0
stew *(Freezer Queen* Single Serve), 9 oz.	5.0
stew *(Stouffer's),* 10 oz.	16.0
Stroganoff *(Light & Elegant),* 9 oz.	6.0
Stroganoff *(Stouffer's),* 9¾ oz.	21.0
Szechuan *(Benihana),* 1 serving	14.0
Szechuan, and vegetable *(Van de Kamp's* Chinese Classics), 11 oz.	15.0
teriyaki *(Dining Lite),* 8⅝ oz.	3.0
teriyaki *(Light & Elegant),* 8 oz.	3.0
teriyaki *(Stouffer's),* 9¾ oz.	9.0
Beef gravy, canned *(Franco-American),* 2 oz.	1.0
Beef, ground, seasoning mix *(Durkee),* 1.1-oz. pkg.	.9
Beef loaf, jellied *(Hormel* Perma-Fresh), 2 slices	4.0
Beef luncheon meat:	
(Eckrich Calorie Watcher Slender Sliced), 1-oz. slice	2.0
(Hormel), 1 oz.	3.0
roasted *(Boar's Head),* 2 oz.	1.0
smoked *(Carl Buddig),* 1 oz.	2.0
Beef pie, frozen:	
(Banquet), 8 oz.	34.0
(Stouffer's), 10 oz.	37.0
(Swanson), 8 oz.	21.0
(Swanson Chunky), 10 oz.	28.0
(Swanson Hungry-Man), 16 oz.	34.0
steak burger *(Swanson Hungry-Man),* 16 oz.	44.0
Beef, roast, croissant sandwich, frozen:	
in wine sauce *(Sara Lee Le San-Wich),* 4 oz.	15.0
Beef, roast, hash, canned:	
(Mary Kitchen), 7½-oz. can	23.0
(Mary Kitchen, 15-oz. can), 7½ oz.	22.0

Beef, roast, spread, canned *(Hormel)*, 1/2 oz.	2.0
Beef stew, see "Beef entrée"	
Beef stew seasoning mix:	
(Durkee), 1.7-oz. pkg.	.5
(French's), 1/6 pkg.	0
Beef sticks, see "Sausage sticks"	
Beer, ale and malt liquor (all brands), 12-fl.-oz.	0
Beerwurst, see "Salami, beer"	
Beet:	
fresh, raw, whole, 1 beet, 2" diam.	.1
fresh, boiled, drained, 1 cup or 2 beets, 2" diam.	.1
canned or frozen, plain, Harvard or pickled (all	
brands), 1/2 cup	0
Beet greens, fresh:	
raw, pieces, 1" pieces, 1 cup	< .1
boiled, drained, 8 oz.	.5
Berliner, pork and beef, 1 oz.	4.9
Berry drink, canned, frozen* or mix* (all brands), 6	
fl. oz.	< .1
Biscuit:	
(Wonder), 1 biscuit	1.0
refrigerated, 2 biscuits:	
(Ballard Ovenready)	1.0
(1869 Brand Butter Tastin')	10.0
(Pillsbury Big Country Butter Tastin')	8.0
(Pillsbury Country)	1.0
baking powder *(1869 Brand)*	10.0
baking powder, dinner *(Pillsbury* Tenderflake)	5.0
butter *(Pillsbury)*	1.0
buttermilk *(Ballard Ovenready)*	1.0
buttermilk *(1869 Brand)*	10.0
buttermilk *(Hungry Jack* Extra Rich)	3.0
buttermilk *(Pillsbury)*	1.0
buttermilk *(Pillsbury Big Country)*	8.0
buttermilk *(Pillsbury* Deluxe Heat 'n Eat)	15.0
buttermilk *(Pillsbury* Heat 'n Eat)	5.0
buttermilk *(Pillsbury* Tenderflake)	5.0
buttermilk, flaky *(Hungry Jack)*	7.0

* *Prepared according to package directions*

Biscuit, refrigerated, continued
    buttermilk, flaky *(Pillsbury Extra Lights)* 4.0
    buttermilk, fluffy *(Hungry Jack)* 8.0
    flaky *(Hungry Jack)* 7.0
    flaky *(Hungry Jack Butter Tastin')* 9.0
    fluffy *(Pillsbury* Good'N Buttery) 10.0
    southern style *(Big Country)* 8.0
Biscuit dough, frozen:
  buttermilk *(Bridgford),* 1-oz. piece 3.0
  buttermilk *(Bridgford),* 2-oz. piece 6.0
Biscuit mix:
  (Bisquick), 2 oz. 8.0
  (Martha White Bixmix), 1 pkg. 22.0
Blackberry:
  fresh, 1 cup 6
  canned or frozen (all brands), 1/2 cup . . . .   < .4
Blackeye peas, canned or frozen (all brands), 1/2 cup   < 1.0
Blintz, frozen:
  all varieties, except potato *(Golden),* 1 piece 5
  potato *(Golden),* 1 piece 4.0
Blood sausage, 1 oz. 9.8
Bloody Mary drink mixer (all brands), 1 fl. oz.   0
Blue cheese dip:
  (Kraft Premium), 1 oz. 4.0
  (Nalley), 1 oz. 11.5
Blueberry:
  fresh, 1 cup 6
  canned or frozen (all brands), 1/2 cup . . . .   < .5
Blueberry fruit square, frozen *(Pepperidge Farm),* 1
  piece 11.0
Blueberry turnover:
  frozen *(Pepperidge Farm),* 1 piece 19.0
  refrigerated *(Pillsbury),* 1 piece 8.0
Bluefish fillets, raw, meat only, 1 lb. 15.0
Bockwurst *(Usinger's),* 2-oz. link 13.0
Bologna:
  (Armour), 1 oz. 8.0
  (Ballpark), 1 slice 10.1
  (Boar's Head), 1 oz. 6.3
  (Eckrich), 1 slice 8.0

Bologna, continued
 (Eckrich German Brand), 1 slice or 1 oz. 7.0
 (Eckrich Smorgas Pac), 1 slice 8.0
 (Eckrich Thick Slice), 1 slice 14.0
 (Eckrich Thin Slice, 8-oz. pkg.), 2 slices 9.0
 (Eckrich Thin Slice, 12-oz. pkg.), 2 slices 10.0
 (Grillmaster), 1 slice 7.3
 (Hormel Coarse Ground), 2 oz. 14.0
 (Hormel Fine Ground), 2 oz. 16.0
 (Light & Lean), 2 slices 12.0
 (Light & Lean Thin Slice), 2 slices 6.0
 (Oscar Mayer), 4/5-oz. slice 6.8
 (Usinger's), 1 oz. 8.0
 beef *(Eckrich),* 1 slice 8.0
 beef *(Eckrich Smorgas Pac),* 1 slice 6.0
 beef *(Eckrich* Thick Sliced), 1 slice 12.0
 beef *(Hormel* Coarse Ground), 2 oz. 14.0
 beef *(Hormel* Perma-Fresh), 2 slices 16.0
 beef *(Kahn's),* 1 oz. 8.2
 beef *(Oscar Mayer),* 4/5-oz. slice 6.9
 beef, Lebanon *(Oscar Mayer),* 1.6 oz. 3.3
 with cheese *(Eckrich),* 1 slice 8.0
 cheese *(Oscar Mayer),* 4/5-oz. slice 6.7
 garlic *(Eckrich),* 1 slice 8.0
 garlic *(Oscar Mayer),* 4/5-oz. slice 6.8
 lunch, chub *(Eckrich),* 1 oz. 9.0
 meat *(Armour),* 1 oz. 8.0
 meat *(Hormel* Perma-Fresh), 2 slices 16.0
 pickled ring or sandwich *(Eckrich),* 1 slice or 1 oz.   8.0
Bonito, raw, meat only, 4 oz. 8.3
Borage, fresh:
 raw, 1" pieces, 1 cup 6
 boiled, drained, 4 oz. 9
Bouillon, beef, chicken, onion, or vegetable, packet,
 cube or powder (all brands), 1 serving . . . .   < 1.0
Boysenberry:
 fresh, see "Blackberry"
 canned in heavy syrup, 1 cup 3
 frozen, unsweetened, 1 cup 4
Boysenberry juice *(Smucker's),* 8 fl. oz.   0

Brains, all varieties, raw, 8 oz. 19.5
Bran, see "Wheat bran"
Bratwurst:
  (Kahn's), 2-oz. link 17.0
  cooked *(Hillshire Farms),* 1 oz. 7.7
  hot or precooked *(Usinger's),* 3-oz. link 29.0
  smoked *(Usinger's* Smoki), 3-oz. link 28.0
Braunschweiger:
  (Hormel), 1 oz.   7.0
  (Oscar Mayer), 1-oz. slice 8.6
  chub *(Eckrich),* 1 oz. 6.0
  chub *(Jones Dairy Farm),* 1 oz. 7.7
  chub *(Oscar Mayer),* 1 oz. 8.4
  sliced *(Jones Dairy Farm),* 1 oz. 7.9
  tube *(Oscar Mayer),* 1 oz. 8.7
Brazil nuts:
  shelled, 1 cup 92.7
  shelled, 6 large nuts 18.8
Bread, 2 slices, except as noted:
  (Arnold Bran'nola) 3.0
  bran, honey *(Pepperidge Farm)* 2.0
  cinnamon *(Pepperidge Farm)* 4.0
  corn, see "Bread mix"
  date nut loaf *(Thomas'),* 1 oz. 1.4
  French *(DiCarlo* Parisian) 2.0
  French *(Francisco),* 2 oz. 2.0
  French *(Gonnella),* 1 oz. 5
  French *(Wonder)* 2.0
  French Vienna *(Francisco),* 2 oz. 2.0
  (Hillbilly/Hollywood Dark or Light) 2.0
  Italian *(Wonder* Family) 2.0
  (Monk's Hi-Fibre), 1 oz. 1.0
  multi-grain *(Home Pride* 7 Grain) 2.0
  multi-grain, very thin *(Pepperidge Farm)* 1.0
  nut *(Brownberry* Health Nut) 3.0
  oat *(Arnold Bran'nola* Country) 4.0
  oatmeal *(Pepperidge Farm)* 3.0
  pita *(Sahara* Mini), 1-oz. piece 1.0
  pita *(Toufayan's),* ½ piece or 1 oz. 1.0
  pita, whole wheat *(Sahara),* 1-oz. piece 7

Bread, continued

protein *(Thomas' Fresh)*	.8
protein *(Thomas' Frozen)*	1.0
pumpernickel *(Arnold)*	1.0
pumpernickel *(Levy)*	2.0
pumpernickel *(Pepperidge Farm Family)*	2.0
raisin *(Arnold Tea)*	3.0
raisin-cinnamon *(Pepperidge Farm)*	3.0
raisin-nut *(Brownberry)*	6.0
rye *(Arnold Melba Thin)*	1.0
rye *(Pepperidge Farm Family)*	2.0
rye, Dijon *(Pepperidge Farm)*	2.0
rye, dill or Jewish, seeded or unseeded *(Arnold)*	2.0
rye, Jewish, seeded or unseeded *(Levy)*	2.0
rye, seedless *(Pepperidge Farm)*	2.0
sourdough, French *(Boudin)*, 2 slices or 1¾ oz.	.7
sourdough *(DiCarlo)*	2.0
sourdough *(Parisian)*, 1.8 oz.	.6
Vienna *(Gonnella)*, 1 oz.	< 1.0
wheat *(Arnold Bran'nola Hearty)*	4.0
wheat *(Fresh Horizons)*	2.0
wheat *(Fresh & Natural)*	2.0
wheat *(Home Pride Butter Top/Wheatberry)*	2.0
wheat *(Pepperidge Farm)*	3.0
wheat *(Wonder Family)*	2.0
wheat, apple honey *(Brownberry)*	1.0
wheat, cracked *(Pepperidge Farm)*	2.0
wheat, cracked *(Wonder)*	2.0
wheat, honey *(Arnold Wheatberry)*	2.0
wheat, sprouted *(Arnold)*	2.0
wheat, whole *(Arnold Brick Oven)*	3.0
wheat, whole *(Arnold Brick Oven, 32 oz.)*	4.0
wheat, whole *(Arnold Measure Up)*	2.0
wheat, whole *(Pepperidge Farm)*	3.0
wheat, whole, regular or soft *(Wonder 100%)*	2.0
wheat, whole, very thin *(Pepperidge Farm)*	2.0
white *(Arnold Bran'nola Old Style)*	2.0
white *(Arnold Brick Oven)*	2.0
white *(Arnold Brick Oven, 32 oz.)*	3.0
white *(Arnold Country/Hearthstone)*	3.0

Bread, continued

white *(Arnold Measure Up)*	2.0
white *(Fresh Horizons)*	2.0
white *(Home Pride Butter Top)*	2.0
white *(Pepperidge Farm)*	3.0
white *(Pepperidge Farm Sandwich/Toasting)*	2.0
white, regular or buttermilk *(Wonder)*	2.0
white, very thin *(Pepperidge Farm)*	1.0
Bread, canned, brown *(S&W New England)*, 2 slices, 12 per can	0

Bread mix*:

applesauce spice *(Pillsbury)*, 1/12 loaf	3.0
apricot nut *(Pillsbury)*, 1/12 loaf	4.0
banana *(Duncan Hines)*, 1/2" slice	5.0
banana *(Pillsbury)*, 1/12 loaf	5.0
blueberry nut *(Pillsbury)*, 1/12 loaf	4.0
carrot nut *(Duncan Hines)*, 1/2" slice	5.0
carrot nut *(Pillsbury)*, 1/12 loaf	4.0
cherry nut *(Pillsbury)*, 1/12 loaf	5.0
corn *(Dromedary)*, 2" × 2" piece	3.0
corn, Mexican *(Martha White)*, 1/4 bread	7.0
cranberry or date *(Pillsbury)*, 1/12 loaf	3.0
date-nut roll *(Dromedary)*, 1/2" slice	2.0
French *(Home Hearth)*, 2 slices, 3/8"	3.0
honey granola *(Pillsbury)*, 1/12 loaf	4.0
nut *(Duncan Hines)*, 1/2" slice	6.0
nut *(Pillsbury)*, 1/12 loaf	6.0
raisin-cinnamon *(Duncan Hines)*, 1/2" slice	4.0
rye *(Home Hearth)*, 2 slices, 3/8"	1.0
white *(Home Hearth)*, 2 slices, 3/4"	1.0

Bread crumbs:

dry, grated, 1 oz.	1.3
seasoned *(Contadina)*, 1 cup	3.6
seasoned *(Contadina)*, 1 tbsp.	< 1.0
toasted *(Old London)*, 2 oz.	2.0

Bread dough:

frozen, French *(Bridgford)*, 2 slices	1.0
frozen, honey wheat *(Bridgford)*, 2 slices	2.0

* *Prepared according to package directions*

Bread dough, continued
frozen, white *(Bridgford)*, 2 slices	2.0
frozen, white *(Rich's)*, 2 slices	1.1
refrigerated, French *(Pipin' Hot)*, 1″ slice	1.0
refrigerated, wheat or white *(Pipin' Hot)*, 1″ slice	2.0
refrigerated, white *(Pipin' Hot)*, 1″ slice	2.0

Bread stuffing, see "Stuffing"

Breadfruit, fresh, raw, peeled and seeded, 1 cup 5

Breadfruit seeds:
raw, shelled, 1 oz.	1.6
boiled, shelled, 1 oz.	.7
roasted, shelled, 1 oz.	.8

Breadnut tree seeds, raw, 1 oz. 3
dried, 1 oz.	.5

Breadsticks:
plain, regular or dietetic *(Stella D'Oro)*, 1 piece	1.3
onion *(Stella D'Oro)*, 1 piece	1.1
salt sticks, plain, 1 oz.	.8
sesame *(Stella D'Oro)*, 1 piece	2.2
sesame, dietetic *(Stella D'Oro)*, 1 piece	2.3
soft *(Pillsbury)*, 1 piece	2.0
wheat *(Stella D'Oro)*, 1 piece	1.3

Breakfast bar (see also "Granola and similar snack bars"):
chocolate or chocolate chip *(Carnation Slender)*, 2 bars	14.0
chocolate chip or honey nut *(Carnation)*, 1 bar . . .	11.0
chocolate crunch *(Carnation)*, 1 bar	10.0
chocolate peanut butter *(Carnation Slender)*, 2 bars	15.0
peanut butter, crunch or chocolate chip *(Carnation)*, 1 bar	11.0
vanilla *(Carnation Slender)*, 2 bars	15.0

Breakfast strips, see "Bacon, substitute"

Broad beans, raw, 1 cup 7
boiled, drained, 4 oz.	.6

Broccoli:
fresh, raw, 1 spear, 8.7 oz.	.5
fresh, boiled, drained, 1 spear, 6.3 oz.	.5
fresh, boiled, drained, chopped, 1 cup	.4

Broccoli, continued
  frozen:
    plain (all brands), 3.3 oz. . . . . < .1
    with almonds *(Birds Eye)*, 3.3 oz. 3.0
    in butter sauce, spears *(Green Giant)*, ½ cup 2.0
    with cheddar cheese sauce *(Stouffer's)*, 4½ oz. 10.0
    with cheese sauce *(Birds Eye)*, 5 oz. 7.0
    in cheese-flavored sauce *(Green Giant)*, ½ cup 2.0
    with creamy Italian cheese sauce *(Birds Eye)*, 4.5
      oz. 7.0
    in white cheddar-cheese-flavored sauce *(Green
      Giant)*, ½ cup 3.0
    and carrots, in butter sauce *(Green Giant)*, ½
      cup 1.0
    and carrots, in cheese-flavored sauce *(Green
      Giant)*, ½ cup 2.0
    and carrots and pasta twists *(Birds Eye)*, 3.3 oz. 4.0
    and cauliflower, with creamy Italian cheese sauce
      (Birds Eye), 4.5 oz. 7.0
    and cauliflower medley, with sauce *(Green Giant
      Valley Combination)*, ½ cup 2.0
    and cauliflower and carrots, with cheese sauce
      (Birds Eye), 5 oz. 7.0
    fanfare, with sauce *(Green Giant Valley
      Combination)*, ½ cup 2.0
Broccoli with cheese, in pastry, frozen:
  (Pepperidge Farm), 1 piece 16.0
  croissant *(Sara Lee Le San-Wich)*, 4-oz. piece . . . 18.0
Brown gravy:
  canned *(Heinz Home Style)*, 2 oz. 2.3
  canned, with onions *(Franco-American)*, 2 oz. . . . 1.0
  mix *(Durkee)*, .8-oz. pkg. 4
  mix *(French's)*, ¼ cup* 1.0
  mix *(Pillsbury French's)*, ¼ cup* 0
  mix *(Spatini Family Style)*, 1 fl. oz.* 0
  mix, with mushrooms or onions *(Durkee)*, .8-oz.
    pkg. 5

---

* *Prepared according to package directions*

Brownies (see also "Cookies"):

fudge walnut *(Tastykake)*, 1 piece 18.5

mix*:

    (Duncan Hines Moist, Regular or Family Size), 1

      piece 7.0

    black forest *(Pillsbury)*, 2″ square 6.0

    chocolate chip *(Betty Crocker)*, 1/24 pkg. 5.0

    fudge *(Betty Crocker)*, 1/16 pkg. 6.0

    fudge *(Betty Crocker* Family Size), 1/24 pkg. . . .   5.0

    fudge *(Betty Crocker* Supreme), 1/24 pkg. 3.0

    fudge, frosted *(Betty Crocker)*, 1/24 pkg. 5.0

    fudge or double fudge *(Pillsbury)*, 2″ square . . .   6.0

    fudge *(Pillsbury* Family Size), 2″ square 7.0

    golden *(Betty Crocker)*, 1/24 pkg. 5.0

    rocky road, fudge *(Pillsbury)*, 2″ square 7.0

    walnut *(Betty Crocker)*, 1/16 pkg. 7.0

    walnut *(Betty Crocker* Family Size), 1/24 pkg.   6.0

    walnut *(Pillsbury* Family Size), 2″ square 8.0

refrigerated, fudge *(Pillsbury)*, 1 bar 5.0

Browning sauce *(Gravymaster)*, 1 tsp. . . . .   < .1

Brussels sprouts:

fresh, raw, 4 average sprouts 2

fresh, boiled, drained, 4 average sprouts 4

frozen, plain (all brands), 3.3 oz. . . . .   < .1

frozen, in butter sauce *(Green Giant)*, 1/2 cup 1.0

frozen, baby, with cheese sauce *(Birds Eye)*, 4.5 oz.   6.0

frozen, baby, in cheese-flavored sauce *(Green*

    Giant), 1/2 cup 2.0

Bulgur (parboiled wheat):

club wheat, dry, 8 oz. 3.2

hard red winter wheat, dry, 8 oz. 3.4

white wheat, dry, 8 oz. 2.7

canned, hard red winter wheat, unseasoned, 8 oz.   1.6

canned, hard red winter wheat, seasoned, 8 oz. . . .   7.5

Buns, honey:

glazed *(Hostess)*, 1 bun 27.0

frozen, all varieties *(Morton)*, 2.3-oz. bun 12.0

Burdock root, raw, 1 root, 7.3 oz. 2

---

* *Prepared according to package directions*

Burger King:
  sandwiches, 1 serving:
    bacon double cheeseburger, 7.13 oz. 35.0
    cheeseburger, 4.7 oz. 16.0
    cheeseburger, double, 6.7 oz. 28.0
    chicken, 7.3 oz. 42.0
    ham and cheese, 7.8 oz. 30.0
    hamburger, 4.3 oz. 12.0
    hamburger, double, 5.8 oz. 21.0
    Whaler, 7.23 oz. 24.0
    Whaler with cheese, 7.66 oz. 28.0
    Whopper, 9.9. oz. 38.0
    Whopper with cheese, 10.8 oz. 45.0
    Whopper double beef, 12.6 oz. 53.0
    Whopper double beef, with cheese, 13.5 oz. 61.0
    Whopper Jr., 5.3 oz. 18.0
    Whopper Jr. with cheese, 5.7 oz. 21.0
  side dishes, 1 serving:
    French fries, regular, 2.4 oz. 11.0
    onion rings, regular, 2.7 oz. 16.0
  dessert and shakes, 1 serving:
    apple pie, 4.5 oz. 14.0
    chocolate shake, 10 oz. 10.0
    vanilla shake, 10 oz. 11.0
Burrito, frozen:
  beef *(Hormel)*, 1 piece 8.0
  beef and bean *(Patio)*, 1-oz. piece 9.0
  beef and bean *(Patio)*, 6-oz. piece 22.0
  beef and bean, with red chili *(Patio)*, 1-oz. piece . . 8.0
  beef and bean, with red chili *(Patio)*, 6-oz. piece . . 19.0
  beef and bean, with green chili *(Patio)*, 1-oz. piece . 8.0
  beef and bean, with green chili *(Patio)*, 6-oz. piece . 20.0
  cheese *(Hormel)*, 1 piece 5.0
  chicken and rice *(Hormel)*, 1 piece 4.0
  chili, hot *(Hormel)*, 1 piece 8.0
Burrito dinner, frozen:
  bean and beef *(Swanson)*, 15¼ oz. 32.0
  Grande, with rice and corn *(Van de Kamp's)*, 14¾
    oz. 20.0

Burrito entrée, frozen:

fried, crispy *(Van de Kamp's* Mexican Classics), 6
oz. 15.0

Grande *(Hormel),* 5½ oz. 16.0

sirloin Grande *(Van de Kamp's* Mexican Classics),
11 oz. 15.0

Burrito sauce, canned *(Del Monte* Salsa), ¼ cup . . . 0

Butter, salted or unsalted:

regular, 4 oz. or 1 stick 92.0

regular, 1 tbsp. 11.5

regular, 1 pat, 1″ × ⅓″ 4.1

whipped, ½ cup or 1 stick 61.3

whipped, 1 tbsp. 7.6

whipped, 1 pat, 1¼″ × ⅓″ 3.1

Butter oil, 1 tbsp. 12.7

Butterbeans:

canned *(Joan of Arc),* ½ cup . . . . < 1.0

canned *(Van Camp's),* ½ cup 1.4

dry, cooked *(S&W Tender),* ½ cup 1.0

frozen *(Frosty Acres),* 3.3 oz. 0

Butterbur (Fuki), raw or boiled, 1 cup . . . . < .1

Butterfish, fresh:

raw, gulf, meat only, 4 oz. 3.3

raw, northern, meat only, 4 oz. 11.6

Buttermilk dip *(Kraft),* 2 tbsp. 6.0

Butternuts, dried, shelled, 4 oz. 64.7

	C

	fat grams
Cabbage, fresh:	
raw, one head, 5¾″ diam.	1.6
raw, shredded, 1 cup	.1
boiled, drained, shredded, 1 cup	.4
Cabbage, Chinese, fresh:	
bok choy or pe-tsai, raw, whole, 1 lb.	.8
bok choy, raw, shredded, 1 cup	.1
bok choy, boiled, drained, shredded, 1 cup	.3
pe-tsai, raw or boiled, shredded, 1 cup	.2
Cabbage, red, fresh:	
raw, whole, 1 lb.	.9

Cabbage, red, continued
raw, shredded, 1 cup	.2
boiled, drained, shredded, 1 cup	.3
canned (all brands), 1/2 cup	0
Cabbage, savoy, fresh:	
raw, whole, 1 lb.	.4
raw or boiled, 1 cup	.1
Cabbage, stuffed, dinner, frozen:	
(Classic Lite), 12 oz.	8.0
(Lean Cuisine), 10 3/4 oz.	9.0
Cake, frozen:	
black forest *(Sara Lee)*, 2.5 oz.	8.0
Boston cream *(Pepperidge Farm)*, 2 7/8 oz.	14.0
butterscotch pecan layer *(Pepperidge Farm)*, 1 5/8 oz.	7.0
carrot, with cream cheese icing *(Pepperidge Farm)*, 1 3/8 oz.	8.0
cheese *(Sara Lee Classic Elegant Endings)*, 4 oz.	22.0
cheese, chocolate chip *(Sara Lee Elegant Endings)*, 4 oz.	27.0
cheese, cream, French *(Sara Lee)*, 3 oz.	17.0
cheese, pecan praline *(Sara Lee Elegant Endings)*, 4 oz.	30.0
cheese, strawberry, French *(Sara Lee)*, 3.3 oz.	16.0
chocolate *(Pepperidge Farm Supreme)*, 2 7/8 oz.	17.0
chocolate, Dutch *(Pepperidge Farm Supreme)*, 1 3/4 oz.	10.0
chocolate, German, layer *(Pepperidge Farm)*, 1 5/8 oz.	10.0
chocolate fudge layer *(Pepperidge Farm)*, 1 5/8 oz.	10.0
chocolate mint layer *(Pepperidge Farm)*, 1 5/8 oz.	9.0
chocolate mousse *(Sara Lee)*, 2.7 oz.	16.0
coconut layer *(Pepperidge Farm)*, 1 5/8 oz.	9.0
coffee cake, pecan *(Sara Lee)*, 1.45 oz.	8.0
coffee, walnut *(Sara Lee)*, 1.45 oz.	9.0
devil's food or golden layer *(Pepperidge Farm)*, 1 5/8 oz.	9.0
Grand Marnier *(Pepperidge Farm Supreme)*, 1 1/2 oz.	18.0
lemon coconut *(Pepperidge Farm Supreme)*, 3 oz.	13.0
peach Melba *(Pepperidge Farm Supreme)*, 3 1/8 oz.	7.0

Cake, frozen, continued

pineapple cream *(Pepperidge Farm* Supreme), 2 oz.	7.0
pound cake, butter *(Pepperidge Farm)*, 1 oz.	7.0
pound cake, butter *(Sara Lee)*, 1.1 oz.	7.0
pound cake, chocolate chip *(Sara Lee)*, 1.3 oz. . . .	5.0
pound cake, walnut raisin *(Sara Lee)*, 1.4 oz.	5.0
raspberry mocha *(Pepperidge Farm* Supreme), 3⅛ oz.	14.0
strawberry cream *(Pepperidge Farm* Supreme), 2 oz.	7.0
strawberry shortcake *(Sara Lee)*, 2.5 oz.	8.0
vanilla layer *(Pepperidge Farm)*, 1⅝ oz.	8.0

Cake, mix:

angel food *(Duncan Hines)*, 1/12 cake*	0
angel food, all varieties *(Betty Crocker)*, 1/12 pkg.	0
apple *(Duncan Hines* Deluxe), 1/12 cake*	12.0
apple, Dutch *(Betty Crocker Cake Lovers Collection)*, 1/12 pkg.	4.0
apple, Dutch *(Streusel Swirl)*, 1/16 cake*	11.0
apple-cinnamon *(Betty Crocker Supermoist)*, 1/12 pkg.	3.0
applesauce-raisin *(Betty Crocker Snackin' Cake)*, 1/9 pkg.	6.0
applesauce-spice or banana *(Pillsbury Plus)*, 1/12 cake*	11.0
banana supreme *(Duncan Hines* Deluxe), 1/12 cake*	11.0
banana-walnut *(Betty Crocker Snackin' Cake)*, 1/9 pkg.	7.0
Boston cream *(Pillsbury Bundt)*, 1/16 cake*	10.0
Boston cream pie *(Betty Crocker* Classics), 1/8 pkg.	4.0
butter *(Betty Crocker Supermoist Brickle)*, 1/12 pkg.	3.0
butter pecan *(Betty Crocker Supermoist)*, 1/12 pkg.	4.0
butter recipe *(Pillsbury Plus)*, 1/12 cake*	12.0
carrot *(Betty Crocker Supermoist)*, 1/12 pkg.	4.0
carrot *(Betty Crocker Cake Lovers Collection)*, 1/12 pkg.	5.0
carrot *(Duncan Hines* Deluxe), 1/12 cake*	11.0
carrot, with cream cheese frosting *(Betty Crocker Stir N' Frost)*, 1/6 pkg.	6.0

---
* *Prepared according to package directions*

Cake, mix, continued

    carrot and spice *(Pillsbury Plus)*, 1/12 cake* 11.0

    cheese *(Royal No Bake)*, 1/8 cake* 10.0

    cheese, real *(Royal No Bake)*, 1/8 cake* 9.0

    cherry chip *(Betty Crocker Supermoist)*, 1/12 pkg.   3.0

    cherry supreme *(Duncan Hines)*, 1/12 cake* 11.0

    chocolate, dark *(Pillsbury Plus)*, 1/12 cake* 12.0

    chocolate, deep *(Duncan Hines* Deluxe), 1/12 cake*   15.0

    chocolate, double *(Betty Crocker Cake Lovers

        Collection)*, 1/12 pkg. 7.0

    chocolate, German *(Betty Crocker Supermoist)*, 1/12

        pkg. 3.0

    chocolate, German *(Pillsbury Plus)*, 1/12 cake* . . .   11.0

    chocolate, German, coconut pecan *(Betty Crocker

        Snackin' Cake)*, 1/9 pkg. 5.0

    chocolate, milk *(Betty Crocker Supermoist)*, 1/12

        pkg. 3.0

    chocolate, Swiss *(Duncan Hines* Deluxe), 1/12 cake*   15.0

    chocolate almond *(Betty Crocker Cake Lovers

        Collection)*, 1/12 pkg. 9.0

    chocolate chip *(Betty Crocker Supermoist)*, 1/12 pkg.   4.0

    chocolate chip *(Duncan Hines* Deluxe), 1/12 cake*   12.0

    chocolate chip *(Pillsbury Plus)*, 1/12 cake* 14.0

    chocolate chip, with chocolate frosting *(Betty

        Crocker Stir N' Frost)*, 1/6 pkg. 6.0

    chocolate chip, chocolate *(Betty Crocker

        Supermoist)*, 1/12 pkg. 4.0

    chocolate chip, chocolate, with chocolate chocolate

        chip frosting *(Betty Crocker Stir N' Frost)*, 1/6

        pkg. 6.0

    chocolate fudge *(Betty Crocker Supermoist)*, 1/12

        pkg. 3.0

    chocolate fudge, with vanilla frosting *(Betty Crocker

        Stir N' Frost)*, 1/6 pkg. 5.0

    chocolate fudge chip *(Betty Crocker Snackin' Cake)*,

        1/9 pkg. 6.0

    chocolate macaroon *(Pillsbury Bundt)*, 1/16 cake*   11.0

---

* *Prepared according to package directions*

Cake, mix, continued

chocolate mousse *(Pillsbury Bundt)*, 1/16 cake* 9.0
chocolate pudding *(Betty Crocker* Classics), 1/6 pkg. 4.0
chocolate-mint *(Pillsbury Plus)*, 1/12 cake* 12.0
cinnamon *(Streusel Swirl)*, 1/16 cake* 11.0
coconut macaroon *(Betty Crocker* Classics), 1/24
pkg. 4.0
coffee cake *(Aunt Jemima* Easy), 1.3 oz. dry 4.4
coffee cake *(Pillsbury)*, 1/8 cake* 7.0
date bar *(Betty Crocker* Classics), 1/32 pkg. 2.0
devil's food *(Betty Crocker Supermoist)*, 1/12 pkg. 5.0
devil's food *(Duncan Hines* Deluxe), 1/12 cake* . . . 15.0
devil's food *(Pillsbury Plus)*, 1/12 cake* 14.0
devil's food, chocolate, with chocolate frosting
 (Betty Crocker Stir N' Frost), 1/6 pkg. 6.0
fudge *(Duncan Hines* Butter Recipe), 1/12 cake* 13.0
fudge *(Pillsbury Bundt Tunnel of Fudge)*, 1/16 cake* 12.0
fudge marble *(Duncan Hines* Deluxe), 1/12 cake* 11.0
fudge marble *(Pillsbury Plus)*, 1/12 cake* 12.0
fudge peanut butter chip *(Betty Crocker Snackin'*
 Cake), 1/9 pkg. 7.0
gingerbread *(Betty Crocker* Classics), 1/9 pkg. 6.0
gingerbread *(Dromedary)*, 2" × 2" piece* 2.0
gingerbread *(Pillsbury)*, 3" square* 4.0
golden *(Duncan Hines* Butter Recipe), 1/12 cake* 13.0
golden chocolate chip *(Betty Crocker Snackin'*
 Cake), 1/9 pkg. 5.0
golden pound *(Betty Crocker* Classics), 1/12 pkg. 8.0
golden vanilla *(Duncan Hines* Deluxe), 1/12 cake* 11.0
lemon *(Betty Crocker Supermoist)*, 1/12 pkg. 3.0
lemon *(Pillsbury Bundt Tunnel of Lemon)*, 1/16
cake* 9.0
lemon *(Pillsbury Plus)*, 1/12 cake* 9.0
lemon *(Streusel Swirl)*, 1/16 cake* 11.0
lemon chiffon *(Betty Crocker* Classics), 1/12 pkg. 3.0
lemon pudding *(Betty Crocker* Classics), 1/6 pkg. 4.0
lemon supreme *(Duncan Hines* Deluxe), 1/12 cake* 11.0
lemon-blueberry *(Pillsbury Bundt)*, 1/16 cake* 8.0

---

* *Prepared according to package directions*

Cake, mix, continued

marble *(Betty Crocker Supermoist)*, 1/12 pkg.	3.0
mocha *(Pillsbury Plus)*, 1/12 cake*	12.0
oats'n brown sugar *(Pillsbury Plus)*, 1/12 cake* . . .	12.0
orange, pineapple or strawberry supreme *(Duncan Hines* Deluxe), 1/12 cake*	11.0
pecan brown sugar *(Streusel Swirl)*, 1/16 cake* . . .	11.0
pineapple cream *(Pillsbury Bundt)*, 1/16 cake*	10.0
pineapple upside-down, with topping *(Betty Crocker* Classics), 1/9 pkg.	6.0
pound *(Dromedary)*, 1/2" slice*	6.0
pound *(Pillsbury Bundt)*, 1/16 cake*	9.0
sour cream chocolate *(Betty Crocker Supermoist)*, 1/12 pkg.	3.0
sour cream chocolate *(Duncan Hines* Deluxe), 1/12 cake*	15.0
sour cream white *(Betty Crocker Supermoist)*, 1/12 pkg.	3.0
spice *(Betty Crocker Supermoist)*, 1/12 pkg.	4.0
spice *(Duncan Hines* Deluxe), 1/12 cake*	11.0
spice, with vanilla frosting *(Betty Crocker Stir N' Frost)*, 1/6 pkg.	9.0
strawberry *(Pillsbury Plus)*, 1/12 cake*	11.0
Vienna dream bar *(Betty Crocker* Classics), 1/24 pkg.	4.0
white *(Betty Crocker Supermoist)*, 1/12 pkg.	4.0
white *(Duncan Hines* Deluxe/*Pillsbury Plus)*, 1/12 cake*	10.0
yellow *(Betty Crocker Supermoist)*, 1/12 pkg.	4.0
yellow *(Betty Crocker Supermoist* Butter Recipe), 1/12 pkg.	2.0
yellow *(Duncan Hines* Deluxe/*Pillsbury Plus)*, 1/12 cake*	11.0
yellow, with chocolate frosting *(Betty Crocker Stir N' Frost)*, 1/6 pkg.	8.0
Cake, snack, 1 piece:	
banana *(Hostess Suzy Q's)*	9.0
banana *(Tastykake* Banana Treats)	4.3
butterscotch *(Tastykake Krimpets)*	5.0

* *Prepared according to package directions*

Cake, snack, continued

(Hostess Big Wheels/Ding Dongs)	9.0
(Hostess Chip Flips)	16.0
(Hostess Choco-Diles)	11.0
(Hostess Ding Dongs)	9.0
(Hostess Ho Hos)	6.0
(Hostess Suzy Q's)	10.0
(Tastykake Creamie*)*	9.2
(Tastykake Kandy Kake*)*	4.3
(Tastykake Tempty*)*	3.7
coconut covered *(Hostess Sno Balls)*	4.0
creme filled *(Drake's Devil Dogs)*	8.0
creme filled *(Drake's Ring Ding Jr.)*	9.0
creme filled *(Drake's Yankee Doodles)*	5.0
creme filled *(Tastykake Junior)*	11.5
creme filled *(Tastykake Krimpets)*	6.7
fudge bar *(Tastykake)*	10.5
coconut *(Tastykake Junior)*	7.1
coconut *(Tastykake* Kandy Kake*)*	4.8
coffee cake *(Tastykake* Koffee Kake*)*	11.8
coffee cake, creme filled *(Tastykake* Koffee Kake*)*	5.7
coffee cake, small *(Drake's)*	9.0
cupcake, buttercream, creme filled *(Tastykake)*	5.1
cupcake, chocolate *(Hostess)*	6.0
cupcake, chocolate *(Tastykake)*	3.5
cupcake, chocolate, creme filled *(Tastykake)*	5.8
cupcake, creme *(Tastykake* Kreme Kups*)*	5.4
cupcake, orange *(Hostess)*	5.0
cupcake, vanilla *(Tastykake)*	4.6
(Drake's Funny Bones)	9.0
(Hostess L'il Angels)	2.0
(Hostess O's)	11.0
(Hostess Tiger Tails)	6.0
(Hostess Twinkies)	5.0
jelly *(Tastykake Krimpets)*	2.1
oatmeal raisin bar *(Tastykake)*	8.0
orange *(Tastykake Junior)*	11.0
peanut *(Hostess Peanut Putters)*	21.0
peanut, filled *(Hostess Peanut Putters)*	15.0
peanut butter *(Tastykake* Kandy Kake*)*	5.6

Cake, snack, continued
    vanilla *(Tastykake* Creamie) 9.8
    vanilla, creme filled *(Tastykake Krimpets)* 6.6
Candy, 1 oz., except as noted:
    (Baby Ruth) 6.0
    bridge mix *(Nabisco)* 6.0
    (Butterfinger) 6.0
    (Butternut), 2-oz. bar 13.0
    butterscotch chips *(Nestlé* Morsels) 7.0
    caramel *(Kraft),* 1 piece 1.0
    caramel, chocolate coated *(Milk Duds)* 4.4
    caramel, chocolate coated *(Pom Poms)* 3.0
    caramel, chocolate coated *(Rolo),* 8 pieces or 1.55
      oz. 10.0
    caramel, chocolate coated, with cookies *(Twix)* . . .   7.0
    cherries, in dark or milk chocolate *(Cortina),* 2
      pieces. 5.0
    chocolate, with almonds or Brazil nuts *(Cadbury),* 2
      oz. 18.0
    chocolate, candy coated *(M & M's),* 1.7 oz. pkg. . . . 10.0
    chocolate, with caramel *(Cadbury Caramello),* 2 oz. 13.0
    chocolate, dark *(Hershey's Special Dark),* 1.35-oz.
      bar 12.0
    chocolate, with fruit and nuts *(Cadbury),* 2 oz. . . . 16.0
    chocolate, with hazelnuts *(Cadbury),* 2 oz. 17.0
    chocolate, milk *(Cadbury Dairy Milk),* 2 oz. 16.0
    chocolate, milk *(Hershey's),* 1.45-oz. bar 13.0
    chocolate, milk *(Hershey's Kisses),* 8 or 1.3 oz. . . . 11.0
    chocolate, milk *(Nestlé)* 9.0
    chocolate, milk, with almonds *(Hershey's),* 1.45-oz.
      bar 14.0
    chocolate, milk, with almonds *(Nestlé)* 10.0
    chocolate, milk, with crisps *(Krackel),* 1.45-oz. bar 12.0
    chocolate, milk, with crisps *(Nestlé Crunch)* 1 1/16
      oz. 8.0
    chocolate, milk, with fruit and nuts *(Chunky)* . . .   8.0
    chocolate, milk, with fruit and nuts (Deluxe Nut
      Chunky) 10.0
    chocolate, milk, with peanuts *(Mr. Goodbar),* 1.65-
      oz. bar 17.0

Candy, continued

(Clark Bar)	5.0
coconut, chocolate coated *(Mounds)*, 1.65 oz.	12.0
coconut, chocolate coated, with almonds *(Almond Joy)*, 1.55-oz.	12.0
fruit chews *(Starburst)*, 2.1 oz.	5.0
granola bars, see "Granola and similar snack bars"	
gum *(Big Red/Doublemint/Juicy Fruit/Wrigley's)*, 1 stick	1.5
gum *(Beach-Nut/Fruit Stripe/care*free/Bubble Yum)*, 1 stick	0
halvah *(Sahadi)*	10.0
hard candy, all varieties *(Life Savers)*	0
honey *(Bit-O-Honey)*, 1.7 oz.	4.0
jellied candy, fruit flavors *(Chuckles)*	0
jellied candy, spiced or spearmint leaves *(Chuckles)*	1.0
licorice *(Switzer/Y&S Twizzlers)*	< .1
licorice, candy coated *(Good & Fruity)*	.1
licorice, candy coated *(Good & Plenty)*	< .1
lollipops, all flavors *(Life Savers)*, 1 piece	0
(Mars), 1.8-oz. bar	11.0
marshmallow, plain (all brands)	0
(Milkshake), 2-oz. bar	8.0
(Milky Way), 2.1-oz. bar	10.0
mint *(Junior Mints)*	3.0
mint, plain or butter *(Kraft)*, 1 piece	0
mint, chocolate coated *(York* Peppermint Pattie)*, 1.25 oz.	4.0
(My Buddy), 1.8-oz. bar	13.0
nougat, all flavors, chocolate coated *(Charleston Chew)*	3.0
(Nutcracker)	10.1
nut-fruit bar, almond/apricot or peanut/raisin *(Planters)*	7.0
nut-fruit bar, almond/pineapple *(Planters)*	6.0
nut-fruit bar, walnut/apple *(Planters)*	8.0
nut fudge square *(Nabisco)*, 2 pieces	5.0
(Oh Henry!), 2 oz.	14.0
(100 Grand), 1.5-oz. bar	8.0
(Park Avenue), 1.8-oz. bar	9.0

Candy, continued

(Pay Day), 1.9-oz. bar	12.0
peanut *(Munch)*, 1.4-oz. bar	14.0
peanut *(Planters* Bar), 1.6-oz. bar	14.0
peanut, chocolate coated *(Goobers)*	10.0
peanut, chocolate coated *(Nabisco)*	9.0
peanut, chocolate coated, candy covered *(M & M's)*, 1.7 oz.	12.0
peanut brittle *(Kraft)*	5.0
peanut butter, candy coated *(Reese's Pieces)*, 1.75-oz. pkg.	10.0
peanut butter chips *(Nestlé* Morsels)	10.0
peanut butter chips *(Reese's)*, 1.5 oz. or ¼ cup	13.0
peanut butter, chocolate coated *(Reese's* Cups), 2 pieces or 1.6 oz.	15.0
peanut butter, chocolate coated, with cookies *(Twix* Bar), .9 oz.	8.0
popcorn, plain or flavored, see "Popcorn"	
popcorn, caramel *(Orville Redenbacher's Gourmet Crunch)*	6.0
popcorn, caramel, with peanuts *(Cracker Jacks)*	3.0
(Powerhouse), 2 oz.	11.0
raisins, chocolate coated *(Nabisco)*	5.0
raisins, chocolate coated *(Raisinets)*	4.0
(Snickers), 2-oz. bar	13.0
(3 Musketeers), 2.1-oz. bar	8.0
toffee *(Kraft)*, 1 piece	1.0
toffee *(Skor)*, 1.2-oz. bar	12.0
(Tootsie Roll)	2.5
(Treasure), 2-oz. bar	13.0
wafer bar, chocolate coated *(Kit Kat)*, 1.5-oz. bar	12.0
(Whatchamacallit), 1.4-oz. bar	12.0
(Wispa)	8.0
(Zagnut)	4.4
(Zero), 2-oz. bar	10.0
Cannelloni dinner, frozen, beef and pork or cheese *(Lean Cuisine)*, 9⅝ oz.	10.0
Cannelloni entrée, frozen:	
cheese *(Dining Lite)*, 9 oz.	6.8
veal and vegetable *(Dining Lite)*, 9 oz.	8.0

Cantaloupe, fresh:
  1/2 melon, 5" diam. .7
  cubed, 1 cup 4
Capocollo *(Hormel),* 1 oz. 6.0
Carambola, raw, cubed, 1 cup 5
Caraway seeds (all brands), 1 tsp. 3
Cardamom seeds, ground (all brands), 1 tsp. 1
Cardoon, fresh:
  raw, shredded, 1 cup 2
  boiled, drained, 4 oz. 1
Carissas (natal plums), fresh, 1 average 3
Carrot:
  raw, 1 carrot, 71/2" × 11/8" diam. 1
  raw, shredded, 1 cup 2
  boiled, drained, sliced, 1 cup 3
  canned or frozen, plain (all brands), 1/2 cup . . . . . < .1
Carrot juice, canned, 6 fl. oz. 3
Carrot-raisin salad, dairy pack *(Knudsen),* 1/2 cup   5.0
Casaba melon, fresh:
  whole, with rind, 1 lb. 3
  cubed, 1 cup 2
Cashew:
  (Eagle Honey Roast/Planters Honey Roast), 1 oz.   12.0
  (Frito-Lay's), 1 oz. 14.0
  dry-roasted *(Flavor House),* 1 oz. 13.0
  dry-roasted *(Planters),* 1 oz. 13.0
  oil-roasted *(Planters),* 1 oz. 14.0
  and peanuts *(Planters* Honey Roast), 1 oz. 12.0
Cashew butter:
  raw, unsalted *(Hain),* 2 tbsp. 15.0
  toasted, unsalted *(Hain),* 2 tbsp. 16.0
Cassava, fresh, 4 oz. 4
Catfish:
  fresh, freshwater, raw, fillets, 4 oz. 3.5
  frozen, fillets *(Taste o 'Sea),* 4 oz. 2.0
  frozen, breaded, fillets *(Mrs. Paul's),* 1 fillet 12.0
  frozen, breaded, fingers *(Mrs. Paul's),* 4 oz. 14.0
Catsup (all brands), 2 tbsp. . . . . < .1
Cauliflower:
  fresh, raw, whole, 1 lb. 3

Cauliflower, continued

fresh, raw or boiled, pieces, 1 cup	.2
frozen, plain (all brands), 3.3 oz.	< .1
frozen, with almonds *(Birds Eye)*, 3.3 oz.	2.0
frozen, in butter sauce *(Green Giant)*, 1/2 cup	1.0
frozen, with cheese sauce *(Birds Eye)*, 5 oz.	7.0
frozen, in cheese-flavored sauce *(Green Giant)*, 1/2 cup	2.0
frozen, in white cheddar-cheese-flavored sauce *(Green Giant)*, 1/2 cup	3.0
frozen, and carrot bonanza *(Green Giant Harvest Get Togethers)*, 1/2 cup	3.0

Cauliflower and cheese sauce, in pastry, frozen *(Pepperidge Farm)*, 1 piece ... 13.0

Caviar, sturgeon:

granular, 1 oz.	4.3
pressed, 1 oz.	4.7

Celeriac, fresh:

raw, pared, 1 cup	.5
boiled, drained, 4 oz.	.2

Celery, fresh:

raw, 1 large stalk or 1 cup diced	.1
boiled, drained, diced, 1 cup	.2

Celery seed (all brands), 1 tsp. 5

Celtus, raw, trimmed, 4 oz. 3

Cereal, ready-to-eat:

bran *(All-Bran/Bran Buds)*, 1 oz.	1.0
bran *(Kellogg's Bran Flakes/Post 40%)*, 1 oz.	0
bran *(Nabisco 100%)*, 1 oz.	2.0
bran, with fruit *(Kellogg's Fruitful Bran)*, 1 oz.	0
bran, with raisins *(Kellogg's Raisin Bran)*, 1 oz.	1.0
bran, with raisins *(Post Raisin Bran)*, 1 oz.	0
bran, with raisins, honey *(Post Honey Nut Crunch)*, 1 oz.	1.0
bran, with raisins, nuts *(Raisin Nut Bran)*, 1 oz.	3.0
corn *(Country Corn Flakes)*, 1 oz.	0
corn *(Honeycomb)*, 1 oz.	1.0
corn *(Kellogg's Corn Flakes/Frosted Flakes)*, 1 oz.	0
corn *(Kix/Post Toasties/Total)*, 1 oz.	1.0
corn bran *(Quaker)*, 1 oz.	.9

Cereal, ready-to-eat, continued
  (*Fiber One/Golden Grahams*), 1 oz. 1.0
  granola or natural style (*C.W. Post* Hearty), 1 oz. 4.0
  granola or natural style (*Heartland*), 1 oz. 4.0
  mixed grain (*Apple Jacks/Grape Nuts/Product 19*),
    1 oz. 0
  mixed grain (*Grape Nuts* Flakes), 1 oz. 1.0
  mixed grain (*Special K*), 1 oz. 0
  oats (*Cheerios*), 1 oz. 2.0
  oats (*Honey Nut Cheerios*), 1 oz. 1.0
  oats (*Life*), 1 oz. 1.8
  oats (*Post* Fortified Oat Flakes), 1 oz. 1.0
  oat bran (*Cracklin' Oat Bran*), 1/2 cup 4.0
  rice (*Kellogg's Rice Krispies*), 1 oz. 0
  rice (*Quaker* Puffed Rice), 1 oz. 1
  wheat (*Quaker* Puffed Wheat), 1 oz. 2
  wheat (*Total/Wheaties*), 1 oz. 1.0
  wheat, shredded (*Nabisco*), 5/6-oz. biscuit 1.0
  wheat, shredded (*Nabisco Spoon Size*), 1 oz. 0
  wheat, shredded (*Quaker*), 2 biscuits 4
  wheat, shredded, and bran (*Nabisco*), 1 oz. 1.0
Cereal, cooked:
  oat (*Instant Quaker*), 3/4 cup 1.7
  oat (*Quaker* Quick/Old Fashioned), 2/3 cup 1.9
  wheat (*Wheat Hearts*), 3/4 cup 1.0
  wheat, farina (*Pillsbury*), 2/3 cup . . . . < 1.0
  wheat, whole (*Quaker* Natural), 2/3 cup 6
Cereal beverage, mix* (*Postum/Postum* Coffee
    Flavor), 6 fl. oz. 0
Cervelat (*Hormel* Viking Chub), 1 oz. 8.0
Chard, Swiss, fresh:
  raw, whole, 1 lb. 8
  raw or boiled, chopped, 1 cup 1
Chayote, fresh:
  raw, 1 chayote, 53/4″ × 27/8″ 6
  boiled, drained, pieces, 1 cup 8
Cheddarwurst (*Hillshire Farms*), 1-oz. slice 8.9

———————
* *Prepared according to package directions*

Cheese, 1 oz., except as noted:

American, regular or sharp (all brands)	9.0
American, hot pepper *(Sargento)*	8.9
(Bel Paese)	7.4
(Bel Paese Madallion Processed)	5.9
blue *(Dorman's)*	8.3
blue *(Frigo)*	8.0
blue *(Kraft)*	9.0
blue *(Sargento)*	8.2
brick *(Dorman's)*	8.2
brick *(Kraft)*	9.0
brick *(Sargento)*	8.4
Brie *(Sargento)*	7.9
Camembert *(Sargento)*	6.9
caraway *(Kraft)*	8.0
cheddar *(Dorman's)*	9.2
cheddar *(Frigo/Kraft)*	9.0
cheddar *(Sargento)*	9.4
colby *(Dorman's)*	8.6
colby *(Kraft)*	9.0
colby *(Sargento)*	9.1
cottage *(Borden)*, 1/2 cup	5.0
cottage, dry curd *(Crowley)*, 1/2 cup	1.0
cottage, large curd *(Knudsen* Velvet), 1/2 cup	5.0
cottage, 4% fat *(Crowley)*, 1/2 cup	5.0
cottage, low fat, 1% *(Crowley)*, 1/2 cup	1.0
cottage, chive *(Knudsen)*, 1/2 cup	5.0
cottage, fruit cocktail *(Knudsen)*, 1/2 cup	5.0
cottage, with garden or fruit salad *(Crowley)*, 1/2 cup	4.0
cottage, with pineapple *(Crowley)*, 1/2 cup	4.0
cream, regular, soft or whipped *(Philadelphia Brand)*	10.0
cream, with chives or pimento *(Philadelphia Brand)*	9.0
cream, soft, with chives and onion *(Philadelphia Brand)*	9.0
cream, soft, with fruit *(Philadelphia Brand)*	8.0
cream, whipped, with bacon and horseradish, chives, blue cheese, or smoked salmon *(Philadelphia Brand)*	9.0

Cheese, continued

cream, whipped, with onions or pimentos *(Philadelphia Brand)*	8.0
Edam *(Dorman's)*	7.8
Edam *(Kraft)*	7.0
Edam *(Sargento)*	7.9
farmer's *(Sargento)*	8.0
feta *(Frigo)*	8.0
feta *(Sargento)*	6.0
fontina *(Frigo)*	9.0
fontina *(Sargento)*	8.8
gjetost *(Sargento)*	8.4
Gorgonzola *(Sargento)*	8.2
Gouda *(Kraft)*	9.0
Gouda *(Sargento)*	7.8
Gruyère *(Sargento)*	9.2
havarti *(Casino)*	11.0
havarti *(Sargento)*	10.6
Italian blend, grated *(Kraft)*	7.0
Italian style, grated *(Sargento)*	7.6
jalapeño, processed *(Kraft)*	6.0
Jarlsberg *(Norseland/Sargento)*	7.0
limburger *(Mohawk Valley Little Gem)*	8.0
limburger *(Sargento)*	7.7
Monterey Jack *(Dorman's)*	8.0
Monterey Jack *(Kraft)*	9.0
Monterey Jack *(Sargento)*	8.6
Monterey Jack, with jalapeño or mild peppers *(Kraft)*	9.0
mozzarella *(Casino)*	7.0
mozzarella, whole milk *(Frigo/Sargento)*	7.0
mozzarella, part skim *(Frigo/Kraft)*	5.0
mozzarella, part skim *(Sargento)*	4.9
mozzarella, part skim, with jalapeño pepper *(Kraft)*	5.0
mozzarella, with pizza spices *(Sargento)*	4.9
Muenster *(Dorman's/Kraft)*	9.0
Muenster *(Sargento Red Rind)*	8.5
nacho *(Sargento)*	8.9
Neufchâtel *(Kraft)*	7.0
nokkelost *(Norseland)*	7.4

Cheese, continued

Parmesan *(Frigo/Kraft)*	7.0
Parmesan *(Sargento)*	7.3
Parmesan, grated *(Frigo/Kraft)*	9.0
Parmesan, grated *(Sargento)*	8.5
Parmesan and Romano, grated *(Frigo)*	9.0
Parmesan and Romano, grated *(Sargento)*	7.5
pizza *(Frigo)*	6.0
pot cheese *(Sargento)*	.2
Port du Salut	8.0
provolone *(Dorman's)*	7.3
provolone *(Frigo/Kraft)*	7.0
provolone *(Sargento)*	7.6
queso blanco *(Sargento)*	8.5
queso de papa *(Sargento)*	9.4
ricotta, whole milk *(Frigo/Sargento)*	4.0
ricotta, whole milk and whey *(Sargento)*	2.6
ricotta, part skim *(Frigo)*	3.0
ricotta, part skim *(Sargento)*	1.9
Romano *(Casino Natural)*	7.0
Romano *(Frigo)*	8.0
Romano *(Sargento)*	7.6
Romano, grated *(Frigo/Kraft)*	9.0
Roquefort	8.7
Scamorze, part skim *(Kraft)*	5.0
Slim-Jack *(Dorman's)*	7.0
smoked *(Sargento Smokestik)*	7.1
string cheese, regular or smoked *(Sargento)*	4.9
Swiss *(Dorman's/Frigo/Kraft)*	8.0
Swiss *(Sargento)*	7.8
Swiss, processed *(Borden)*	8.0
Swiss, processed *(Deluxe)*	7.0
taco cheese *(Frigo)*	9.0
taco cheese *(Sargento)*	8.8
taco cheese, shredded *(Kraft)*	9.0
Tilsiter or tybo *(Sargento)*	7.4

Cheese, spreads, 1 oz.:

all varieties *(Cheez Whiz/Velveeta/Easy Cheese)*	6.0
all varieties *(Squeez-a-Snak)*	7.0
American, pimento *(Sargento)*	8.8

Cheese, spreads, continued

American, sharp *(Sargento)* 8.9
and bacon *(Kraft)* 7.0
blue *(Roka)* 6.0
brick *(Sargento)* 8.6
cream cheese, see "Cheese"
with garlic *(Kraft)* 6.0
garlic and herb *(Pub Cheese)* 8.0
jalapeño pepper *(Kraft)* 5.0
limburger *(Mohawk Valley)* 6.0
olive and pimento *(Kraft)* 5.0
pimento, pineapple or relish *(Kraft)* 5.0
sharp *(Old English)* 7.0
Swiss *(Sargento)* 7.1
Cheese and bacon dip *(Nalley)*, 1 oz. 12.4
Cheese croissant *(Sara Lee L'Original)*, 1.5-oz. piece   8.0
Cheese danish, frozen *(Sara Lee)*, 1.3-oz. piece 8.0
Cheese dip, see specific listings
Cheese food, 1 oz.:
American *(Borden/Kraft Singles)* 7.0
American *(Dorman's)* 9.0
American *(Sargento Burger cheese)* 8.9
American grated *(Kraft)* 4.0
with bacon *(Cheez 'n Bacon Singles/Kraft/Cracker
  Barrel)* 7.0
cheddar, sharp, extra sharp, or port wine *(Cracker
  Barrel)* 7.0
with garlic or jalapeño *(Kraft)* 7.0
Monterey Jack or pimento *(Kraft Singles)* 7.0
sharp *(Kraft Singles)* 8.0
smoked *(Smokelle)* 7.0
Swiss *(Kraft Singles)* 7.0
Cheese nuggets, breaded, frozen:
cheddar *(Banquet)*, 3 oz. 30.0
mozzarella *(Banquet)*, 3 oz. 16.0
Cheese-nut logs, 1 oz.:
cheddar with almonds *(Sargento)* 7.5
port wine, sharp or smoky, with almonds *(Cracker
  Barrel)* 6.0
port wine with almonds *(Sargento)* 7.5

Cheese-nut logs, continued

Swiss with almonds *(Sargento)*	7.4
Cheese sauce mix, *(Durkee)*, 1.1-oz. pkg.	8.4
Cheese soufflé, frozen *(Stouffer's)*, 6 oz.	29.0
Cheese straws or sticks:	
(Farm Rich Fiesta), 3 oz.	18.0
with bacon *(Farm Rich)*, 3 oz.	19.0
cheddar *(Farm Rich)*, 3 oz.	21.0
cheddar *(Flavor Tree)*, 1 oz.	11.0
hot pepper *(Farm Rich)*, 3 oz.	17.0
mozzarella *(Farm Rich)*, 3 oz.	13.0
Cherimoyas, raw, whole, 1 lb.	1.2
Cherry:	
fresh, sour, whole, with pits, 1 lb.	1.2
fresh, sweet, whole, with pits, 1 lb.	3.9
fresh, sweet, 10 cherries	.7
candied, 1 oz.	.1
canned or frozen (all brands), 1 cup	< .5
Cherry, maraschino, bottled, with liquid, 1 oz.	.1
Cherry drink, canned, mix* or frozen* (all brands), 8 fl. oz.	< .1
Cherry fruit square, frozen *(Pepperidge Farm)*, 1 square	12.0
Cherry turnover:	
frozen *(Pepperidge Farm)*, 1 piece	19.0
refrigerated *(Pillsbury)*, 1 piece	8.0
Chervil:	
fresh, raw, 1 oz.	.3
dried, 1 tsp.	< .1
Chestnut flour, 4 oz.	4.2
Chestnuts:	
Chinese, raw, shelled, 4 oz.	1.3
Chinese, boiled or steamed, shelled, 4 oz.	.9
Chinese, roasted, 4 oz.	1.4
Chinese, dried, 1 oz.	.5
European, raw, peeled, 4 oz.	1.4
European, boiled or steamed, peeled, 4 oz.	1.6
European, roasted, 4 oz.	2.5

* *Prepared according to package directions*

Chestnuts, continued

European, dried, peeled, 1 oz.	1.1
Japanese, raw, in shell, 1 lb.	1.6
Japanese, boiled or steamed, 4 oz.	.2
Japanese, roasted, 4 oz.	.9
Japanese, dried, 1 oz.	.4

Chewing gum, see "Candy"

Chicken, fresh:

broilers or fryers, roasted:

with skin, 1/2 chicken or 10.5 oz.	40.7
meat only, 4 oz.	8.4
breast, with skin, 1/2 breast or 3.5 oz.	7.6
drumstick, with skin, 1 drumstick or 1.8 oz.	5.8
thigh, with skin, 1 thigh or 2.2 oz.	9.6
wing, with skin, 1 wing or 1.2 oz.	6.6
capon, roasted, with skin, 1/4 capon or 11.2 oz.	37.1

roaster, roasted:

with skin, 1/2 chicken or 16.9 oz.	64.3
meat only, 4 oz.	7.5
light meat, meat only, 4 oz.	4.6
dark meat, meat only, 4 oz.	9.9

stewing, stewed:

with skin, 1/2 chicken or 9.2 oz.	49.2
meat only, 4 oz.	13.5
light meat, meat only, 4 oz.	9.1
dark meat, meat only, 4 oz.	17.3

Chicken, canned:

breast, chunk *(Hormel)*, 6¾ oz.	20.0
chunk style *(Swanson* Mixin')*, 2½ oz.	8.0
dark, chunk *(Hormel)*, 6¾ oz.	18.0
white *(Swanson)*, 2½ oz.	2.0
white and dark *(Swanson)*, 2½ oz.	3.0
white and dark, chunk *(Hormel)*, 6¾ oz.	20.0
white and dark, chunk *(Hormel* No Salt)*, 6¾ oz.	18.0

Chicken bologna *(Weaver)*, 3 oz. | 24.9

Chicken breast:

(Eckrich Calorie Watcher)*, 2 slices	1.0
(Oscar Mayer), 1-oz. slice	.5
oven roasted *(Louis Rich)*, 1-oz. slice	1.8

Chicken and broccoli in croissant, frozen *(Sara Lee Le San-Wich),* 4-oz. piece 19.0
Chicken and fish seasoning *(Lawry's Natural Choice for Chicken and Fish),* 1 tsp. 2
Chicken crepes, with mushroom sauce, frozen *(Stouffer's),* 8¼ oz. 21.0
Chicken dinner, frozen:
à la king *(Le Menu),* 10¼ oz. 13.0
à l'orange *(Lean Cuisine),* 8 oz. 5.0
and vegetables *(Lean Cuisine),* 12¾ oz. 7.0
baked, and dressed *(Banquet Extra Helpings),* 19 oz. 34.0
boneless *(Morton),* 11 oz. 11.8
boneless *(Morton),* 17 oz. 22.9
boneless *(Morton Lite),* 11 oz. 7.0
boneless *(Swanson Hungry-Man),* 17½ oz. 27.0
breast, medallions Marsala *(Classic Lite),* 11 oz.   7.0
breast, roast *(Classic Lite),* 11 oz. 9.0
Burgundy *(Classic Lite),* 11¼ oz. 5.0
cacciatore *(Lean Cuisine),* 10⅞ oz. 10.0
chow mein *(Classic Lite),* 10½ oz. 4.0
chow mein *(La Choy),* 12 oz. 4.0
chow mein *(Lean Cuisine),* 11¼ oz. 5.0
chow mein *(Morton Lite),* 11 oz. 5.0
cordon bleu *(Le Menu),* 11 oz. 19.0
Florentine *(Le Menu),* 12½ oz. 23.0
fricassee *(Dinner Classics),* 11¾ oz. 12.0
fried *(Banquet American Favorites),* 11 oz. 11.0
fried *(Morton),* 11 oz. 6.9
fried, barbecue *(Swanson),* 9¼ oz. 30.0
fried, breast *(Swanson),* 10¾ oz. 33.0
fried, breast *(Swanson Hungry-Man),* 14 oz. 49.0
fried, dark meat *(Swanson),* 10¼ oz. 32.0
fried, dark meat *(Swanson Hungry-Man),* 14 oz.   46.0
glazed *(Lean Cuisine),* 8½ oz. 8.0
Hawaiian *(Dinner Classics),* 11½ oz. 9.0
Milano *(Dinner Classics),* 11½ oz. 12.0
Parmigiana *(Swanson Hungry-Man),* 20 oz. 51.0
Parmigiana, breast *(Le Menu),* 11½ oz. 18.0
sweet and sour *(Classic Lite),* 11 oz. 3.0

Chicken dinner, continued

sweet and sour *(Dinner Classics)*, 11 oz.	17.0
sweet and sour *(Le Menu)*, 11¼ oz.	22.0
teriyaki *(Dinner Classics)*, 10½ oz.	15.0

Chicken entrée, canned:

à la king *(Swanson)*, 5¼ oz.	12.0
chow mein *(Chun King* Stir-Fry), 6 oz. with chicken	11.0
chow mein *(La Choy)*, ¾ cup	2.0
chow mein *(La Choy* Bi-Pack), ¾ cup*	3.0
chow mein, drained *(Chun King* Divider Pak—4 servings), 7.14 oz.	3.6
chow mein, drained *(Chun King* Divider Pak—2 servings), 8.11 oz.	3.8
and dumplings *(Swanson)*, 7½ oz.	12.0
Oriental sweet and sour *(La Choy)*, ¾ cup	1.0
stew *(Dinty Moore)*, 7½ oz.	16.0
stew *(Swanson)*, 7⅝ oz.	7.0
stew, with dumplings *(Heinz)*, 7½ oz.	9.0

Chicken entrée, freeze-dried *(Mountain House)*, 1 cup — 8.0

Chicken entrée, frozen:

à la king *(Banquet Cookin' Bag)*, 5 oz.	7.0
à la king *(Dining Lite)*, 9.5 oz.	9.6
à la king *(Freezer Queen* Boil-in-Pouch), 5 oz.	2.0
à la king *(Freezer Queen* Single Serve), 9.5 oz.	7.0
à la king *(Morton* Lite), 8 oz.	10.0
à la king *(Stouffer's)*, 9½ oz.	11.0
almond Cantonese, with rice *(Van de Kamp's* Chinese Classics), 11 oz.	15.0
au gratin *(The Budget Gourmet)*, 9.1 oz.	10.0
barbecue *(Light & Elegant)*, 8 oz.	6.0
breaded croquettes, gravy and *(Freezer Queen*, 2 lb.), 10.67 oz.	14.0
breaded patties *(Banquet Entree Express)*, 3 oz.	14.0
breaded patties, barbecue *(Banquet Entree Express)*, 3 oz.	9.0
breaded sticks *(Banquet Entree Express)*, 3 oz.	13.0
broccoli *(Light & Elegant)*, 9½ oz.	11.0

* *Prepared according to package directions*

Chicken entrée, frozen, continued

cacciatore *(Freezer Queen* Single Serve), 9.5 oz.	5.0
cacciatore *(Tyson)*, 10.5 oz.	12.0
cashew *(Stouffer's)*, 9½ oz.	17.0
chow mein *(Chun King* Boil-in-Bag), 10 oz.	4.8
chow mein *(Dining Lite)*, 11.3 oz.	1.3
chow mein *(La Choy)*, ⅔ cup	2.0
chow mein *(Morton* Lite), 8 oz.	3.0
chow mein *(Stouffer's)*, 8 oz.	5.0
chow mein, Mandarin *(Van de Kamp's* Chinese Classics), 11 oz.	10.0
cordon bleu *(Beatrice* International Entrees), 6 oz.	18.0
cordon bleu *(Tyson Chick'N Quick)*, 5 oz.	15.0
creamed *(Stouffer's)*, 6½ oz.	24.0
divan *(Stouffer's)*, 8½ oz.	22.0
and dumplings *(Banquet Family Entrees)*, 8 oz.	25.0
escalloped *(Stouffer's)*, 5¾ oz.	16.0
with fettuccine *(The Budget Gourmet)*, 1 serving	21.0
fiesta *(Tyson)*, 10.5 oz.	20.0
Francais *(Tyson)*, 8¾ oz.	16.0
French recipe *(The Budget Gourmet)*, 10 oz.	11.0
fried *(Swanson)*, 7¼ oz.	21.0
fried, breast *(Swanson Hungry-Man)*, 11¾ oz.	37.0
fried, dark meat *(Swanson Hungry-Man)*, 11 oz.	36.0
glazed *(Dining Lite)*, 8.5 oz.	6.0
glazed *(Light & Elegant)*, 8 oz.	4.0
Kiev *(Beatrice* International Entrees), 6 oz.	24.0
Kiev *(Tyson Chick'N Quick)*, 5 oz.	31.0
l'orange *(Tyson)*, 8¼ oz.	8.0
Lucerne *(Beatrice* International Entrees), 6 oz.	18.0
Mandarin *(The Budget Gourmet)*, 10 oz.	7.0
marsala *(Tyson)*, 10.5 oz.	11.0
Mexican, Suiza, with rice *(Van de Kamp's* Combinations), 14¾ oz.	20.0
nibbles *(Swanson)*, 5 oz.	25.0
and noodles, broccoli *(The Budget Gourmet)*, 1 serving	26.0
Oriental *(Chun King* Boil-in-Bag), 10 oz.	3.7
Oriental, and mushrooms *(Benihana)*, 1 serving	6.0
Oriental, and snow peas *(Benihana)*, 1 serving	7.0

Chicken entrée, frozen, continued

Oriental, with vegetables and rice *(Tyson)*, 10¼ oz.	8.0
paprikash *(Stouffer's)*, 10½ oz.	15.0
Parmigiana *(Banquet Family Entrees)*, 6.4 oz.	5.0
Parmigiana *(Beatrice* International Entrees), 6 oz.	11.0
Parmigiana *(Light & Elegant)*, 8 oz.	6.0
Parmigiana *(Tyson)*, 11¾ oz.	18.0
patties, Italian flavored *(Banquet Entree Express)*, 3 oz.	9.0
picatta *(Tyson)*, 9 oz.	9.0
Romanoff *(Beatrice* International Entrees), 6 oz.	16.0
royale *(Beatrice* International Entrees), 6 oz.	15.0
sliced, gravy and *(Freezer Queen* Boil-in-Pouch), 5 oz.	4.0
sliced, gravy and *(Morton* Lite), 8 oz.	9.0
sweet and sour *(Benihana)*, 1 serving	3.0
sweet and sour *(The Budget Gourmet)*, 1 serving	7.0
sweet and sour *(Chun King* Boil-in-Bag), 10 oz.	2.3
sweet and sour *(Freezer Queen* Single Serve), 9.5 oz.	4.0
sweet and sour *(La Choy)*, ⅔ cup	< 1.0
sweet and sour *(Tyson)*, 11 oz.	17.0
in teriyaki sauce *(Benihana)*, 1 serving	8.0
with vegetables *(Freezer Queen*, 2 lb.), 8 oz.	3.0
with vegetables, country *(The Budget Gourmet)*, 1 serving	10.0
with vegetables and vermicelli *(Dining Lite)*, 12.8 oz.	6.8
walnut chicken, chunky *(Chun King* Boil-in-Bag), 10 oz.	9.9

Chicken entrée, mix*

and dumpling *(Chicken Helper)*, ⅕ pkg.	26.0
and mushroom *(Chicken Helper)*, ⅕ pkg.	25.0
potato and gravy *(Chicken Helper)*, ⅕ pkg.	32.0
stuffing *(Chicken Helper)*, ⅕ pkg.	33.0
teriyaki *(Chicken Helper)*, ⅕ pkg.	24.0

Chicken frankfurter:

(Grillmaster), 1 link	11.0
(Weaver), 1 link	10.6

* *Prepared according to package directions*

Chicken frankfurter, continued
cheese *(Grillmaster)*, 1 link 11.9
with cheese *(Weaver)*, 1 link 13.0

Chicken, fried, frozen:
(Banquet Regular or Spicy), 6.4 oz. 19.0
(Swanson/Swanson Take-Out), 3¼ oz. 17.0
(Weaver Crispy Light), 2.9 oz. 9.4
(Weaver Party Pack), 3.5 oz. 16.9
(Weaver Variety Pack), 3.5 oz. 15.0
in batter, breasts *(Weaver)*, 3.5 oz. 15.5
in batter, drumsticks and thighs *(Weaver)*, 3.5 oz. 16.0
breaded drum nuggets *(Banquet)*, 12 oz. 38.0
breaded nuggets *(Banquet)*, 3 oz. 14.0
breaded winglets *(Banquet)*, 12 oz. 38.0
breast *(Swanson)*, 4½ oz. 21.0
breast *(Weaver* Dutch Frye), 3.5 oz. 14.2
cutlets *(Swanson)*, 3½ oz. 13.0
dipsters *(Swanson)*, 3 oz. 14.0
drumlets *(Swanson)*, 3 oz. 13.0
drumsticks and thighs *(Weaver* Dutch Frye), 3.5 oz. 15.1
nibbles, wings *(Swanson)*, 3¼ oz. 20.0
thighs and drumsticks *(Banquet)*, 5 oz. 16.0
thighs and drumsticks *(Swanson)*, 3¼ oz. 19.0
wings *(Banquet)*, 6¾ oz. 22.0

Chicken gravy:
canned *(Franco-American)*, 2 oz. 4.0
canned *(Heinz* Home Style), 2 oz. 2.3
giblet, canned *(Franco-American)*, 2 oz. 2.0
mix *(Durkee)*, 1-oz. pkg. 1.2
mix *(Durkee Roastin' Bag)*, 1.5-oz. pkg. 1.0
mix *(French's/French's* Gravy for Chicken), ¼
cup* 1.0
mix, creamy *(Durkee)*, 1.2-oz. pkg. 9.0
mix, creamy *(Durkee Roastin' Bag)*, 2-oz. pkg. . . . 12.0
mix, Italian style *(Durkee Roastin' Bag)*, 1.5-oz.
pkg. 1.0

Chicken pie, frozen:
(Banquet), 8 oz. 30.0

---
* *Prepared according to package directions*

Chicken pie, continued
(Stouffer's), 10 oz.	34.0
(Swanson), 8 oz.	24.0
(Swanson Chunky), 10 oz.	33.0
(Swanson Hungry-Man), 16 oz.	37.0

Chicken sausage:
(Grillmaster), 1 link	13.6
(Grillmaster Rope), 4 oz.	25.6
canned *(Hormel)*, 4 links	16.0

Chicken, smoked *(Carl Buddig)*, 1 oz. 2.8

Chicken spread, canned:
(Hormel), 1/2 oz.	2.0
(Swanson), 1 oz.	4.0
salad *(The Spreadables)*, 1.9 oz.	9.0

Chick-peas (garbanzos):
dry, raw, 8 oz.	10.9
canned *(Progresso)*, 8 oz.	4.0
canned, regular or marinated *(S&W)* 1/2 cup	1.0

Chicory, witloof, see "Endive, French or Belgian"

Chicory greens, fresh:
untrimmed, 1 lb.	1.1
chopped, 1 cup	.5

Chicory root, raw:
1 root, 2.6 oz.	.1
1″ pieces, 1 cup	.2

Chili con carne, canned:
with beans *(Hormel,* 15 oz.), 7 1/2 oz.	17.0
with beans *(Hormel,* 25 oz.), 8 1/3 oz.	20.0
with beans *(Hormel* Short Order), 7 1/2 oz.	14.0
with beans *(Van Camp's)*, 1 cup	23.2
with beans *(Wolf)*, 7 1/2 oz.	22.0
with beans, hot *(Heinz)*, 7 3/4 oz.	16.0
with beans, hot *(Hormel/Hormel* Short Order), 7 1/2 oz.	16.0
with beans, spicy *(Wolf)*, 7 1/2 oz.	20.6
without beans *(Hormel)*, 10 1/2 oz. can	41.0
without beans *(Hormel,* 15 oz.), 7 1/2 oz.	28.0
without beans *(Hormel,* 25 oz.), 8 1/3 oz.	33.0
without beans *(Hormel* Short Order), 7 1/2 oz.	27.0
without beans *(Nalley)*, 3 1/2 oz.	9.0

Chili con carne, continued

without beans *(Nalley Big Chunk)*, 3½ oz.	12.0
without beans *(Van Camp's)*, 1 cup	33.5
without beans *(Wolf)*, 7½ oz.	26.6
without beans, hot *(Hormel)*, 7½ oz.	28.0
without beans, spicy *(Wolf)*, 7½ oz.	24.9
and franks *(Van Camp's Chilee Weenee)*, 1 cup	15.7
and macaroni *(Heinz)*, 7½ oz.	12.0
and macaroni *(Hormel Short Order)*, 7½ oz.	10.0
and macaroni *(Wolf Chili Mac)*, 7½ oz.	19.9
mild, hot or thick *(Nalley)*, 3½ oz.	6.0

Chili con carne, freeze-dried:

with beans *(Mountain House)*, 1 cup	16.0
with macaroni and beef *(Mountain House)*, 1 cup	8.0

Chili con carne, frozen *(Stouffer's)*, 8¾ oz. — 11.0

Chili con carne spread, concentrate *(Oscar Mayer)*, 1 oz. — 5.8

Chili peppers, see "Pepper, chili"

Chili powder, seasoned, 1 tbsp. — 1.3

Chili sauce, canned:

(Del Monte), ¼ cup	0
(Heinz), 1 tbsp.	< .1
(S&W Chili Makin's), ½ cup	1.0
green, mild *(Del Monte Chile Salsa)*, ¼ cup	0
hot dog sauce *(Wolf)*, ⅙ cup	2.3

Chili seasoning mix:

(Durkee Con Carne), 1.7-oz. pkg.	1.6
(Durkee Texas), 1.8-oz. pkg.	4.4
regular or with onion *(French's Chili-O)*, ⅙ pkg.	0

Chinese snacks, crispy *(Mother's TV)*, 1 oz. — 7.0

Chives:

fresh, whole, 1 lb.	2.7
fresh or freeze-dried, chopped, 1 tbsp.	< .1

Chocolate, see "Candy"

Chocolate, baking:

(Nestlé Choco-Bake), 1 oz.	15.0
milk *(Nestlé Morsels)*, 1 oz.	9.0
semi-sweet *(Borden Chips)*, 1 oz.	7.0
semi-sweet, regular or miniature *(Hershey's)*, ¼ cup	12.0
semi-sweet *(Nestlé Toll House Morsels)*, 1 oz.	8.0

Chocolate, baking, continued
  unsweetened *(Hershey's)*, 1 oz. 16.0
Chocolate drink mix, dry:
  (Hershey's Instant), 3 tbsp. or .75 oz. 1.0
  (Quik), 2 tsp. 1.0
Chocolate syrup *(Hershey's)*, 1 oz. or 2 tbsp. 1.0
Chocolate topping, see "Toppings, dessert"
Chop suey seasoning mix *(Durkee)*, 1.5-oz. pkg. . . .   2.1
Chorizo:
  pork and beef, 1 oz. 10.9
  pork and beef, 1 link, 4" long 23.0
Chrysanthemum garland, fresh:
  raw, whole, 1 lb. 8
  raw or boiled, 1" pieces, 1 cup 1
Church's:
  catfish, fried, ¾-oz. piece 4.0
  chicken, fried:
    breast, 4.3-oz. piece 17.3
    breast-wing, 4.8-oz. piece 19.7
    leg (drumstick), 2.9-oz. piece 8.6
    thigh, 4.2-oz. piece 21.6
  chicken nuggets:
    regular, .63-oz. piece 3.1
    spicy, .63-oz. piece 2.9
  corn on cob, 6-oz. ear 9.3
  French fries, 3-oz. serving 5.5
  hush puppy, .82-oz. piece 2.9
Cinnamon, ground (all brands), 1 tsp. 1
Citron, candied, 1 oz.   .1
Citrus drink, canned, frozen,* or mix* (all brands), 6
  fl. oz. . . . .   < .1
Clam:
  fresh, raw, hard or round, meat only, 8 oz. 2.0
  fresh, raw, soft, meat only, 8 oz. 4.3
  canned, chopped, minced or chowder *(S&W)*, 2 oz.   0
  canned, minced *(Gorton's)*, ½ can 1.0
  canned, minced *(Snow's)*, 6½ oz. 1.0
  frozen, in batter *(Mrs. Paul's)*, 2½ oz. 13.0

* *Prepared according to package directions*

Clam, continued
  frozen, French fried *(Taste o' Sea* Crispy Light), 5
    oz. 20.0
  frozen, strips, fried *(Gorton's* Crunchy), ½ pkg. . . 15.0
Clam chowder, see "Soup"
Clam dinner, frozen *(Taste o' Sea* Platter), 6½ oz. 29.0
Clam dip:
  (Kraft), 2 tbsp. or 1 oz. 4.0
  (Nalley), 1 oz. 10.4
Clam juice, canned *(Snow's),* 3 fl. oz. 0
Cloves, ground, (all brands), 1 tsp. 4
Coating mix, see "Seasoned coating mix"
Cocktail sauce:
  (Nalley), 3½ oz. 1.0
  (Sauceworks/Stokely's Finest), 1 tbsp. 0
Cocoa, dry:
  (Alba), .7 oz. .5
  (Hershey's), 1 oz. or ⅓ cup 4.0
  (Nestlé Superior Quality), 1.3 oz. 4.0
  chocolate, double rich or milk *(Swiss Miss),* 1 pkg. 3.0
  chocolate, milk or rich *(Carnation* Instant), 1-oz.
    pkg. 1.0
  chocolate, with mini marshmallows *(Swiss Miss),* 1
    pkg. 3.0
Coconut:
  fresh, shelled, meat only, 4 oz. 38.0
  fresh, shelled, meat only, 1 piece, 2" × 2" × 2½" 15.1
  fresh, shredded or grated, 1 cup 26.8
  canned, shredded *(Durkee),* 1 cup 28.0
Coconut cream:
  fresh (from grated coconut meat), 1 cup 83.2
  canned, 1 tbsp. 3.4
Coconut milk (from grated coconut water and meat),
  1 cup 57.2
Coconut water (coconut liquid), 1 cup 5
Cod:
  fresh, raw, fillets, 8 oz. 7
  canned, 4 oz. 3
  dehydrated, lightly salted, 4 oz. 3.2
  dried, salted, 4 oz. 8

Cod, continued
frozen *(Gorton's Fishmarket Fresh)*, 4 oz.	1.0
frozen *(Van de Kamp's* Today's Catch), 4 oz.	0
frozen, fillets *(Booth* Light & Tender), 4 oz.	1.0
frozen, fillets *(Taste o' Sea)*, 4 oz.	1.0
frozen, breaded *(Van de Kamp's)*, 5 oz.	20.0
frozen, breaded, fillets *(Certi-Fresh Light &* *Crunchy)*, 5 oz.	16.0
frozen, seasoned *(Booth* Light & Tender), 3 oz. . . .	4.0
Cod dinner, frozen, almondine *(Dinner Classics)*, 12 oz.	15.0
Cod entrée, frozen:	
fillets *(Dining Lite)*, 10 oz.	5.8
Florentine *(Certi-Fresh)*, 9 oz.	15.0
in shrimp sauce *(Certi-Fresh)*, 9 oz.	15.0
Coffee, plain, regular or instant (all brands), 1 tbsp.	< .1
Coffee, flavored, prepared,* 6 fl. oz.:	
cafe Amaretto *(General Foods* International)	2.0
café Francais *(General Foods* International)	3.0
cafe Irish creme *(General Foods* International) . . .	3.0
cafe Vienna *(General Foods* International)	2.0
Irish mocha mint *(General Foods* International) . . .	2.0
orange cappuccino *(General Foods* International)	2.0
Suisse mocha *(General Foods* International)	2.0
Colada drink mixer:	
piña *(Freeze & Serve)*, 1 oz.	0
piña or strawberry *(Holland-House)*, 1 pouch	0
piña, bottled *(Coco Casa)*, 1 fl. oz.	2.0
piña, bottled *(Holland House)*, 1 fl. oz.	0
piña, mix* *(Bar-Tender's)*, 5 fl. oz. with alcohol	3.0
Cole slaw, dairy pack *(Knudsen)*, ½ cup	16.0
Collard greens:	
fresh, raw, with stems, 1 lb.	.6
fresh, boiled, drained, chopped, 1 cup	.3
frozen (all brands), 3.3 oz.	< .1
Collins drink mixer (all brands), 6 fl. oz.	0
Cookies:	
almond *(Pepperidge Farm* Supreme), 2 pieces	10.0

* Prepared according to package directions

Cookies, continued

animal crackers *(Barnum's Animals)*, 11 or 1 oz.	4.0
apple *(Apple Newtons)*, 1½ or 1 oz.	2.0
apple, iced *(Almost Home* Dutch Sticks), ⅔-oz. piece	1.0
applesauce-raisin, iced *(Nabisco)*, 2 pieces	8.0
apricot-raspberry *(Pepperidge Farm* Fruit), 3 pieces	6.0
arrowroot *(National)*, 6 or 1 oz.	4.0
blueberry *(Blueberry Newtons)*, 1½ or 1 oz.	2.0
blueberry *(Pepperidge Farm* Fruit Cookies), 3 pieces	6.0
brown edge wafer *(Nabisco)*, 5 or 1 oz.	6.0
brownie, chocolate-nut *(Pepperidge Farm)*, 3 pieces	10.0
brownie cream sandwich *(Pepperidge Farm* Capri), 2 pieces	9.0
brownie, fudge and nut *(Almost Home)*, 1¼-oz. piece	7.0
butter flavor *(Nabisco)*, 6 pieces	5.0
butter flavor *(Nabisco* Danish), 5 or 1 oz.	8.0
butter flavor *(Pepperidge Farm* Chessmen), 3 pieces	6.0
butter flavor *(Sunshine)*, 2 pieces	2.0
cherry *(Cherry Newtons)*, 1½ or 1 oz.	2.0
chocolate *(Famous* Wafers), 5 pieces	4.0
chocolate *(Nabisco* Snaps), 7 pieces	4.0
chocolate chip *(Almost Home* Real), 2 pieces	5.0
chocolate chip *(Chewy Chips Ahoy!)*, 2 pieces	6.0
chocolate chip *(Chip-A-Roos)*, 1 piece	3.0
chocolate chip *(Chips 'n More)*, 2 pieces	7.0
chocolate chip *(Duncan Hines)*, 1 piece	2.5
chocolate chip *(Keebler* Chips Deluxe), 1 piece . . .	4.0
chocolate chip *(Keebler* Rich 'n Chips), 1 piece	4.0
chocolate chip *(Nabisco* Snaps), 6 pieces	4.0
chocolate chip *(Pepperidge Farm)*, 3 pieces	8.0
chocolate chip *(Sunshine Nuggets)*, 3 pieces	3.0
chocolate chip, chocolate *(Pepperidge Farm)*, 3 pieces	9.0
chocolate chip, mocha *(Pepperidge Farm)*, 3 pieces	6.0
chocolate chunk pecan *(Pepperidge Farm)*, 2 pieces	7.0
chocolate macadamia *(Pepperidge Farm)*, 2 pieces	7.0
chocolate sandwich *(Pepperidge Farm* Brussels), 3 pieces	8.0

Cookies, continued

chocolate sandwich *(Pepperidge Farm* Lido), 2 pieces	11.0
chocolate sandwich *(Pepperidge Farm* Milano), 3 pieces	10.0
chocolate mint sandwich *(Pepperidge Farm* Brussels Mint), 3 pieces	10.0
cinnamon raisin *(Almost Home),* 2 or 1 oz.	7.0
coconut, chocolate filled *(Pepperidge Farm* Tahiti), 2 pieces	11.0
coconut macaroon *(Nabisco),* 1⅓-oz. piece	9.0
coffee, chocolate-praline filled *(Pepperidge Farm* Cappucino), 3 pieces	9.0
creme sandwich *(Frito-Lay's* Duplex), 2½ oz.	13.0
creme sandwich *(Hydrox),* 1 piece	2.0
creme sandwich *(Vienna Fingers),* 1 piece	3.0
creme sandwich, chocolate *(Oreo),* 3 or 1 oz.	6.0
creme sandwich, chocolate *(Oreo Double Stuf),* 2 or 1 oz.	7.0
creme sandwich, fudge *(Keebler),* 1 piece	3.0
creme sandwich, fudge *(Almost Home),* 1⅛-oz. piece	6.0
creme sandwich, oatmeal *(Almost Home),* 1⅛-oz. piece	5.0
creme sandwich, peanut butter *(Almost Home),* 1⅛-oz. piece	6.0
creme sandwich, vanilla *(Cameo),* 3 or 1 oz.	5.0
custard sandwich *(Sunshine Cup Custard),* 1 piece	3.0
date-nut granola *(Pepperidge Farm* Kitchen Hearth), 3 pieces	9.0
date-nut pecan *(Pepperidge Farm* Kitchen Hearth), 3 pieces	8.0
devil's food *(Nabisco* Cakes), 1⅓-oz. piece	1.0
fig bars *(Fig Newtons),* 2 pieces	2.0
fig bars *(Sunshine Fig Chewies),* 1 piece	1.0
fruit, all varieties, without icing *(Almost Home* Fruit Sticks), ⅔-oz. piece	2.0
fudge stripes *(Keebler),* 1 piece	3.0
ginger *(Nabisco* Snaps), 4 or 1 oz.	3.0
ginger *(Pepperidge Farm* Gingerman), 3 pieces	4.0

Cookies, continued

ginger *(Sunshine* Snaps), 3 pieces	2.0
graham crackers *(Honey Maid/Nabisco),* 2 or ½ oz.	1.0
graham crackers *(Sunshine* Honey), 4 pieces	2.0
graham crackers, chocolate *(Nabisco),* 3 or 1 oz.	7.0
graham crackers, fudge *(Keebler* Deluxe), 2 pieces	4.0
hazelnut *(Pepperidge Farm),* 3 pieces	9.0
lemon *(Sunshine Lemon Coolers),* 3 pieces	4.0
lemon nut crunch *(Pepperidge Farm),* 3 pieces	10.0
marshmallow *(Mallomars),* 2 pieces	6.0
marshmallow *(Mallo Puffs),* 1 piece	2.0
marshmallow *(Nabisco* Puffs), 1 piece	4.0
marshmallow *(Nabisco* Twirls), 1 piece	5.0
marshmallow *(Pinwheels),* 1-oz. piece	5.0
marshmallow sandwich *(Nabisco),* 4 pieces	3.0
mint sandwich, chocolate-filled *(Pepperidge Farm* Mint Milano), 3 pieces	13.0
molasses *(Pepperidge Farm* Crisps), 3 pieces	5.0
oatmeal *(Drake's),* 3 pieces	7.0
oatmeal *(Keebler* Old Fashioned), 1 piece	3.0
oatmeal *(Pepperidge Farm* Irish), 3 pieces	7.0
oatmeal *(Sunshine* Country Style), 1 piece	2.0
oatmeal peanut sandwich *(Sunshine),* 1 piece	3.0
oatmeal raisin *(Almost Home),* 2 or 1 oz.	5.0
oatmeal raisin *(Pepperidge Farm),* 3 pieces	8.0
oatmeal raisin, iced *(Almost Home),* 2 or 1 oz.	5.0
oatmeal sandwich *(Keebler),* 1 piece	3.0
orange, chocolate-filled *(Pepperidge Farm* Orange Milano), 3 pieces	13.0
peanut, chocolate filled *(Pepperidge Farm* Nassau), 2 pieces	10.0
peanut butter *(Almost Home),* 2 or 1 oz.	8.1
peanut butter *(Sunshine* Wafers), 2 pieces	4.0
peanut butter, chocolate chip *(Pepperidge Farm),* 3 pieces	8.0
peanut butter creme patties *(Nutter Butter),* 4 or 1 oz.	8.0
peanut butter fudge *(Almost Home),* 2 or 1 oz.	7.0
peanut butter sandwich *(Nutter Butter),* 2 or 1 oz.	6.0

Cookies, continued

raisin bran *(Pepperidge Farm* Kitchen Hearth), 3
   pieces 8.0
(Social Tea Biscuit), 6 or 1 oz. 4.0
shortbread *(Lorna Doone),* 4 or 1 oz. 7.0
shortbread *(Pepperidge Farm),* 2 pieces 8.0
shortbread, fudge striped *(Nabisco),* 3 or 1 oz. . . . 7.0
shortbread, pecan *(Nabisco),* 2 or 1 oz. 9.0
shortbread, pecan *(Pecan Sandies),* 1 piece 5.0
strawberry *(Pepperidge Farm* Fruit), 3 pieces 7.0
sugar *(Bisco* Wafers), 8 or 1 oz. 7.0
sugar *(Bisco* Waffle Cremes), 3 or 1 oz. 7.0
sugar *(Pepperidge Farm),* 3 pieces 8.0
sugar *(Sunshine* Wafers), 2 pieces 4.0
vanilla *(Nilla* Wafers), 7 or 1 oz. 4.0
vanilla *(Pepperidge Farm* Bordeaux), 3 pieces 5.0
vanilla *(Pepperidge Farm* Pirouettes), 3 pieces 7.0
vanilla *(Sunshine* Wafers), 4 pieces 4.0
vanilla, chocolate coated *(Pepperidge Farm*
   Orleans), 3 pieces 6.0
vanilla, chocolate nut coated *(Pepperidge Farm*
   Geneva), 3 pieces 10.0

Cookie, mix*:

brownie, see "Brownies"
chocolate chip *(Betty Crocker Big Batch),* 2 pieces 6.0
chocolate chip *(Duncan Hines),* 2 pieces 8.0
chocolate chip, double *(Duncan Hines),* 2 pieces 7.0
oatmeal raisin *(Duncan Hines),* 2 pieces 6.0
peanut butter *(Duncan Hines),* 2 pieces 7.0
sugar *(Betty Crocker Big Batch),* 2 pieces 5.0
sugar, golden *(Duncan Hines),* 2 pieces 6.0

Cookie, refrigerator:

chocolate chip *(Pillsbury),* 3 pieces 10.0
oatmeal raisin *(Pillsbury),* 3 pieces 8.0
peanut butter *(Pillsbury),* 3 pieces 8.0
sugar *(Pillsbury),* 3 pieces 8.0

Cookie crumbs:

graham cracker *(Nabisco),* 2 tbsp. or ½ oz. 1.0

---

* *Prepared according to package directions*

Cookie crumbs, continued

graham cracker *(Sunshine)*, 1 cup	14.0
Coriander, fresh raw, 1/4 cup	< .1
Coriander seed, ground, (all brands), 1 tsp.	.3

Corn:

fresh, raw, on cob, with husks, 1 lb.	1.9
fresh, kernels, cut from 1 average ear, boiled, drained	1.0
fresh, boiled, drained, cut, 1 cup	2.1
canned or frozen, regular or cream (all brands), 1/2 cup	1.0
frozen, in butter sauce *(Green Giant)*, 1/2 cup	2.0
frozen, with green beans and pasta *(Birds Eye)*, 3.3 oz.	5.0

Corn chips, puffs, and similar snacks, 1 oz.:

(Bachman)	9.0
(Diggers Corn Snack)	8.0
(Fritos/Fritos Light Corn Chips)	10.0
(Fritos King Size Dip Chips)	9.0
(Planters Corn Chips/Wise Corn Crunchies)	10.0
barbecue flavored *(Bachman/Fritos)*	9.0
(Bugles)	8.0
cheese flavored *(Cheese 'N Crunch)*	11.0
cheese flavored *(Chee·tos/Cheez Doodles)*	10.0
cheese flavored *(Cheez Waffies)*	8.0
cheese flavored *(Doo Dads)*, 1/2 cup or 1 oz.	6.0
cheese flavored *(Jax)*	8.0
cheese flavored *(Jax Crunchy)*	11.0
cheese flavored *(Planters Cheez Balls or Curls)*	11.0
cheddar flavored *(Chee·tos)*	10.0
cheddar flavored, all varieties *(Doo Dads)*	6.0
cheddar flavored, sharp *(Chee·tos Cheddar Valley)*	9.0
chili cheese *(Fritos)*	10.0
onion flavored *(Funyuns)*	6.0
pizza or sour cream and onion *(Planters)*	10.0
sticks, buttered, popped *(Flavor Tree)*	10.0
toasted, all varieties *(Cornnuts)*	4.0
tortilla chips *(Bachman)*	8.0
tortilla chips *(Doritos)*	7.0
tortilla chips *(Eagle/Planters/Tostitos)*	8.0

Corn chips, puffs, and similar snacks, continued
tortilla chips, nacho *(Bachman)*	6.0
tortilla chips, nacho *(Bravos/Eagle/Planters)*	8.0
tortilla chips, taco *(Doritos)*	7.0
Corn fritter, frozen *(Mrs. Paul's)*, 2 fritters	12.0

Corn grits:
dry, white or yellow *(Quaker/Aunt Jemima* Regular or Quick), 3 tbsp.	.2
dry, white *(Quaker* Instant), 1 packet	.1
dry, yellow *(Quaker/Aunt Jemima* Quick), 3 tbsp.	.2
dry, with imitation bacon bits *(Quaker* Instant), 1 packet	.4
dry, with imitation ham bits *(Quaker* Instant), 1 packet	.3
dry, with real cheddar flavor *(Quaker* Instant), 1 packet	1.0
canned *(Van Camp's* Golden Hominy), 1 cup	.6
canned *(Van Camp's* White Hominy), 1 cup	.7
canned, with red and green pepper *(Van Camp's* Golden), 1 cup	.5

Corn meal, dry:
white or yellow, whole ground, unbolted, 8 oz.	8.8
white or yellow, bolted, 8 oz.	7.7
white or yellow, degermed, 8 oz.	2.7
white or yellow, self-rising, whole-ground, 8 oz.	7.3
white or yellow, self-rising, degermed, 8 oz.	2.5
white *(Aunt Jemima* Self-rising), 1/6 cup	.5
white or yellow *(Quaker/Aunt Jemima)*, 3 tbsp.	.5
white, bolted *(Aunt Jemima* Mix), 1/6 cup	.7
white, bolted *(Aunt Jemima* Self-rising), 1/6 cup	.9
white, buttermilk *(Aunt Jemima* Self-rising Mix), 3 tbsp.	1.1
yellow, bolted *(Aunt Jemima* Mix), 1/6 cup	.4

Corn soufflé, frozen *(Stouffer's)*, 4 oz.	7.0
Corn syrup, dark or light *(Karo)*, 1 tbsp.	0
Cornstarch, *(Argo/Kingsford's)*, 1 tbsp.	0

Cottonseed kernels, roasted:
1 cup	54.1
1 tbsp.	3.6

Cottonseed flour:
partially defatted, 1 cup	5.8
partially defatted, 1 tbsp.	.3
lowfat, 4 oz.	1.6

Cottonseed meal, partially defatted, 4 oz. — 5.4

Couscous pilaf mix *(Casbah),* 1 oz. dry — 0

Cowpeas:
raw, shelled, 1 cup	1.2
boiled, drained, 1 cup	1.3
young pods, with seeds, raw or boiled, 1 cup	.3
leafy-tips, fresh, raw or boiled, chopped, 1 cup	.1

Crab:
fresh, steamed in shell, 1 lb.	4.1
fresh, steamed, meat only, 8 oz.	4.3
canned *(Louisiana Brand),* 4 oz.	3.0
canned, Dungeness *(S&W),* 3¼ oz.	2.0
frozen, au gratin *(Gorton's Light Recipe),* 1 pkg.	13.0
frozen, deviled *(Mrs. Paul's),* 3-oz. piece	6.0
frozen, deviled, miniature *(Mrs. Paul's),* 3½ oz.	10.0
frozen, king or snow *(Wakefield),* 3 oz.	< 1.0
frozen, stuffed, Imperial *(Gorton's Light Recipe),* 1 pkg.	20.0

Crab and shrimp, frozen *(Wakefield),* 3 oz. — < 1.0

Crabapple, raw, with skin, sliced, 1 cup — .3

Crackers:
bacon flavored *(Great Crisps!* Real), 9 or ½ oz.	4.0
bacon flavored *(Nabisco* Thins), 7 or ½ oz.	4.0
butter flavor *(Escort),* 3 or ½ oz.	4.0
butter flavor *(Hi-Ho),* 4 pieces	5.0
butter flavor *(Keebler Club),* 4 pieces	2.0
butter flavor *(Pepperidge Farm* Thins), 4 pieces	3.0
butter flavor *(Ritz/Ritz* Low Salt), 4 or ½ oz.	4.0
butter flavor *(Town House),* 5 pieces	5.0
cheese *(A & Eagle),* 1 oz.	6.0
cheese *(Cheese Nips),* 13 or ½ oz.	3.0
cheese *(Cheese Tid-Bit),* 16 or ½ oz.	4.0
cheese *(Cheez-It),* 12 pieces	4.0
cheese *(Pepperidge Farm* Snack Sticks), 8 pieces	6.0
cheese *(Pepperidge Farm* Thins), 4 pieces	3.0
cheese *(Planters),* 1 oz.	7.0

Crackers, continued

cheese *(Ritz Cheese)*, 5 or 1/2 oz.	3.0
cheese *(Wheat Thins Cheese)*, 9 or 1/2 oz.	3.0
cheese, blue *(Better Blue)*, 10 or 1/2 oz.	4.0
cheese, cheddar *(American Heritage)*, 5 pieces . . .	4.0
cheese, cheddar *(Better Cheddar)*, 11 or 1/2 oz. . . .	4.0
cheese, cheddar or Parmesan *(Pepperidge Farm Goldfish)*, 45 pieces	6.0
cheese and chive *(Dip in a Chip/Great Crisps!)*, 1/2 oz.	4.0
cheese, nacho *(Better Nacho/Great Crisps!)*, 1/2 oz.	4.0
cheese, Parmesan *(American Heritage)*, 4 pieces	4.0
cheese sandwich *(Nabisco)*, 2 or 1/2 oz.	3.0
cheese–peanut butter sandwich *(Nabisco)*, 2 or 1/2 oz.	3.0
chicken flavored *(Chicken in a Biskit)*, 7 or 1/2 oz.	4.0
cinnamon *(Nabisco Treats)*, 2 or 1/2 oz.	1.0
(Finn Crisp Dark/Dark with Caraway), 4 pieces	0
(Finn Crisp Light), 4 pieces	1.0
garlic *(Great Crisps! Savory)*, 8 or 1/2 oz.	3.0
graham crackers, see "Cookies"	
(Ideal Crisp Bread Extra Thin), 3 pieces	0
(Ideal Fiber Crisp Bread), 2 pieces	0
(Kavli Norwegian Thick), 2 pieces	0
(Kavli Norwegian Thin), 2 pieces	.3
malted milk–peanut butter sandwich *(Nabisco)*, 2 or 1/2 oz.	3.0
(Manischewitz Tam Tams), 10 pieces	8.0
matzo *(Manischewitz Passover)*, 1 piece	.4
matzo *(Manischewitz Unsalted)*, 1 oz.	.3
matzo, egg *(Manischewitz Passover)*, 1.2-oz. piece	2.0
matzo, egg and onion *(Manischewitz)*, 1-oz. piece	1.0
matzo, tea, thin *(Manischewitz)*, .9-oz. piece	.3
matzo, wheat *(Manischewitz)*, 10 pieces	1.0
matzo, whole wheat, bran *(Manischewitz)*, 1.1-oz. piece	1.0
(Nabisco Country Crackers), 5 or 1/2 oz.	4.0
melba, bacon or cheese *(Old London Rounds)*, 5 pieces	2.0

Crackers, continued

melba, garlic, onion or salty rye *(Old London* Rounds), 5 pieces	1.0
melba, pumpernickel, rye or white *(Old London)*, 3 pieces	0
melba, sesame *(Old London* Rounds), 5 pieces	2.0
melba, whole grain *(Old London)*, 3 slices	1.0
onion *(Great Crisps!* French), 7 or ½ oz.	4.0
oyster and soup *(Dandy)*, 20 or ½ oz.	1.0
oyster and soup *(Oysterettes)*, 18 or ½ oz.	1.0
oyster and soup *(Sunshine)*, 16 pieces	2.0
peanut butter sandwich, toasted *(Nabisco)*, 5 or ½ oz.	2.0
peanut butter and cheese sandwich *(Handi-Snacks)*, 1 pkg.	13.0
(Pepperidge Farm Goldfish), 45 pieces	7.0
(Pepperidge Farm Snack Sticks), 8 pieces	5.0
pizza flavored *(Pepperidge Farm Goldfish)*, 45 pieces	7.0
pumpernickel *(Pepperidge Farm* Snack Sticks), 8 pieces	5.0
rye *(Keebler* Toasted), 5 pieces	4.0
rye *(Pepperidge Farm* Snack Sticks), 8 pieces	4.0
rye *(Wasa* Crisp Bread, Golden, Lite or Sport) 1 piece	0
rye *(Wasa* Hearty Rye Crisp Bread), 1 piece	1.0
rye-bran *(Kavli)*, 2 pieces	15.0
saltine *(Krispy/Krispy* Unsalted Tops), 5 pieces	1.0
saltine *(Premium/Premium* Unsalted Tops), 5 or ½ oz.	2.0
saltine *(Zesta)*, 5 pieces	2.0
sesame *(American Heritage)*, 4 pieces	4.0
sesame *(Great Crisps!)*, 9 or ½ oz.	4.0
sesame *(Keebler* Toasted), 5 pieces	4.0
sesame *(Meal Mates)*, 3 or ½ oz.	3.0
sesame *(Pepperidge Farm)*, 4 pieces	3.0
sesame *(Pepperidge Farm* Snack Sticks), 8 pieces	6.0
sesame *(Wasa* Sesame Crisp Bread), 1 piece	1.5
sesame and cheese *(Twigs)*, 5 or ½ oz.	4.0
soda or water *(Crown Pilot)*, ½-oz. piece	1.0
soda or water *(Pepperidge Farm* English), 4 pieces	1.0

Crackers, continued

soda or water *(Royal Lunch/Sea Rounds)*, ½-oz. piece	2.0
soda or water *(Sailor Boy* Pilot), .9-oz. piece	2.5
toast *(Holland Rusk)*, ½-oz. piece	1.0
toast *(Planters)*, 1 oz.	7.0
toast *(Uneeda* Unsalted Tops), 3 or ½ oz.	2.0
toast *(Nabisco* Zwieback), 2 or ½ oz.	1.0
tomato and celery *(Great Crisps!)*, 9 or ½ oz.	4.0
vegetable *(Nabisco* Thins), 7 or ½ oz.	4.0
(Wasa Breakfast Crisp Bread), 1 piece	1.5
(Wasa Extra Crisp Crackerbread), 1 piece	.7
(Wasa Fiber Plus Crisp Bread), 1 piece	1.0
wheat *(Keebler* Harvest), 3 pieces	4.0
wheat *(Keebler* Toasted), 5 pieces	4.0
wheat *(Pepperidge Farm* Hearty), 4 pieces	4.0
wheat *(Rich/Rich* No Salt Added) 8 or 1 oz.	5.0
wheat *(Wheatsworth* Stoneground), 5 or ½ oz.	3.0
wheat *(Wheat Thins/Wheat Thins* Low Salt), 8 or ½ oz.	3.0
wheat *(Triscuit/Triscuit* Low Salt), 3 or ½ oz.	2.0
wheat *(Sociables)*, 6 or ½ oz.	3.0
wheat *(Sunshine* Wafers), 8 pieces	4.0
wheat, cheese and garlic *(Hain)*, 11 or 1 oz.	8.0
wheat, cracked *(Pepperidge Farm)*, 4 pieces	4.0
wheat, nutty *(Wheat Thins)*, 7 or ½ oz.	5.0
wheat, onion *(Hain/Hain* No Salt Added), 11 or 1 oz.	6.0
wheat, pumpernickel *(Hain/Hain* No Salt Added), 10 or 1 oz.	6.0
wheat, sesame *(Hain/Hain* No Salt Added), 11 or 1 oz.	7.0
wheat, sour cream & chive *(Hain)*, 11 or 1 oz.	6.0
wheat, sourdough *(Hain/Hain* No Salt Added), 11 or 1 oz.	5.0
wheat, toasted, with onion *(Pepperidge Farm)*, 4 pieces	3.0
wheat, vegetable *(Hain/Hain* No Salt Added), 11 or 1 oz.	5.0

Crackers, continued

wheat and rye *(Hain/Hain* No Salt Added), 11 or 1 oz.	4.0
whole grain *(Ideal* Crisp Bread No Salt), 2 pieces	0
Cracker crumbs and meal:	
cracker *(Nabisco)*, 2 tbsp. or ½ oz.	0
matzo *(Manischewitz Farfel)*, 1 cup	.8
matzo meal *(Manischewitz)*, 1 cup	1.4
Cranberry:	
fresh, whole, with stems, 1 lb.	.9
whole or chopped, 1 cup	.2
fresh *(Ocean Spray)*, 4 oz.	< 1.0
sauce, whole or jellied (all brands), ½ cup	< 1.0
Cranberry drink, with blended juices *(Ocean Spray Crantastic)*, 8 fl. oz.	< 1.0
Cranberry juice:	
(Smucker's), 8 fl. oz.	0
cocktail, canned or frozen* (all brands), 8 fl. oz.	< .1
Cranberry-orange relish *(Ocean Spray)*, 1 oz.	< 1.0
Crayfish, fresh:	
raw, in shell, 1 lb.	.3
raw, meat only, 4 oz.	.6
Cream:	
half and half, 1 cup	27.8
half and half, 1 tbsp.	1.7
heavy, whipping, 1 cup unwhipped or 2 cups whipped	88.1
heavy, whipping, 1 tbsp. unwhipped or 2 tbsp. whipped	5.6
light, coffee or table, 1 cup	46.3
light, coffee or table, 1 tbsp.	2.9
light, whipping, 1 cup unwhipped or 2 cups whipped	73.9
light, whipping, 1 tbsp. unwhipped or 2 tbsp. whipped	4.6
medium, 25% fat, 1 cup	59.8
medium, 25% fat, 1 tbsp.	3.8
sour, 1 cup	48.2

* *Prepared according to package directions*

Cream, continued

sour, 1 tbsp.	2.5
sour, half and half, 1 tbsp.	1.8
whipped, topping, pressurized, 1 cup	13.3
whipped, topping, pressurized, 1 tbsp.	.7

Cream, imitation (non-dairy):

powdered, 1 cup	33.4
powdered, 1 tbsp.	2.1
powdered, 1 tsp.	.7
frozen, 1 cup	23.9
frozen, 1 fl. oz.	3.0
sour, 1 cup	44.9
whipping, pressurized, 1 cup	15.6
whipping, pressurized, 1 tbsp.	.9
whipped topping, semisolid, 1 cup	19.0
whipping, semisolid, 1 tbsp.	1.0

Cream puff, frozen:

Bavarian *(Rich's)*, 1 puff	7.6
chocolate *(Rich's)*, 1 puff	7.8

Cress, garden, fresh:

raw, 1/2 cup	.2
boiled, drained, 1 cup	.8

Cress, water, see "Watercress"

Croaker, fresh:

Atlantic, raw, meat only, 4 oz.	2.5
white or yellow, raw, meat only, 4 oz.	.9

Croissants (see also specific listings), 1 piece:

(Pepperidge Farm), 1.63 oz.	9.0
frozen, all butter *(Sara Lee L'Original)*, 1.5 oz.	9.0
frozen, chocolate *(Sara Lee Le Pastrie)*, 2.6 oz.	18.0
frozen, cinnamon-nut-raisin *(Sara Lee Le Pastrie)*, 3.3 oz.	17.0
frozen, wheat 'n honey *(Sara Lee L'Original)*, 1.5 oz.	9.0

Croutons:

buttery or cheddar cheese *(Brownberry)*, 1 oz.	6.0
Caesar salad *(Brownberry)*, 1 oz.	5.0
cheese and garlic *(Pepperidge Farm)*, 1/2 oz.	3.0
cheese, sexton *(Brownberry)*, 1 oz.	5.0
onion and garlic *(Brownberry)*, 1 oz.	5.0

Croutons, continued

onion and garlic *(Pepperidge Farm)*, ½ oz.	3.0
ranch style *(Brownberry)*, 1 oz.	5.0
seasoned *(Brownberry)*, 1 oz.	6.0
seasoned *(Pepperidge Farm)*, ½ oz.	3.0
toasted *(Brownberry)*, 1 oz.	4.0
Crowder peas, frozen *(Southland)*, 3.3 oz.	1.0
Cucumber, fresh:	
with skin, 1 large, 8¼″ × 2⅛″	.4
with skin, sliced, 1 cup	.1
Cumin seed (all brands), 1 tsp.	.4
Cupcake, see "Cake, snack"	
Currant:	
fresh, black, trimmed, 1 cup	.5
fresh, red or white, trimmed, 1 cup	.2
dried, Zante *(Del Monte)*, ½ cup	0
Curry powder (all brands), 1 tsp.	.3
Curry sauce, dry, 1.2-oz. packet	8.2
Cusk, fresh:	
raw, meat only, 4 oz.	.2
steamed, meat only, 4 oz.	.8

	fat grams
Daiquiri drink mixer (all brands), 1 fl. oz.	0
Dairy Queen/Brazier:	
sandwiches, 1 piece:	
chicken, 7.9 oz.	41.0
fish, 6 oz.	17.0
fish, with cheese, 6.3 oz.	21.0
hamburger, single, 5.3 oz.	16.0
hamburger, double, 7.5 oz.	28.0
hamburger, triple, 9.7 oz.	45.0
hamburger with cheese, single, 5.8 oz.	20.0

Dairy Queen/Brazier, sandwiches, continued

hamburger with cheese, double, 8.5 oz.	37.0
hamburger with cheese, triple, 10.8 oz.	50.0
hot dog, plain, 3.5 oz.	16.0
hot dog, with cheese, 4 oz.	21.0
hot dog, with chili, 4.6 oz.	20.0
hot dog, super, plain, 6.3 oz.	27.0
hot dog, super, with cheese, 7 oz.	34.0
hot dog, super, with chili, 7.8 oz.	32.0
side dishes, 1 serving:	
French fries, regular, 2.5 oz.	10.0
French fries, large, 4 oz.	16.0
onion rings, 3 oz.	16.0
desserts and shakes, 1 serving:	
banana split, 13.7 oz.	11.0
Buster Bar, 5.3 oz.	29.0
cone, small, 3 oz.	4.0
cone, regular, 5.1 oz.	7.0
cone, large, 7.6 oz.	10.0
cone, dipped, chocolate, small, 3.3 oz.	9.0
cone, dipped, chocolate, regular, 5.6 oz.	16.0
cone, dipped, chocolate, large, 8.4 oz.	24.0
Dairy Queen frozen dessert, 4 oz.	6.0
Dilly bar, 3 oz.	13.0
Double Delight, 9.1 oz.	20.0
DQ sandwich, 2.1 oz.	4.0
float, 14.2 oz.	7.0
freeze, 14.2 oz.	12.0
hot fudge *Brownie Delight,* 9.5 oz.	25.0
malt, chocolate, small, 10.4 oz.	13.0
malt, chocolate, regular, 14.9 oz.	18.0
malt, chocolate, large, 21 oz.	25.0
Mr. Misty, any size serving	0
Mr. Misty float, 14.7 oz.	7.0
Mr. Misty freeze, 14.7 oz.	12.0
Mr. Misty Kiss, 3.2 oz.	0
parfait, 10.1 oz.	8.0
Peanut Butter Parfait, 10.9 oz.	34.0
shake, chocolate, small, 10.4 oz.	13.0
shake, chocolate, regular, 14.9 oz.	19.0

Dairy Queen/Brazier, desserts and shakes, continued

shake, chocolate, large, 21 oz.	26.0
strawberry shortcake, 11.4 oz.	11.0
sundae, chocolate, small, 3.8 oz.	4.0
sundae, chocolate, regular, 6.3 oz.	8.0
sundae, chocolate, large, 8.8 oz.	10.0

Dandelion greens, fresh:

raw, 1 lb.	3.2
boiled, drained, chopped, 1 cup	.6

Danish pastry (see also specific listings), 1 piece:

butterhorn *(Hostess)*	18.0
frozen, cinnamon-raisin *(Sara Lee)*, 1.3-oz. roll . . .	8.0
refrigerator, caramel, with nuts *(Pillsbury)*	8.0
refrigerator, cinnamon raisin, with icing *(Pillsbury)*	7.0

Dates, domestic:

natural and dry, whole, 10 average	.4
pitted *(Dromedary)*, 5 whole dates or ¼ cup chopped	0
pitted *(Bordo)*, 2 oz.	1.2
diced *(Bordo)*, 2 oz.	1.1

Dill pickle dip *(Nalley)*, 1 oz. 9.0

Dill sauce mix, creamy, for fish *(Durkee Roastin' Bag)*, 1.1-oz. pkg. 14.0

Dips, see specific listings

Dock, fresh:

raw, with stems, 1 lb.	2.2
boiled, drained, 8 oz.	1.5

Domino's Pizza:

cheese, 2 slices or ¼ of 12″ pie	6.0
cheese, 2 slices or ⅙ of 16″ pie	8.0
pepperoni, 2 slices or ¼ of 12″ pie	12.0
pepperoni, 2 slices or ⅙ of 16″ pie	14.0

Doughnut, 1 piece:

cinnamon *(Hostess)*	6.0
cinnamon *(Tastykake)*	9.7
chocolate coated *(Hostess)*	8.0
chocolate coated, mini *(Hostess Donettes)*	3.0
coated, mini *(Tastykake)*	4.9
fudge iced *(Tastykake* Premium)	17.9
honey wheat *(Tastykake* Premium)	13.5

Doughnut, continued
honey wheat, mini *(Tastykake)* 2.7
krunch *(Hostess)* 4.0
old-fashioned *(Hostess)* 10.0
old-fashioned, glazed *(Hostess)* 12.0
orange glazed *(Tastykake* Premium) 16.4
plain *(Hostess)* 7.0
plain *(Tastykake)* 10.9
powdered sugar *(Hostess)* 5.0
powdered sugar *(Tastykake)* 11.2
powdered sugar *(Tastykake,* 12 oz.) 5.9
powdered sugar, mini *(Hostess Donettes)* 2.0
powdered sugar, mini *(Tastykake)* 2.7
Drum, fresh:
freshwater, raw, meat only, 4 oz. 5.9
red, raw, meat only, 4 oz. 5
Duck:
domestic, raw, meat only, 4 oz. 6.7
domestic, roasted, meat only, 4 oz. 12.7
wild, raw, breast meat only, 4 oz. 4.8
Dutch brand loaf, pork and beef, 1-oz. slice 5.1

	fat grams
Eclair, frozen, chocolate *(Rich's),* 1 piece	9.7
Eel:	
domestic, raw, meat only, 4 oz.	20.8
smoked, 4 oz.	31.5
Egg, chicken:	
raw, large, 1 whole egg	5.6
raw, large, white of 1 egg	< .1
raw, large, yolk of 1 egg	5.6
hard boiled or poached, large, 1 whole egg	5.6
dried, whole, 1 oz.	11.9

Egg, chicken, continued
dried, whole, 1/2 cup sifted	17.8
dried, whole, 1 tbsp.	2.1
dried, white, flakes or powder, stabilized, 1 oz.	< .1
dried, yolk, 1 oz.	17.4
dried, yolk, 1 tbsp.	2.5
Egg, duck, raw, 1 whole egg	9.6
Egg, goose, raw, 1 whole egg	19.1
Egg, quail, raw, 1 whole egg	1.0
Egg, turkey, raw, whole, 1 egg	9.4

Egg, mix:
scrambled *(Durkee)*, .8-oz. pkg.	10.0
scrambled, with bacon *(Durkee)*, 1.3-oz. pkg.	13.0
omelet, Western *(Durkee)*, 1.3-oz. pkg.	5.0
freeze-dried, with real bacon *(Mountain House)*, 1/2 pkg.	10.0
freeze-dried, omelet, cheese *(Mountain House)*, 1/2 pkg.	9.0
freeze-dried, precooked, with bacon *(Mountain House)*, 1/2 pkg.	12.0
freeze-dried, scrambled, with butter *(Mountain House)*, 1/2 pkg.	8.0

Egg, substitute:
frozen, 1 cup	26.7
liquid, 1 cup	8.3
powder, 1 cup	2.6
(Fleischmann's Egg Beaters), 1/4 cup	0
99% real egg, with cheese *(Fleischmann's Egg Beaters)*, 1/2 cup	6.0

Egg breakfast, frozen:
omelet with cheese sauce and ham *(Swanson)*, 7 oz.	31.0
omelet, Spanish *(Swanson)*, 7 3/4 oz.	17.0
scrambled, and sausage, with hash brown potatoes *(Swanson)*, 6 1/4 oz.	33.0
Egg foo yung dinner mix *(La Choy)*, 1/6 pkg.	0

Egg roll, frozen:
chicken *(Chun King)*, .65-oz. roll with sauce*	1.5
chicken *(La Choy)*, 1 roll	1.0

---

* *Mustard packet prepared with water*

Egg roll, continued
lobster *(La Choy)*, 7/16-oz. roll	.7
lobster *(La Choy)*, 3-oz. roll	5.0
meat-shrimp *(Chun King)*, .65-oz. roll with sauce*	1.7
meat-shrimp *(Chun King)*, 2.6-oz. roll with sauce*	6.3
meat-shrimp *(La Choy, 15 pack)*, 1 roll	.7
meat-shrimp *(La Choy, 30 pack)*, 1 roll	.5
shrimp *(Chun King)*, .65-oz. roll with sauce*	1.4
shrimp *(La Choy)*, 7/16-oz. roll	.7
shrimp *(La Choy)*, 3-oz. roll	4.0

Egg roll entrée, frozen, Cantonese *(Van de Kamp's Chinese Classic)*, 5¼ oz. ... 5.0

Eggnog:
(Flav-O-Rich), 8 fl. oz.	17.0
(Land o' Lakes), 8 fl. oz.	15.0

Eggplant:
fresh, raw, whole, 1 lb.	.4
fresh, boiled, drained, cubed, 1 cup	.2
frozen, sticks *(Mrs. Paul's)*, 3½ oz.	12.0

Eggplant entrée, frozen, Parmigiana *(Mrs. Paul's)*, 11 oz. ... 34.0

Elderberry, fresh:
without stems, 1 lb.	2.3
1 cup	.7

Enchilada, frozen:
beef *(Hormel)*, 1 piece	5.0
beef *(Patio)*, 2 pieces	12.0
beef, and chili gravy *(Patio Boil-in-Bag)*, 2 pieces	12.0
cheese *(Hormel)*, 1 piece	6.0
cheese *(Patio)*, 2 pieces	5.0
cheese, and chili gravy *(Patio Boil-in-Bag)*, 2 pieces	5.0

Enchilada dinner, frozen:
beef *(Banquet International Favorites)*, 12 oz.	15.0
beef *(Patio)*, 13 oz.	23.0
beef *(Swanson)*, 15 oz.	23.0
beef *(Van de Kamp's Mexican Holiday)*, 12 oz.	15.0
beef, chili 'n beans *(Patio)*, 16 oz.	50.0
beef and cheese, chili 'n beans *(Patio)*, 16 oz.	40.0

* *Mustard packet prepared with water*

Enchilada dinner, continued

cheese *(Banquet International Favorites)*, 12 oz.	19.0
cheese *(Patio)*, 12¾ oz.	14.0
cheese *(Van de Kamp's* Mexican Holiday), 12 oz.	20.0

Enchilada dip *(Fritos)*, 3⅛ oz. 4.0

Enchilada entrée, frozen:

beef *(Banquet Family Entrees)*, 8 oz.	8.0
beef *(Swanson)*, 11¼ oz.	20.0
beef *(Swanson Hungry-Man)*, 16 oz.	35.0
beef *(Van de Kamp's* Mexican Holiday), 7½ oz.	15.0
beef *(Van de Kamp's* Mexican Holiday, 4 pack), 8½ oz.	15.0
beef and cheese, with rice and beans *(Van de Kamp's* Mexican Combination), 14¾ oz.	20.0
beef, shredded *(Van de Kamp's* Mexican Classics), 5½ oz.	10.0
beef, shredded, with rice and corn *(Van de Kamp's* Mexican Combination), 14¾ oz.	15.0
cheese *(Van de Kamp's* Mexican Holiday), 7½ oz.	15.0
cheese *(Van de Kamp's* Mexican Holiday, 4 pack), 8½ oz.	20.0
cheese, with rice and beans *(Van de Kamp's* Mexican Combination), 14¾ oz.	30.0
chicken *(Van de Kamp's* Mexican Holiday), 7½ oz.	10.0
chicken Suiza *(Van de Kamp's* Mexican Classic), 5½ oz.	10.0
Ranchero *(Van de Kamp's* Mexican Classic), 5½ oz.	15.0

Enchilada sauce, canned:

(Rosarita), 3 oz.	< 1.0
hot or mild *(Del Monte* Cooking Sauce), ½ cup	0
mix *(Durkee)*, 1.1-oz. pkg.	1.8

Endive, curly, fresh, trimmed, 18.9-oz. head 1

Endive, French or Belgian, fresh, 1 cup or 1.9-oz. head 1

Escarole, see "Endive, curly"

Eulachon (smelt), raw, meat only, 4 oz. 7.0

F

	fat grams
Falafel mix *(Casbah)*, 1 oz. dry	2.0
Fancy loaf *(Usinger's)*, 1 oz.	6.0
Fat, see specific listings	
Fat substitute *(Rokeach Neutral Nyafat)*, 1 tbsp. . . .	0
Fennel leaves, raw, 1 lb.	1.8
Fennel seed ground (all brands), 1 tsp.	.3
Fettuccine entrée, frozen:	
Alfredo *(Stouffer's)*, 5 oz.	20.0
and meat sauce *(The Budget Gourmet)*, 10 oz. . . .	10.0
primavera *(Stouffer's)*, 5 1/3 oz.	21.0

Field peas, with snaps, frozen *(Southland)*, 3.3 oz. — 1.0

Figs:

fresh, raw, 1 large . . . . — .2

candied, 1 oz. . . . . — .2

canned (all brands), 1/2 cup . . . . — < .1

dried, uncooked, 10 figs . . . . — 2.2

Filberts:

dried, shelled, 4 oz. . . . . — 71.0

dried, shelled, chopped, 1 cup . . . . — 72.0

dry-roasted, 1 oz. . . . . — 18.8

Finnan haddie, meat only, 4 oz. . . . . — .5

Fish, see specific listings

Fish, frozen:

cakes *(Mrs. Paul's)*, 2 cakes . . . . — 8.0

cakes, French fried *(Taste o' Sea* Crispy Light), 4 oz. . . . . — 8.0

cakes, thin *(Mrs. Paul's)*, 2 cakes . . . . — 15.0

fillets *(Gorton's* Crunchy), 2 fillets . . . . — 26.0

fillets *(Gorton's* Potato Crisp), 2 fillets . . . . — 24.0

fillets *(Van de Kamp's* Light & Crispy), 1 fillet . . . — 15.0

fillets, in batter *(Gorton's* Crispy), 1 fillet . . . . . — 16.0

fillets, in batter *(Mrs. Paul's)*, 2 fillets . . . . — 19.0

fillets, in batter *(Mrs. Paul's* Crunchy Light), 2 fillets . . . . — 16.0

fillets, in batter *(Mrs. Paul's* Supreme Light), 1 fillet — 10.0

fillets, in batter *(Van de Kamp's)*, 1 fillet . . . . . . — 10.0

fillets, breaded *(Certi-Fresh* Light & Crunchy), 5 oz. — 12.0

fillets, breaded *(Gorton's* Light Recipe), 1 fillet . . . — 7.0

fillets, breaded *(Mrs. Paul's* Crispy Crunchy), 2 fillets . . . . — 16.0

fillets, breaded *(Mrs. Paul's* Light & Natural), 1 fillet . . . . — 13.0

fillets, buttered *(Mrs. Paul's)*, 2 fillets . . . . — 13.0

fillets, country seasoned *(Van de Kamp's)*, 1 fillet — 10.0

fillets, tempura batter *(Gorton's* Light Recipe), 1 fillet . . . . — 12.0

kabobs, in batter *(Van de Kamp's)*, 4 oz. . . . . — 15.0

nuggets *(Taste o' Sea)*, 3 oz. . . . . — 15.0

nuggets *(Van de Kamp's* Light & Crispy), 2 oz. — 10.0

Fish, frozen, continued

nuggets, breaded *(Certi-Fresh Light & Crunchy)*,
    4.5 oz. 12.0
portions, in batter *(Taste o' Sea Batter Dipt)*, 3 oz.   13.0
sticks *(Booth)*, 4 oz. 8.0
sticks *(Gorton's Crunchy)*, 4 sticks 15.0
sticks *(Gorton's Value Pack)*, 4 sticks 11.0
sticks *(Gorton's Potato Crisp)*, 4 sticks 20.0
sticks *(Van de Kamp's Light & Crispy)*, 4 sticks   20.0
sticks, in batter *(Gorton's Crispy)*, 4 sticks 14.0
sticks, in batter *(Mrs. Paul's Crunchy Light)*, 4
    sticks 13.0
sticks, in batter *(Taste o' Sea Batter Dipt)*, 4 oz.   18.0
sticks, in batter *(Van de Kamp's)*, 4 oz. 15.0
sticks, breaded *(Certi-Fresh Light & Crunchy)*, 4.5
    oz. 14.0
sticks, breaded *(Gorton's)*, 4 sticks 9.0
sticks, breaded *(Mrs. Paul's Crispy Crunchy)*, 4
    sticks 10.0
Fish and Chips, frozen:
(Taste o' Sea Batter Dipt), 4 oz. fish and 4 oz. chips   30.0
in batter *(Van de Kamp's)*, 7 oz. 25.0
Fish dinner, frozen:
(Banquet American Favorites), 8¾ oz. 33.0
(Morton), 10 oz. 7.1
(Taste o' Sea), 9 oz. 23.0
cake *(Taste o' Sea)*, 8 oz. 20.0
and chips *(Swanson)*, 10½ oz. 28.0
and chips *(Swanson Hungry-Man)*, 14¾ oz. 36.0
English Country *(Taste o' Sea)*, 9 oz. 26.0
fillet *(Van de Kamp's)*, 12 oz. 10.0
fillet divan *(Lean Cuisine)*, 12⅜ oz. 9.0
fillet, Florentine *(Lean Cuisine)*, 9 oz. 9.0
fillet, jardiniere *(Lean Cuisine)*, 11¼ oz. 10.0
Italian, mild *(Taste o' Sea)*, 9 oz. 24.0
New England cheddar *(Taste o' Sea)*, 9 oz. 25.0
Fish entrée, frozen:
Dijon *(Mrs. Paul's Light)*, 8½ oz. 14.0
fillet and broccoli Florentine *(Freezer Queen)*, 9 oz.   9.0
fillet, Newburg sauce *(Wakefield)*, 8 oz. 5.0

Fish entrée, continued
Florentine *(Mrs. Paul's* Light), 9 oz.	5.0
Mornay *(Mrs. Paul's* Light), 10 oz.	10.0
Parmesan *(Mrs. Paul's* Light), 5 oz.	11.0
Fish flakes, canned, 1 oz.	.2

Fish flour:
from whole fish, 1 oz.	.1
from fish fillets, 1 oz.	< .1
Fish, gefilte (all brands), 1 average piece	1.0
Flounder, fresh, raw, fillets, 4 oz.	.9

Flounder, frozen:
(Gorton's Fishmarket Fresh), 4 oz.	1.0
breaded *(Van de Kamp's),* 5 oz.	15.0
fillets *(Booth* Light & Tender), 4 oz.	1.0
fillets *(Gorton's* Light Recipe), 1 fillet	11.0
fillets *(Taste o' Sea),* 4 oz.	1.0
fillets, in batter *(Mrs. Paul's* Crunchy Light), 2 fillets	17.0
fillets, breaded *(Mrs. Paul's* Crispy Crunchy), 2 fillets	15.0
fillets, breaded *(Mrs. Paul's* Light & Natural), 1 fillet	16.0
with lemon and herbs *(Booth* Light & Tender), 3 oz.	9.0
stuffed *(Gorton's Light Recipe),* 1 pkg.	14.0

Flounder dinner, frozen:
(Taste o' Sea), 9 oz.	27.0
fillet, with salmon mousse *(Le Menu),* 10½ oz.	18.0
provencale *(Taste o' Sea* Gourmet), 12 oz.	15.0

Flour (see also specific listings):
all purpose, white, 4 oz.	1.1
bread, white, 4 oz.	1.2
buckwheat, whole grain, 4 oz.	2.7
buckwheat, dark, 4 oz.	2.8
buckwheat, light, 4 oz.	1.4
cake or pastry, 4 oz.	.9
carob (Saint-John's-bread), 4 oz.	1.6
corn, 4 oz.	2.9
gluten (45%), 4 oz.	2.2
rye, dark, 4 oz.	2.9

Flour, continued

rye, light, 4 oz.	1.0
rye, medium, 4 oz.	1.9
self-rising, 4 oz.	1.1
soybean, full-fat, 4 oz.	23.0
soybean, low-fat, 4 oz.	7.6
soybean, defatted, 4 oz.	1.0
whole wheat, hard wheat, 4 oz.	2.3
Frankfurter wrap, refrigerator *(Wiener Wrap),* 1 wrap	2.0

Frankfurters and wieners:

(Armour Star Jumbo), 2-oz. link	18.0
(Armour Star Jumbo Lower Salt), 2-oz. link	15.0
(Ballpark), 1 link	16.5
(Eckrich, 12 oz.), 1 link	11.0
(Eckrich, 1 lb.), 1 link	13.0
(Eckrich Jumbo), 1 link	17.0
(Kahn's Jumbo Wieners), 2-oz. link	18.0
(Kahn's Wieners), 1.6-oz. link	14.0
(Oscar Mayer Little Wieners), 1/3-oz. link	2.6
(Oscar Mayer Wieners), 1.6-oz. link	13.4
(Usinger's), 3-oz. link	24.0
(Usinger's Wieners), 2-oz. link	16.0
bacon and cheddar *(Oscar Mayer* Hot Dogs), 1.6-oz. link	12.7
beef *(Armour Star),* 1.6-oz. link	13.0
beef *(Armour Star),* 2-oz. link	17.0
beef *(Armour Star* Jumbo), 2-oz. link	18.0
beef *(Armour* Jumbo Lower Salt), 2-oz. link	15.0
beef *(Ballpark),* 1 link	15.6
beef *(Eckrich,* 12 oz.), 1 link	10.0
beef *(Eckrich,* 1 lb.), 1 link	13.0
beef *(Eckrich* Jumbo), 1 link	17.0
beef *(Hillshire Farms* Old Fashioned), 1-oz. link	7.7
beef *(Hormel* Wieners, 12 oz.), 1 link	10.0
beef *(Hormel* Wieners, 1 lb.), 1 link	13.0
beef *(Kahn's),* 1.6-oz. link	17.0
beef *(Kahn's* Jumbo), 2-oz. link	17.0
beef *(Oscar Mayer),* 1.6-oz. link	13.3
beef *(Usinger's),* 3-oz. link	24.0
cheese *(Eckrich),* 1 link	17.0

Frankfurters and wieners, continued
cheese *(Oscar Mayer* Hot Dogs), 1.6-oz. link 13.2
cheese, nacho style *(Oscar Mayer* Hot Dogs), 1.6-
   oz. link 12.5
chili *(Hormel* Frank 'n Stuff), 1 link 15.0
meat *(Hormel* Wieners, 12 oz.), 1 link 10.0
meat *(Hormel* Wieners, 1 lb.), 1 link 13.0
smoked *(Hormel Range Brand Wranglers)*, 1 link 16.0
smoked, beef *(Hormel Wranglers)*, 1 link 15.0
smoked, with cheese *(Hormel Wranglers)*, 1 link 16.0
French toast, frozen, 2 slices:
(Aunt Jemima), 3 oz. 3.9
cinnamon swirl *(Aunt Jemima)*, 3 oz. 6.0
raisin *(Aunt Jemima)*, 3 oz. 4.2
French toast breakfast, frozen:
cinnamon swirl, with sausage *(Swanson)*, 6½ oz. 29.0
with sausage *(Swanson)*, 6½ oz. 26.0
Frog's legs, raw, whole, with bone, 4 oz. 9
Frosting, cake, ready-to-spread, 1/12 cake or can:
butter pecan *(Betty Crocker Creamy Deluxe)* 7.0
caramel pecan *(Pillsbury Frosting Supreme)* 8.0
chocolate *(Betty Crocker Creamy Deluxe)* 8.0
chocolate *(Duncan Hines)* 7.0
chocolate, Dutch or fudge *(Pillsbury Frosting
   Supreme)* 6.0
chocolate, milk *(Betty Crocker Creamy Deluxe)* 7.0
chocolate, milk *(Duncan Hines)* 7.0
chocolate, milk *(Pillsbury Frosting Supreme)* 6.0
chocolate, mint *(Pillsbury Frosting Supreme)* 7.0
chocolate chip *(Betty Crocker Creamy Deluxe)* . . . 7.0
chocolate chip *(Pillsbury Frosting Supreme)* 5.0
chocolate chip chocolate *(Betty Crocker Creamy
   Deluxe)* 8.0
chocolate fudge, dark *(Betty Crocker Creamy
   Deluxe)* 7.0
chocolate fudge, dark *(Duncan Hines)* 7.0
chocolate nut *(Betty Crocker Creamy Deluxe)* . . . 8.0
coconut almond *(Pillsbury Frosting Supreme)* 9.0
coconut pecan *(Betty Crocker Creamy Deluxe)* . . . 10.0
coconut pecan *(Pillsbury Frosting Supreme)* 10.0

Frosting, cake, ready-to-spread, continued

cream cheese *(Betty Crocker/Pillsbury)*	6.0
fruit flavors *(Betty Crocker Creamy Deluxe)*	6.0
fruit flavors *(Pillsbury Frosting Supreme)*	6.0
mocha *(Pillsbury Frosting Supreme)*	6.0
sour cream *(Betty Crocker Creamy Deluxe)*	8.0
sour cream, vanilla or white *(Betty Crocker/ Pillsbury)*	6.0
vanilla *(Betty Crocker Creamy Deluxe)*	6.0
vanilla *(Duncan Hines)*	7.0
vanilla *(Pillsbury Frosting Supreme)*	6.0
Fructose *(Estee),* 1 tsp.	0
Fruit cocktail, canned (all brands), ½ cup	< .1
Fruit, mixed:	
canned or frozen (all brands), ½ cup	< .1
dried (all brands), 2 oz.	< .1
dried, tropical, with nuts *(Carnation),* .9-oz. pouch	3.0
Fruit bars, frozen:	
all flavors *(Good Humor* Lite Stix), 1.5-oz. bar	0
all flavors *(Life Savers* Flavor Pops), 1 bar	0
banana *(Dole Fruit'njuice),* 2½-fl.-oz. bar	< .1
banana and cream *(Shamitoff's),* 3-fl.-oz. bar	3.0
blueberry *(Dole Fruit'ncream),* 2½-fl.-oz. bar	1.4
cherry, pineapple, or raspberry *(Shamitoff's),* 3-fl.- oz. bar	0
chocolate coconut *(Shamitoff's),* 2½-fl.-oz. bar	10.0
coconut *(Shamitoff's),* 3-fl.-oz. bar	8.0
lemon *(Shamitoff's),* 2½-fl.-oz. bar	< .1
lemon *(Shamitoff's),* 3-fl.-oz. bar	0
orange *(Dole Fruit'njuice),* 2½-fl.-oz. bar	< .1
orange or lemon *(Sunkist),* 3-fl.-oz. bar	0
orange, Mandarin *(Dole Fruit'njuice),* 2½-fl.-oz. bar	< .1
peach and cream *(Dole Fruit'ncream),* 2½-fl.-oz. bar	1.4
peach and cream *(Shamitoff's),* 2½-fl.-oz. bar	3.0
pineapple *(Dole Fruit'njuice),* 2½-fl.-oz. bar	< .1
piña colada *(Shamitoff's),* 2½-fl.-oz. bar	4.0
raspberry *(Dole Fruit'njuice),* 2½-fl.-oz. bar	< .1
strawberry *(Dole Fruit'ncream),* 2½-fl.-oz. bar	1.4
strawberry *(Dole Fruit'njuice),* 2½-fl.-oz. bar	< .1

Fruit bars, frozen, continued
    strawberry *(Shamitoff's)*, 2½-fl.-oz. bar 2
    strawberry *(Shamitoff's)*, 3-fl.-oz. bar 0
Fruit drink or juice, blended flavors and punch,
    canned mix* or frozen* (all brands), 6 fl. oz. . . . . < .1
Fruit and nut mix *(Planters)*, 1 oz. 9.0
Fruit rolls, all fruits (all brands), ½-oz. roll . . . . . . < .1

* *Prepared according to package directions*

G

	fat grams
Garden salad, canned:	
(Joan of Arc), ½ cup	< 1.0
marinated *(S&W),* ½ cup	0
Garlic, raw, 1 oz. or 5 cloves	.1
Garlic dip:	
(Kraft), 2 tbsp.	4.0
(Nalley), 1 oz.	12.6
Garlic powder:	
(all brands), 1 tsp.	< .1
with parsley *(Lawry's),* 1 tsp.	< .1

Garlic salt *(Lawry's)*, 1 tsp. . . . . < .1
Garlic spread, concentrate *(Lawry's)*, 1 oz. 1.6
Gelatin, unflavored *(Knox)*, 1 envelope 0
Gelatin dessert, mix,* all flavors (all brands), 1/2 cup 0
Gelatin drink, orange flavor *(Knox)*, 1 envelope 0
Ginger, candied, crystallized, 1 oz. 1
Ginger, ground (all brands), 1 tsp. 1
Ginger root, fresh, 1 oz. or 1/4 cup slices 2
Goose, domestic:
   raw, whole, ready-to-cook, 1 lb. 107.6
   roasted, meat and skin, 4 oz. 24.9
   roasted, meat only, 4 oz. 14.4
Gooseberry:
   fresh, 1 lb. 2.0
   canned (all brands), 1 cup . . . . < 1.0
Gourd, dishcloth (towel gourd):
   raw, 1 gourd, 13 1/4" long 4
   raw, 1" slices, 1 cup 2
   boiled, drained, 1" slices, 1 cup 6
Gourd, white-flowered:
   raw, 1 gourd, 17" × 3 1/8" 2
   raw or boiled, 1" cubes, 1 cup . . . . < .1
Gourmet loaf:
   (Eckrich Calorie Watcher), 1 oz. 1.0
   (Eckrich Smorgas Pac), 1 slice 1.0
Granola and similar snack bars, 1 roll or bar:
   almond *(Nature Valley* Bars) 5.0
   almond *(Nature Valley Clusters)* 4.0
   apple *(Nature Valley* Chewy) 5.0
   apple-cinnamon *(Nature Valley Clusters)* 4.0
   caramel *(Nature Valley Clusters)* 3.0
   caramel, chocolate chip *(Nature Valley* Chewy) . . . 6.0
   caramel nut *(Quaker Dipps)* 6.3
   carob chip, chewy *(Nature's Choice)* 3.0
   chocolate *(Nature Valley Clusters)* 3.0
   chocolate almond *(Nature Valley Dandy Bars)* . . . 8.0
   chocolate, dark or milk *(Nature Valley Dandy Bars)* 7.0
   chocolate chip *(Flavor Kist* Chewy) 5.0

* *Prepared according to package directions*

Granola and similar snack bars, continued

chocolate chip *(Nature Valley* Bars)	4.0
chocolate chip *(Nature Valley* Chewy)	7.0
chocolate chip *(Nature Valley* Clusters)	4.0
chocolate chip *(New Trail)*	10.0
chocolate chip *(Quaker Chewy)*	4.7
chocolate chip, plain or mint *(Quaker Dipps)*	6.4
chocolate graham and marshmallow *(Quaker Chewy)*	4.4
chunky nut and raisin *(Quaker Chewy)*	6.1
cinnamon *(Nature Valley* Bars)	5.0
cinnamon and raisin, chewy *(Nature's Choice)*	3.0
coconut *(Nature Valley* Bars)	7.0
honey and oats *(Quaker Chewy)*	4.4
honey and oats *(Quaker Dipps)*	6.1
oats and honey *(Nature's Choice)*	3.0
oats and honey *(Nature Valley* Bars)	5.0
peanut or peanut butter *(Nature Valley* Bars)	6.0
peanut butter *(Flavor Kist* Chewy)	5.0
peanut butter *(Nature's Choice* Chewy)	4.0
peanut butter *(Nature Valley Dandy Bars*/Chewy)	7.0
peanut butter *(New Trail)*	10.0
peanut butter *(Quaker Chewy)*	5.0
peanut butter *(Quaker Dipps)*	7.0
peanut butter honey crisp *(Peanut Butter Boppers)*	10.0
peanut butter peanut crunch *(Peanut Butter Boppers)*	12.0
peanut butter-chocolate chip *(Flavor Kist* Chewy)	5.0
peanut butter-chocolate chip *(Nature Valley* Chewy)	7.0
peanut butter-chocolate chip *(New Trail)*	10.0
peanut butter-chocolate chip *(Quaker Chewy)*	5.5
peanut butter fudge chip *(Peanut Butter Boppers)*	10.0
raisin *(Flavor Kist* Chewy)	5.0
raisin *(Nature Valley* Clusters)	3.0
raisin almond *(Quaker Dipps)*	6.4
raisin cinnamon *(Quaker Chewy)*	5.1
rocky road *(Quaker Dipps)*	6.3

Grape:

adherent skin, fresh, whole, 1 lb.	2.5
adherent skin, fresh, seeded or seedless, 1 cup	.9

Grape, continued
slipskin, fresh, seeded, whole, 1 lb. 9
slipskin, fresh, seeded, 1 cup 3
canned, seedless (all brands), 1/2 cup . . . . < .1
Grape drink or juice, canned or frozen* (all brands),
6 fl. oz. . . . . < .1
Grapefruit:
fresh, all varieties, 1/2 fruit, 3 3/4" diam. 1
fresh, sections, with juice, 1 cup 2
canned or chilled (all brands), 1/2 cup . . . . < .1
Grapefruit juice:
fresh, all varieties, 1 cup 3
canned or frozen* (all brands), 6 fl. oz. . . . . < .1
Grapefruit peel, candied, 1 oz. 1
Grenadine *(Rose's),* 1 fl. oz. 0
Ground cherry, fresh:
raw, without husks, 1 lb. 3.2
without husks, 1 cup 1.0
Grouper, meat only, 4 oz. 6
Guacamole dip (see also "Avocado dip") *(Nalley),* 1
oz. 12.1
Guava, fresh:
4-oz. guava 5
trimmed, 1 cup 1.0
Guava, strawberry, fresh:
whole, with stems, 1 lb. 2.3
trimmed, 1 cup 1.5
Guava juice cocktail, canned *(Ocean Spray),* 8 fl. oz. 1.0
Guava sauce, cooked, 1 cup 3
Guinea hen, fresh:
raw, whole, ready-to-cook, 1 lb. 23.2
raw, meat and skin, 4 oz. 7.3

* *Prepared according to package directions*

	fat grams
Haddock:	
fresh, raw, whole, 1 lb.	.2
fresh, raw, fillets, 1 lb.	.5
smoked, see "Finnan haddie"	
Haddock, frozen:	
(Gorton's Fishmarket Fresh), 4 oz.	1.0
in batter *(Van de Kamp's)*, 4 oz.	10.0
fillets *(Booth* Light & Tender), 4 oz.	1.0
fillets *(Gorton's Light Recipe)*, 1 fillet	10.0
fillets *(Taste o' Sea)*, 4 oz.	1.0

Haddock, frozen, continued

fillets *(Van de Kamp's* Light & Crispy), 2-oz. fillet	15.0
fillets, in batter *(Mrs. Paul's* Crunchy Light), 2 fillets	17.0
fillets, breaded *(Mrs. Paul's* Crispy Crunchy), 2 fillets	15.0
fillets, breaded *(Mrs. Paul's* Light & Natural), 1 fillet	14.0
with lemon butter sauce *(Gorton's* Light Recipe), 1 pkg.	11.0
portions, in batter *(Taste o' Sea Batter Dipt),* 3 oz.	12.0
sticks *(Taste o' Sea),* 4 oz.	12.0
sticks, with Romano cheese *(Booth* Light & Tender), 3 oz.	10.0
Haddock dinner, frozen *(Taste o' Sea),* 9 oz.	18.0
Halibut:	
fresh, raw, whole, 1 lb.	3.2
raw, fillets, 1 lb.	5.4
smoked, 4 oz.	17.0
Halibut, frozen:	
steaks *(Wakefield),* 8 oz.	1.0
in batter *(Van de Kamp's),* 4 oz.	15.0
Halibut dinner, frozen, teriyaki *(Taste o' Sea Gourmet),* 12 oz.	6.0
Halibut entrée, frozen, in white sauce *(Certi-Fresh),* 9 oz.	13.0
Ham, retail cuts, meat only:	
fresh, leg, roasted with bone, fat and skin:	
lean with fat, 3 oz.	17.6
lean with fat, 1 cup	29.0
lean (fat trimmed), 3 oz.	9.4
lean (fat trimmed), 1 cup	15.4
fresh, rump half, roasted with bone, fat and skin:	
lean with fat, 3 oz.	15.1
lean with fat, 1 cup	24.9
lean (fat trimmed), 3 oz.	9.1
lean (fat trimmed), 1 cup	14.9
fresh, shank half, roasted with bone, fat and skin:	
lean with fat, 3 oz.	18.8
lean with fat, 1 cup	31.0

Ham, fresh, shank half, continued

lean (fat trimmed), 3 oz.	8.9
lean (fat trimmed), 1 cup	14.7
cured, blade roll (shoulder), roasted:	
lean with fat, 13.3 oz. (1 lb. unheated)	88.3
lean with fat, 3 oz. (3.6 oz. unheated)	20.0
cured, picnic (shoulder), roasted with bone, fat and skin:	
lean with fat, 3 oz. (5.4 oz. unheated)	18.2
lean with fat, 1 cup	29.9
lean (fat trimmed), 3 oz. (7.3 oz. unheated)	6.0
lean (fat trimmed), 1 cup	9.9

Ham, boneless:

(Armour Lower Salt), 1 oz.	1.4
(Armour Star Speedy Cut), 1 oz.	2.6
(Oscar Mayer Jubilee), 1 oz.	2.9
(Realean), 1 oz.	1.1
slice *(Oscar Mayer* Jubilee), 1 oz.	1.1
steak *(Oscar Mayer* Jubilee), 2 oz.	2.2

Ham, canned:

(Armour Golden Star), 3 oz.	3.0
(Armour Star), 3 oz.	6.0
(Armour Star Nugget), 3 oz.	3.0
(Black Label), 4 oz.	7.0
(EXL), 4 oz.	4.0
(EXL Deli Ham), 4 oz.	6.0
(Holiday Glaze), 4 oz.	4.0
(Hormel Bone In), 4 oz.	15.0
(Hormel Cure 81), 4 oz.	8.0
(Hormel Curemaster), 4 oz.	5.0
(Light & Lean Boneless), 2 oz.	2.0
(Oscar Mayer Jubilee), 3 oz.	3.4
(Patrick Cudahy), 1 oz.	3.4
chopped *(Armour Star),* 3 oz.	21.0
chopped *(Hormel,* 12 oz.), 2 oz.	9.0
chopped *(Hormel,* 8 lb.), 3 oz.	21.0
chunk *(Hormel),* 6¾ oz.	20.0
deviled *(Hormel),* 1 tbsp.	3.0
roll *(Hormel),* 4 oz.	10.0
spiced *(Hormel),* 3 oz.	21.0

Ham, sliced and luncheon:

(Boar's Head Lower Salt), 1-oz. slice	.6
barbecue *(Light & Lean)*, 2 slices	2.0
black or red peppered *(Light & Lean)*, 2 slices . . .	2.0
boiled *(Boar's Head* Short Cut), 1 oz.	.6
chopped *(Armour)*, 1-oz. slice	6.0
chopped *(Eckrich* Calorie Watcher), 1 slice	2.0
chopped *(Eckrich Smorgas Pac)*, 3/4-oz. slice	2.0
chopped *(Hormel* Perma-Fresh), 2 slices	5.0
chopped *(Light & Lean)*, 2 slices	4.0
chopped *(Oscar Mayer)*, 1-oz. slice	4.3
cooked *(Eckrich* Calorie Watcher)	1.0
cooked *(Light & Lean)*, 2 slices	2.0
cracked black pepper *(Oscar Mayer)*, 1-oz. slice	.9
Danish *(Eckrich)*, 1-oz. slice	1.0
glazed *(Light & Lean)*, 2 slices	2.0
honey *(Oscar Mayer)*, 1-oz. slice	1.0
Italian style *(Oscar Mayer)*, 1-oz. slice	.9
loaf *(Eckrich)*, 1-oz. slice	6.0
minced, 4 oz.	23.4
smoked *(Carl Buddig)*, 1 oz.	2.8
smoked *(Eckrich* Calorie Watcher Slender Sliced), 1 oz.	3.0
smoked, cooked *(Light & Lean)*, 2 slices	2.0
smoked, cooked *(Oscar Mayer)*, 1-oz. slice	.9
sweet *(Eckrich* Calorie Watcher), 1 slice	1.0

Ham and cheese loaf:

(Eckrich), 1-oz. slice	5.0
(Light & Lean), 2 slices	6.0
(Hormel Perma-Fresh), 2 slices	7.0
(Oscar Mayer), 1-oz. slice	6.2
canned *(Hormel)*, 3 oz.	22.0
Ham and cheese patties, canned *(Hormel)*, 1 patty	18.0
Ham and cheese spread *(Oscar Mayer)*, 1 oz.	5.1
Ham and Swiss croissant, frozen *(Sara Lee Le San-Wich)*, 4-oz. piece	17.0

Ham crepes, frozen:

and asparagus *(Stouffer's)*, 6 1/4 oz.	18.0
and Swiss cheese *(Stouffer's)*, 7 1/2 oz.	26.0

Ham dinner, frozen:
  (Banquet American Favorites), 10 oz. 22.0
  (Morton), 10 oz. 4.5
  steak *(Le Menu)*, 9¼ oz. 12.0
Ham patties:
  (Patrick Cudahy Hamdingers), 1 patty 14.1
  canned *(Hormel)*, 1 patty 16.0
Ham salad spread:
  (Oscar Mayer), 1 oz. 4.2
  (The Spreadables), 1.9 oz. 8.0
Hamburger, see "Beef"
Hamburger entrée mix*:
  beef noodle *(Hamburger Helper)*, ⅕ pkg. 15.0
  beef Romanoff *(Hamburger Helper)*, ⅕ pkg. 16.0
  cheeseburger macaroni *(Hamburger Helper)*, ⅕
    pkg. 18.0
  chili tomato *(Hamburger Helper)*, ⅕ pkg. 14.0
  hash *(Hamburger Helper)*, ⅕ pkg. 15.0
  lasagna *(Hamburger Helper)*, ⅕ pkg. 13.0
  pizzabake *(Hamburger Helper)*, ⅙ pkg. 14.0
  pizza dish *(Hamburger Helper)*, ⅕ pkg. 14.0
  potato au gratin or Stroganoff *(Hamburger Helper)*,
    ⅕ pkg. 15.0
  rice Oriental *(Hamburger Helper)*, ⅕ pkg. 14.0
  spaghetti *(Hamburger Helper)*, ⅕ pkg. 15.0
  stew *(Hamburger Helper)*, ⅕ pkg. 14.0
  tacobake *(Hamburger Helper)*, ⅙ pkg. 13.0
  tamale pie *(Hamburger Helper)*, ⅕ pkg. 16.0
Hamburger seasoning, mix *(Durkee)*, 1-oz. pkg. 5.0
Hardee's:
  breakfast, 1 serving:
    bacon and egg biscuit, 4 oz. 25.7
    biscuit, 2.6 oz. 12.4
    biscuit, cinnamon 'n raisin, 2.7 oz. 16.2
    biscuit gravy, 4 oz. 9.5
    Canadian sunrise, 5.7 oz. 29.7
    country ham biscuit, 3.4 oz. 17.8
    egg, 1.2 oz. 6.3

* *Prepared according to package directions*

Hardee's, breakfast, continued

Hash Rounds, 2.5 oz.	13.0
sausage biscuit, 4 oz.	28.7
steak biscuit, 5 oz.	28.3

sandwiches, 1 serving:

bacon cheeseburger, 7.3 oz.	32.8
Big Deluxe, 7.4 oz.	28.9
cheeseburger, 4.1 oz.	12.8
cheeseburger, 1/4 lb., 6.5 oz.	28.2
chicken fillet, 6.8 oz.	26.2
Fisherman's Fillet, 7 oz.	20.1
hamburger, 3.4 oz.	15.3
hot dog, 4.3 oz.	21.9
Hot Ham 'N' Cheese, 5.3 oz.	15.0
Hot Ham 'N' Cheese, with lettuce and tomato, 6.6 oz.	19.9
Mushroom 'N' Swiss, 7.3 oz.	23.4
roast beef, 4.6 oz.	12.4
Turkey Club, 6.9 oz.	22.3

salads and side dishes, 1 serving:

chef salad, 12 oz.	16.1
French fries, small, 2.5 oz.	12.9
French fries, large, 4.3 oz.	21.9
shrimp 'n pasta salad, 11.75 oz.	28.9
side salad, 4.2 oz.	.1

desserts and shake, 1 serving:

apple turnover, 3.1 oz.	13.8
big cookie, 1.9 oz.	15.3
milkshake, 11.6 oz.	10.4

Hazelnut, see "Filberts"

Head cheese *(Oscar Mayer)*, 1-oz. slice	4.1

Hearts, fresh:

beef, lean only, braised, 4 oz.	6.5
calf, braised, 4 oz.	10.3
chicken, simmered, 4 oz.	9.0
hog, braised, 4 oz.	5.7
lamb, braised, 4 oz.	16.3
turkey, simmered, 4 oz.	6.9

Herbs, see specific listings

Herbs, mixed *(Lawry's* Pinch of Herbs), 1 tsp.	.5

110   *Corinne T. Netzer*

Herring:
Atlantic, fresh, raw, meat only, 4 oz.	12.8
Pacific, fresh, raw, meat only, 4 oz.	2.9
canned, plain, with liquid, 4 oz.	15.4
canned, in tomato sauce, 4 oz.	11.9
canned, kippered snacks (*King David Brand*), 3¼ oz.	12.0
pickled, Bismarck, 4 oz.	17.1
pickled, salted or brined, 4 oz.	17.2
smoked, bloaters, 4 oz.	14.1
smoked, hard, 4 oz.	17.9
smoked, kippered, 4 oz.	14.6
Hickory nuts, dried, shelled, 4 oz.	73.0
Hollandaise sauce mix:	
(*Durkee*), 1-oz. pkg.	14.0
(*French's*), 3 tbsp.*	4.0
Homestyle gravy mix:	
(*Durkee*), .7-oz. pkg.	2.0
(*French's*), ¼ cup**	1.0
Honey, strained or extracted, all varieties, 4 oz.	0
Honey loaf:	
(*Eckrich* Calorie Watcher), 1-oz. slice	2.0
(*Eckrich Smorgas Pac*), 1-oz. slice	1.0
(*Hormel* Perma-Fresh), 2 slices	5.0
(*Oscar Mayer*), 1 oz.	1.2
Honey roll sausage, beef, 1 oz.	3.0
Honeydew melon, fresh:	
1 wedge, 7" long × 2", 1/10 melon	.1
cubed, 1 cup	.2
Hominy, see "Corn grits"	
Horseradish:	
leafy tips, fresh, raw, chopped, 1 cup	.3
leafy tips, fresh, boiled, drained, chopped, 1 cup	.4
pods, fresh, raw or boiled, sliced, 1 cup	.2
prepared (all brands), 1 tbsp.	0
Horseradish sauce (*Sauceworks*), 1 tbsp.	5.0
Hot dogs, see "Frankfurters and wieners"	

* *Prepared according to package directions with water*
** *Prepared according to package directions*

Hot sauce, see "Pepper sauce"
Hull peas, purple, frozen (all brands), 3.3 oz. 1.0
Hummus mix *(Casbah)*, 1 oz. dry   0
Hushpuppy, frozen *(SeaPak)*, 4 oz. 13.0
Hyacinth beans, raw, trimmed, 1 cup 2

	fat grams
Ice, flavored, lemon or orange *(Häagen-Dazs),* 4 fl. oz.	0
Ice bars, all flavors (all brands), 1 bar	< 1.0
Ice cream, 1/2 cup, except as noted:	
butter almond *(Flav-O-Rich)*	8.0
butter pecan *(Flav-O-Rich/Good Humor)*	9.0
butter pecan *(Häagen-Dazs)*	29.2
butter pecan *(Lady Borden)*	12.0
carob *(Häagen-Dazs)*	17.9
cherry, black *(Good Humor)*	8.0
cherry vanilla *(Flav-O-Rich)*	6.0

cream, continued

chocolate *(Flav-O-Rich/Good Humor)*	7.0
chocolate *(Häagen-Dazs)*	17.2
chocolate *(Lady Borden)*	10.0
chocolate, with cookies *(Oreo* Cookies'n Cream), 3 fl. oz.	8.0
chocolate, Dutch *(Borden)*	6.0
chocolate, Dutch, almond *(Borden* All Natural)	9.0
chocolate, Swiss, almond *(Häagen-Dazs)*	20.0
chocolate chip *(Flav-O-Rich)*	7.0
chocolate chip *(Good Humor)*	8.0
chocolate chip *(Häagen-Dazs)*	18.0
coconut or coffee *(Flav-O-Rich)*	7.0
coffee *(Häagen-Dazs)*	17.2
coffee, Colombian *(Flav-O-Rich* Rich & Creamy)	15.0
cookies'N cream *(Flav-O-Rich)*	8.0
cookies & cream *(Häagen-Dazs)*	17.2
fudge ripple *(Flav-O-Rich)*	6.0
fudge royal *(Good Humor)*	6.0
heavenly hash *(Flav-O-Rich)*	8.0
honey *(Häagen-Dazs)*	18.0
macadamia nut *(Häagen-Dazs)*	19.2
maple walnut *(Häagen-Dazs)*	23.2
mint *(Oreo* Cookies'n Cream), 3 fl. oz.	8.0
mocha chip *(Häagen-Dazs)*	16.0
Neapolitan or moon pie *(Flav-O-Rich)*	7.0
peach *(Flav-O-Rich)*	6.0
peach *(Flav-O-Rich* Rich & Creamy)	7.0
peach *(Häagen-Dazs)*	16.0
pralines & cream *(Häagen-Dazs)*	16.0
rocky road *(Flav-O-Rich)*	8.0
rum raisin *(Häagen-Dazs)*	16.0
spumoni *(Flav-O-Rich)*	6.0
strawberries 'N cream *(Flav-O-Rich)*	6.0
strawberry *(Borden)*	5.0
strawberry *(Flav-O-Rich/Good Humor)*	6.0
strawberry *(Häagen-Dazs)*	16.0
strawberry cheesecake *(Flav-O-Rich* Rich & Creamy)	7.0
toffee fudge twirl *(Good Humor)*	7.0

Ice cream, continued

vanilla *(Borden/Borden* All Natural/*Flav-O-Rich)*	7.0
vanilla *(Good Humor)*	8.0
vanilla or vanilla chip *(Häagen-Dazs)*	17.2
vanilla, with cookies *(Oreo* Cookies'n Cream)	8.0
vanilla, French *(Borden* All Natural)	8.0
vanilla, French *(Lady Borden)*	9.0
vanilla fudge swirl *(Good Humor)*	8.0
vanilla, old-fashioned *(Flav-O-Rich* Rich & Creamy)	8.0
vanilla, slices *(Good Humor),* 1 slice	6.0
vanilla, Swiss, almond *(Häagen-Dazs)*	24.0
vanilla, Swiss chocolate almond *(Flav-O-Rich* Rich & Creamy)	10.0
walnut, black *(Flav-O-Rich)*	8.0
Ice cream, mix,* all flavors *(Salada),* 1 cup	19.0
Ice cream, non-dairy, ½ cup:	
chocolate chip or toasted almond *(Mocha Mix)*	9.0
Dutch chocolate or mocha almond fudge *(Mocha Mix)*	8.0
Neapolitan or strawberry swirl *(Mocha Mix)*	7.0
vanilla *(Mocha Mix)*	7.0
vanilla chocolate almond *(Mocha Mix)*	9.0
Ice cream bars, 1 bar:	
(Good Humor Fat Frog)	**7.0**
(Good Humor Heart)	12.0
(Nestlé Crunch)	13.0
(Oreo Cookies'n Cream)	15.0
almond, toasted *(Good Humor)*	8.0
assorted *(Good Humor Whammy)*	6.0
caramel, toasted *(Good Humor)*	9.0
chip crunch *(Good Humor)*	14.0
chocolate *(Eskimo Pie),* 3½ fl. oz.	12.0
chocolate *(Eskimo Pie* Jr.), 1¾ fl. oz.	7.0
chocolate, double *(Eskimo* Old Fashioned)	20.0
chocolate, double *(Eskimo Pie* Original)	10.0
chocolate eclair *(Good Humor)*	9.0
chocolate fudge cake *(Good Humor)*	16.0
chocolate malt *(Good Humor)*	13.0

---

* *Prepared according to package directions*

Ice cream bars, continued
　crispy *(Eskimo* Old Fashioned) . . . .　21.0
　crunch *(Eskimo Pie),* 3 fl. oz. . . . .　12.0
　crunch *(Eskimo Pie* Jr.), 1¾ fl. oz. . . . .　8.0
　(Eskimo Dietary), 2.5 fl. oz. . . . .　7.0
　mint *(Eskimo* Thin Mints) . . . .　10.0
　peanut butter caramel nut, chocolate coated
　　(Carnation Heaven) . . . .　13.0
　vanilla *(Eskimo* Old Fashioned) . . . .　21.0
　vanilla *(Eskimo Pie),* 3 fl. oz. . . . .　12.0
　vanilla *(Eskimo Pie* Jr.), 1¾ oz. . . . .　8.0
　vanilla *(Eskimo Pie* Original) . . . .　10.0
　vanilla *(Good Humor)* . . . .　11.0
　vanilla caramel nut, chocolate coated *(Carnation*
　　Heaven) . . . .　13.0
　vanilla fudge nut, chocolate coated *(Carnation*
　　Heaven) . . . .　14.0
Ice cream cones and cups, plain or flavored, cup or
　sugar cone *(Comet),* 1 piece . . . .　0
Ice cream nuggets, 5 pieces:
　chocolate, chocolate coated *(Bon Bons)* . . . .　12.1
　vanilla, chocolate coated *(Bon Bons)* . . . .　12.0
Ice cream sandwich, 1 sandwich:
　(Oreo Cookies'n Cream) . . . .　11.0
　cookie, all flavors *(Good Humor),* 2.7 oz. . . . . . .　11.0
　cookie, all flavors *(Good Humor),* 4 oz. . . . .　16.0
　vanilla *(Good Humor)* . . . .　5.0
Ice milk, ½ cup:
　chocolate, strawberry, or vanilla *(Borden* All
　　Natural). . . . .　3.0
　vanilla *(Knudsen's* Nice 'N Light) . . . .　2.0
Inconnu (sheefish), fresh:
　raw, whole, 1 lb. . . . .　19.4
　raw, meat only, 4 oz. . . . .　7.7
Italian style dinner, frozen *(Banquet International*
　Favorites), 12 oz. . . . .　26.0

	fat grams
Jack-in-the-Box:	
breakfast, 1 serving:	
bacon, 2 slices	6.0
breakfast Jack	13.0
Canadian crescent	31.0
eggs, scrambled, breakfast	44.0
pancake breakfast	27.0
sausage crescent	43.0
supreme crescent	40.0
sandwiches, salads and dinners, 1 serving:	
bacon cheeseburger supreme	46.0

Jack-in-the-Box, sandwiches, salads and dinners, continued

cheeseburger	15.0
chicken strips dinner	30.0
chicken supreme	36.0
club pita	8.0
ham and Swiss burger	38.5
hamburger	12.0
jumbo Jack	26.0
jumbo Jack with cheese	35.0
Moby Jack	25.0
mushroom burger	27.2
pasta seafood salad	22.0
shrimp salad	1.0
sirloin steak dinner	27.0
Swiss and bacon burger	43.0
taco, regular	11.0
taco, super	17.0
taco salad	24.0
nachos and side dishes, 1 serving:	
French fries, regular	12.0
nachos, cheese	35.0
nachos, supreme	40.0
onion rings	23.0
dressings, 1 serving:	
bleu cheese	18.0
buttermilk house dressing	29.0
1000 dressing	24.0
dessert and shakes, 1 serving:	
apple turnover	24.0
shake, chocolate or strawberry	7.0
shake, vanilla	6.0
Jackfruit, fresh, peeled and seeded, 4 oz.	.3
Jack mackerel, raw, meat only, 4 oz.	6.4
Jalapeño dip:	
(Fritos), 3⅛ oz.	4.0
(Kraft), 2 tbsp.	4.0
(Kraft Premium), 1 oz.	5.0
(Nalley), 1 oz.	11.5
Jams and preserves, all varieties (all brands), 1 tbsp.	0
Java plum, fresh, 3 average	< .1

Jelly, all varieties (all brands), 1 tbsp.   0
Jerusalem artichoke, fresh, pared, sliced, 1 cup . . . .   < .1
Jujube (Chinese date):
    fresh, whole, 1 lb.   .8
    fresh, without seeds, 4 oz. 2
    dried, whole, with seeds, 1 lb. 4.4
    dried, seeded, 4 oz. 1.2

	fat grams
Kale:	
fresh, raw, trimmed, 4 oz.	.8
fresh, boiled, drained, chopped, 1 cup	.5
frozen, chopped (all brands), 3.3 oz.	0
Kale, Scotch, fresh:	
raw, chopped, 1 cup	.4
boiled, drained, chopped, 1 cup	.5
Kasha, medium or whole *(Wolff's)*, 1/3 oz. dry or 3/4 cup cooked	0
Kentucky Fried Chicken:	
chicken, original recipe:	
breast, center, 3.8 oz.	13.7

Kentucky Fried Chicken, original recipe, continued

breast, side, 3.4 oz.	17.3
drumstick, 2.1 oz.	8.8
thigh, 3.4 oz.	19.2
wing, 2 oz.	12.3
chicken, extra crispy:	
breast, center, 4.2 oz.	20.9
breast, side, 3.5 oz.	23.7
drumstick, 2.1 oz.	10.9
thigh, 3.9 oz.	26.3
wing, 2 oz.	15.6
chicken, Kentucky nuggets, .6-oz. piece	2.9
Kentucky nugget sauces:	
barbecue, 1 oz.	.6
honey, .5 oz.	tr.
mustard, 1 oz.	.9
sweet and sour, 1 oz.	.6
chicken gravy, 2.8 oz.	3.7
side dishes, 1 serving:	
baked beans, 3.1 oz.	1.2
buttermilk biscuit, 2.6-oz. piece	13.6
cole slaw, 2.8 oz.	5.7
corn on the cob, 5 oz.	3.1
Kentucky fries, 4.2 oz.	12.8
mashed potatoes, 2.8 oz.	.6
mashed potatoes with gravy, 3 oz.	1.4
potato salad, 3.2 oz.	9.3
Kidneys, fresh:	
beef, raw, 8 oz.	15.2
beef, braised, 4 oz.	13.6
calf, raw, 8 oz.	10.4
hog, raw, 8 oz.	8.2
lamb, raw, 8 oz.	7.5
Kielbasa:	
(Hormel Kolbase), 3 oz.	19.0
(Hormel Polish Sausage), 2 sausages	14.0
beef or endless *(Hillshire Farms),* 3½ oz.	30.0
skinless *(Hormel* Kielbasa), ½ link	14.0
Kingfish (whiting), fresh:	
raw, whole, 1 lb.	6.0

Kingfish (whiting), continued
raw, meat only, 4 oz. 3.4
Kiwi, fresh:
whole, with skin, 1 lb. 1.7
1 large fruit 4
Knockwurst:
(Ballpark), 1 link 33.0
(Hillshire Farms), 1 oz. 8.3
beef *(Ballpark),* 1 link 31.2
Kohlrabi, fresh:
raw, pared, 4 oz. or 1 cup slices 1
boiled, drained, sliced, 1 cup 2
Kumquat, fresh:
whole, with seeds, 1 lb. 4
trimmed, with seeds, 4 oz. 1

L

	fat grams
Lake herring (Cisco), fresh:	
raw, whole, 1 lb.	5.4
raw, meat only, 4 oz.	2.6
Lake trout, fresh:	
raw, drawn, 1 lb.	16.8
raw, meat only, 4 oz.	11.3
Lake trout (siscowet), fresh:	
raw, under 6.5 lb., whole, 1 lb.	33.4
raw, under 6.5 lb., meat only, 4 oz.	25.6
raw, over 6.5 lb., whole, 1 lb.	88.8

Lake trout (siscowet), continued
raw, over 6.5 lb., meat only, 4 oz.	61.7

Lamb, choice grade, retail trim, meat only:
leg, boneless, roasted, lean with fat, 4 oz.	21.4
leg, boneless, roasted, lean (fat trimmed), 4 oz.	7.9
loin chops, broiled with bone:	
lean and fat, meat only, 4 oz.	33.3
lean (fat trimmed), 4 oz.	8.5
rib chops, broiled with bone:	
lean with fat, meat only, 4 oz.	40.4
lean (fat trimmed), 4 oz.	11.9
shoulder, boneless, roasted:	
lean with fat, 4 oz.	30.8
lean (fat trimmed), 4 oz.	11.3

Lamb's-quarters, fresh:
raw, trimmed, 1 lb.	3.6
boiled, drained, chopped, 1 cup	1.3

Landjaeger *(Usinger's),* 3-oz. link	26.0

Lard:
1 cup	205.0
1 oz.	28.3
1 tbsp.	12.8

Lasagna, canned:
(Hormel Short Order), 7½ oz.	14.0
(Nalley), 3½ oz.	5.0

Lasagna dinner, frozen:
(Dinner Classics), 10 oz.	17.0
(Swanson), 13 oz.	16.0
(Swanson Hungry-Man), 18¾ oz.	26.0
tuna *(Lean Cuisine),* 9¾ oz.	8.0
vegetable *(Le Menu),* 11 oz.	20.0
zucchini *(Lean Cuisine),* 11 oz.	7.0

Lasagna entrée, frozen:
(Banquet Family Entrees), 8 oz.	13.0
(Freezer Queen, 2 lb.), 8 oz.	9.0
(Stouffer's), 10½ oz.	13.0
(Swanson Main Course), 13¼ oz.	18.0
beef and mushroom *(Van de Kamp's* Italian Classic), 11 oz.	25.0
three cheese *(The Budget Gourmet),* 1 serving	17.0

Lasagna entrée, continued

cheese vegetable *(Dining Lite)*, 11 oz.	7.1
Florentine *(Light & Elegant)*, 11¼ oz.	5.0
Italian sausage *(Van de Kamp's* Italian Classic),	
11 oz.	25.0
with meat sauce *(The Budget Gourmet)*, 10 oz. . . .	10.0
vegetable *(Stouffer's)*, 10½ oz.	25.0
zucchini *(Dining Lite)*, 11 oz.	7.0

Leeks:

fresh, raw, 3 average	1.1
fresh, boiled, drained, 1 average leek	.3
fresh, boiled, drained, chopped, 1 cup	.2
freeze-dried, 1 tbsp.	< .1

Lemon, fresh:

whole, 1 lb.	1.3
peeled, 1 large, 2⅜″ diam.	.3

Lemon butter seasoning mix, for fish *(Durkee Roastin' Bag)*, .9-oz. pkg. 7

Lemon extract *(Virginia Dare)*, 1 tsp. 0

Lemon juice:

fresh, 1 cup	0
reconstituted or frozen (all brands), 2 tbsp.	0

Lemon peel, candied, 1 oz. 1

Lemon pepper *(Lawry's)*, 1 tsp. . . . . < .1

Lemonade, canned, frozen,* or mix* (all brands), 6 fl. oz. . . . . < .1

Lentil:

whole, dry, 8 oz.	2.5
split, without seed coat, dry, 8 oz.	2.0

Lentil pilaf mix, with rice *(Casbah)*, 1 oz. dry 0

Lettuce, fresh:

Boston or bibb, 1 head, 5″ diam.	.4
iceberg, trimmed, 1 head, 6″ diam.	1.0
romaine or loose leaf, untrimmed, 1 lb.	.9
romaine or loose leaf, shredded, 1 cup	.2

Lichee nuts:

raw, in shell, 1 lb.	1.2
raw, shelled, 6 average nuts	.2

---

* *Prepared according to package directions*

Lichee nuts, continued
dried, in shell, 1 lb.	2.9
dried, shelled, 4 oz.	1.4

Lime, fresh:
whole, 1 lb.	.8
pulp only, 2″-diam. lime	.1

Lime juice:
fresh, 1 cup	.3
reconstituted or frozen (all brands), 2 tbsp.	0

Limeade, frozen* or mix* (all brands), 6 fl. oz. · · · · < .1

Ling cod, fresh:
raw, whole, 1 lb.	1.2
raw, meat only, 4 oz.	.9

Linguine dinner, frozen, with clam sauce *(Lean Cuisine)*, 9⅝ oz. · · · · · · · · · · 7.0

Linguine entrée, frozen:
with pesto sauce *(Stouffer's)*, 4⅛ oz.	10.0
with scallops and clams *(The Budget Gourmet)*, 9.5 oz.	11.0
with bay shrimp and clams marinara *(The Budget Gourmet)*, 1 serving	15.0

Liquor, distilled (bourbon, gin, rum, Scotch, vodka, etc.), all proofs (all brands) · · · · · · · · · 0

Liver, fresh:
beef, raw, 1 lb.	17.2
calf, raw, 1 lb.	21.3
chicken, raw, 1 lb.	17.5
chicken, simmered, 1 liver, .7 oz.	.3
chicken, simmered, 1 cup	7.6
goose, raw, 1 lb.	45.4
hog, raw, 1 lb.	16.6
lamb, raw, 1 lb.	17.7
lamb, broiled, 4 oz.	14.1
turkey, raw, 1 lb.	18.0
turkey, simmered, 1 cup	8.3

Liver cheese:
(Oscar Mayer), 1⅜-oz. slice	10.0
(Usinger's Leberkaese), 1-oz. slice	6.0

---

* *Prepared according to package directions*

Liver loaf, *(Hormel* Perma-Fresh), 2 slices 13.0
Liver sausage, see "Braunschweiger"
Liverwurst:
  fresh or goose style *(Usinger's),* 1 oz. 8.0
  hessiche *(Usinger's),* 1 oz. 13.0
  hildesheimer *(Usinger's),* 1 oz. 7.0
  (Armour Star), 1 oz. 8.0
Liverwurst spread, canned *(Hormel),* ½ oz. 3.0
Lobster:
  northern, fresh, raw, in shell, 1 lb. 2.2
  northern, cooked or canned, meat only, 4 oz. 1.7
Lobster paste, canned, 1 oz. 2.7
Lobster newburg, frozen *(Stouffer's),* 6½ oz. 30.0
Loganberry, fresh, trimmed, 4 oz. 7
Longan:
  fresh, shelled and seeded, 4 oz. 1
  dried, shelled and seeded, 4 oz. 5
Loquat, fresh:
  whole, 1 lb. 6
  without seeds, 10 loquats or 4 oz. 2
Lotus seeds:
  raw, 1 oz. 2
  dried, 1 oz. or 1 cup 6
Luncheon meat (see also individual listings):
  (Oscar Mayer), 1-oz. slice 9.2
  (Spam 7 oz.), 1¾ oz. 14.0
  (Spam 12 oz.), 2 oz. 15.0
  (Usinger's), 1 oz. 7.0
  with cheese chunks *(Spam),* 2 oz. 16.0
  deviled *(Spam),* 1 tbsp. 3.0
  smoke flavored *(Spam),* 2 oz. 15.0
  spiced *(Armour),* 1-oz. slice 8.0
  spiced *(Armour Star),* 3 oz. 25.0
  spiced *(Hormel),* 3 oz. 26.0
  spiced *(Hormel* Perma-Fresh), 2 slices 9.0
  spiced *(Light & Lean),* 2 slices 9.0
  spiced, with chicken *(Armour Star),* 3 oz. 24.0
  spiced, loaf *(Grillmaster),* 1 slice 6.6
  turkey, loaf *(Louis Rich),* 1-oz. slice 2.6
Luxury loaf *(Oscar Mayer),* 1 oz. 1.2

	fat grams
Macadamia nuts:	
dried, shelled, 4 oz.	83.6
dried, shelled, 1 cup	98.8
oil-roasted, 1 oz.	21.7
Macaroni:	
dry, 8-oz. pkg.	2.7
plain, cooked 8–10 minutes, firm stage, 4 oz.	.6
plain, cooked 14–20 minutes, tender stage, 4 oz.	.5
Macaroni and beef, canned:	
(Nalley), 3 1/2 oz.	4.0

Macaroni and beef, canned, continued
in tomato sauce *(Heinz Mac'n'Beef)*, 7¼ oz. 8.0
Macaroni and beef dinner, frozen:
  (Morton), 10 oz. 6.1
  (Swanson), 12 oz. 14.0
Macaroni and beef entrée, frozen:
  with tomatoes *(Stouffer's),* 11½ oz. 16.0
Macaroni and cheese, canned:
  (Franco-American), 7⅜ oz. 5.0
  (Heinz), 7½ oz. 8.0
  elbow macaroni *(Franco-American),* 7⅜ oz. 6.0
Macaroni and cheese, frozen:
  (Banquet Casserole), 8 oz. 17.0
  (Banquet Family Entrees), 8 oz. 16.0
  (Freezer Queen, 2 lb.), 8 oz. 7.0
  (Freezer Queen), 8-oz. pkg. 6.0
  (Light & Elegant), 9 oz. 9.0
  (Morton Casserole), 20 oz. 19.9
  (Morton Casserole), 32 oz. 34.4
  (Stouffer's), 6 oz. 12.0
  (Swanson Main Course), 12 oz. 16.0
  pie *(Swanson),* 7 oz. 9.0
Macaroni and cheese, mix*:
  (Kraft Regular and Family Size), ¾ cup 13.0
  (Kraft Deluxe), ¾ cup 8.0
  shells *(Velveeta),* ¾ cup 10.0
  spiral *(Kraft),* ¾ cup 17.0
Macaroni and cheese dinner, frozen:
  (Morton), 11 oz. 7.3
  (Swanson), 12¼ oz. 15.0
Macaroni-cheese loaf:
  (Eckrich), 1 slice 6.0
  (Grillmaster), 1 slice 6.5
Macaroni salad:
  canned *(Joan of Arc),* ½ cup 13.0
  dairy pack *(Knudsen),* ½ cup 9.0
Mace, ground (all brands), 1 tsp. 6

---

* *Prepared according to package directions*

Mackerel:

Atlantic, fresh, raw, fillets, 1 lb. 55.3
Atlantic, canned, with liquid, 4 oz. 12.6
Pacific, fresh, raw, meat only, 4 oz. 8.3
Pacific, canned, with liquid, 4 oz. 11.3
salted, fillets, 4 oz. 26.5
smoked, meat only, 4 oz. 14.7

Mai tai drink mixer (all brands), 1 fl. oz. 0
Malt, dry, 1 oz. 5
Malt extract, dry, 1 oz. . . . . < .1
Mango, fresh:

1 mango, 10.6 oz. .6
sliced, 1 cup 5

Maple syrup, 4 oz. 0
Margarine, salted or unsalted:

hard or soft tub, 1 stick or 4 oz. 91.3
hard or soft tub, 1 tbsp. 11.0
hard or soft tub, 1 tsp. 3.8
whipped, 1 tbsp. 7.0

Margarine, imitation:

1/2 cup 45.0
1 tsp. 1.9

Margarita drink mixer (all brands), 1 fl. oz. 0
Marjoram dried (all brands), 1 tsp. . . . . < .1
Marmalade, all varieties (all brands), 1 tbsp. 0
Mayonnaise (all brands), 1 tbsp. 11.0
McDonald's:

breakfast, 1 serving:

biscuit, plain, 3 oz. 18.2
biscuit, with bacon, egg, cheese, 5.2 oz. 31.6
biscuit, with sausage, 4.3 oz. 30.9
biscuit, with sausage and egg, 6.25 oz. 39.9
Egg McMuffin, 4.9 oz. 15.8
eggs, scrambled, 3.5 oz. 13.0
English muffin with butter, 2.25 oz. 5.3
hash brown potatoes, 2 oz. 7.0
hotcakes with butter and syrup, 7.6 oz. 10.3
sausage, 2 oz. 18.6
Sausage McMuffin, 4.1 oz. 26.3
Sausage McMuffin with egg, 5.8 oz. 32.9

McDonald's, continued

sandwiches and chicken, 1 serving:

Big Mac, 7.1 oz.	35.0
cheeseburger, 4 oz.	16.0
Chicken McNuggets, 3.8 oz.	21.3
barbecue sauce, 1.1 oz.	.4
honey, .5 oz.	< .1
hot mustard sauce, 1.1 oz.	2.1
sweet & sour sauce, 1.1 oz.	.3
Filet-O-Fish, 5.1 oz.	25.7
hamburger, 3.5 oz.	11.3
Quarter Pounder, 5.7 oz.	23.5
Quarter Pounder with cheese, 6.6 oz.	31.6

French fries, regular, 2.4 oz. 11.5

desserts and shakes, 1 serving:

apple pie, 3 oz.	14.3
cherry pie, 3.1 oz.	13.6
cones, 4 oz.	5.2
cookies, chocolate chip, 2.4 oz.	16.3
cookies, *McDonaldland,* 2.4 oz.	10.8
milk shake, chocolate, 10.3 oz.	9.0
milk shake, strawberry, 10.3 oz.	8.7
milk shake, vanilla, 10.3 oz.	8.4
sundae, caramel, 5.8 oz.	10.0
sundae, hot fudge, 5.8 oz.	10.8
sundae, strawberry, 5.8 oz.	8.7

Meat, see specific listings

Meat, potted, canned (*Hormel* Food Product), 1 tbsp. 2.0

Meat-fish-poultry sauce, see "Steak sauce"

Meat loaf, mix,* with ground beef (*Bell's*), 4½ oz. 20.0

Meat loaf dinner, frozen:

(*Banquet American Favorites*), 11 oz.	27.0
(*Morton*), 11 oz.	17.3
(*Swanson*), 11 oz.	26.0

Meat loaf entrée, frozen:

(*Banquet Cookin' Bag*), 5 oz.	17.0
with tomato sauce (*Swanson*), 9 oz.	15.0
tomato sauce and (*Freezer Queen,* 2 lb.), 10.67 oz.	11.0

---

* *Prepared according to package directions*

Meat loaf gravy, mix *(Durkee Roastin' Bag)*, 1.5-oz.
pkg. 1.0
Meat loaf sauce, canned *(Hunt's Meatloaf Fixins)*,
2 oz. 0
Meat marinade, mix *(Durkee)*, 1-oz. pkg. 7
Meat seasoning *(Lawry's Natural Choice* for Meat),
1 tsp. 2
Meatball dinner, frozen:
  stew *(Lean Cuisine)*, 10 oz. 11.0
  Swedish *(Dinner Classics)*, 11½ oz. 28.0
Meatball entrée, frozen:
  with brown gravy *(Swanson)*, 8½ oz. 18.0
  Italian *(The Budget Gourmet)*, 1 serving 12.0
  Swedish *(The Budget Gourmet)*, 1 serving 39.0
  Swedish, in gravy *(Stouffer's)*, 11 oz. 25.0
  tomato sauce and *(Freezer Queen* Cook-in-Pouch),
  5 oz. 10.0
Meatball seasoning mix, Italian *(Durkee)*, 1-oz. pkg. .7
Meatball stew, canned:
  (Dinty Moore), 8 oz. 15.0
  (Nalley), 3½ oz. 7.0
Melon balls (cantaloupe and honeydew), frozen, 1 cup .4
Mettwurst *(Hillshire Farms)*, 1-oz. slice 8.6
Mexican dinner (see also specific listings), frozen:
  (Banquet Extra Helpings), 21¼ oz. 27.0
  (Banquet International Favorites), 12 oz. 18.0
  (Patio), 12¼ oz. 23.0
  (Patio Fiesta), 12¾ oz. 19.0
  (Swanson Hungry-Man), 22 oz. 46.0
  (Van de Kamp's Mexican Holiday), 11½ oz. 20.0
  combination *(Banquet International Favorites)*,
  12 oz. 17.0
  combination *(Patio)*, 11¼ oz. 28.0
  combination *(Swanson)*, 16 oz. 26.0
Milk, fluid, 8 fl. oz., except as noted:
  buttermilk, sweet cream 6.9
  buttermilk, cultured 2.2
  condensed, sweetened 26.6
  evaporated, skim 5
  evaporated, whole 19.1

Milk, fluid, continued

evaporated, canned *(Carnation/Pet)*, 1 fl. oz.	2.4
filled	8.4
lowfat, 1%	2.6
lowfat, 1%, with nonfat milk solids	2.4
lowfat, 1%, protein fortified	2.9
lowfat, 2%	4.7
lowfat, 2%, with nonfat milk solids	4.7
lowfat, 2%, protein fortified	4.9
skim	.4
skim, with nonfat milk solids	.6
skim, protein fortified	.6
whole, 3.3% fat	8.2
whole, 3.5% fat	9.0
whole, low sodium	8.4

Milk, dry:

buttermilk, sweet cream, 1 tbsp.	.4
nonfat, regular, 1 cup	.9
nonfat, instant, 1 envelope, 3.2 oz.	.7
whole, regular, 1 cup	34.2

Milk, goat, 8 fl. oz. — 10.1

Milk, imitation, 1 cup — 8.3

Milk, chocolate, dairy, 8 fl. oz.:

(Crowley)	7.0
(Flav-O-Rich/Farm Best)	8.0
(Flav-O-Rich/Farm Best, 3.5%)	9.0
Dutch *(Borden)*	8.0
lowfat *(Borden* Dutch Brand)	3.0
lowfat *(Crowley,* 1% fat)	3.0
lowfat *(Flav-O-Rich/Farm Best,* 1%)	3.0
lowfat *(Flav-O-Rich/Farm Best,* 2%)	5.0
lowfat *(Hershey's,* 2%)	5.0
lowfat *(Knudsen)*	4.0
nonfat *(Knudsen)*	0

Milk beverages, flavored, canned:

chocolate *(Borden Frosted)*, 8 fl. oz.	11.0
strawberry *(Borden Frosted)*, 8 fl. oz.	10.0

Milk, malted:

natural *(Carnation)*, 3 heaping tsp.	1.7
chocolate *(Carnation)*, 3 heaping tsp.	1.0

Millet, whole grain, 4 oz. 3.3
Mincemeat, see "Pie filling, canned"
Miso, see "Soybean, fermented"
Molasses, green or yellow *(Grandma's)*, 1 tbsp. 0
Mortadella *(Usinger's)*, 1 oz. 8.0
Mostaccioli and meat sauce entrée, frozen *(Banquet Family Entrees)*, 8 oz. 8.0
Muffins, 1 piece:
  blueberry or bran *(Thomas' Toast-r-Cakes)* 3.0
  corn *(Thomas' Toast-r-Cakes)* 4.0
  English *(Pepperidge Farm)* 2.0
  English *(Thomas')*, 2 oz. 1.4
  English *(Wonder)* 1.0
  English, cinnamon raisin *(Pepperidge Farm)* 2.0
  English, honey wheat *(Thomas')*, 2 oz. 1.1
  English, raisin *(Thomas')*, 2.1 oz. 1.5
  English sourdough *(Thomas')*, 2 oz. 1.4
  raisin *(Wonder Raisin Rounds)* 2.0
  sourdough *(Wonder)* 1.0
Muffins, frozen, 1 piece:
  apple spice *(Pepperidge Farm)* 8.0
  cinnamon *(Sara Lee Hearty Fruit)*, 2.5 oz. 8.0
  banana nut *(Sara Lee Hearty Fruit)*, 2.5 oz. 7.0
  blueberry *(Pepperidge Farm)* 7.0
  blueberry *(Sara Lee Hearty Fruit)*, 2.5 oz. 8.0
  bran with raisin *(Pepperidge Farm)* 7.0
  carrot walnut *(Pepperidge Farm)* 4.0
  chocolate chip *(Pepperidge Farm)* 8.0
  cinnamon swirl *(Pepperidge Farm)* 6.0
  corn *(Pepperidge Farm)* 7.0
  oatmeal and fruit *(Sara Lee Hearty Fruit)*, 2.5 oz. 9.0
Muffins, mix,* 1 piece:
  apple cinnamon *(Betty Crocker)*, 1/12 pkg. 4.0
  apple, spicy *(Duncan Hines)* 4.0
  banana-nut *(Betty Crocker)*, 1/12 pkg. 6.0
  banana nut *(Duncan Hines)* 5.0
  blueberry, wild *(Betty Crocker)*, 1/12 pkg. 4.0
  blueberry, wild *(Duncan Hines)* 3.0

---

* Prepared according to package directions

Muffins, mix, continued
    bran and honey *(Duncan Hines)* 4.0
    cherry, tart *(Betty Crocker)*, 1/12 pkg. 4.0
    corn *(Betty Crocker)*, 1/12 pkg. 5.0
    corn *(Dromedary)* 4.0
    corn *(Martha White)*, 2-oz. muffin 3.5
Mulberry, fresh:
    whole, 1 lb. 1.8
    10 mulberries 1
Mullet (see also "Sucker, mullet"), fresh:
    raw, whole, 1 lb.   16.6
    raw, meat only, 4 oz. 7.8
Mushroom:
    fresh, raw, untrimmed, 1 lb. 1.9
    fresh, raw, pieces, 1 cup 3
    canned (all brands), 1 cup . . . .   < .5
Mushroom, Shiitake, dried:
    1 lb. 4.5
    4 mushrooms, .5 oz. 2
    cooked, pieces, 1 cup 3
Mushroom gravy:
    canned *(Franco-American)*, 2 oz. 1.0
    canned *(Heinz* Home Style), 2 oz. 9
    mix *(Durkee)*, .7-oz. pkg. 1.0
    mix *(French's)*, 1/4 cup* 1.0
Mushrooms Dijon, in pastry, frozen *(Pepperidge
    Farm)*, 1 piece 15.0
Muskellunge, fresh:
    raw, whole, 1 lb.   5.6
    raw, meat only, 4 oz. 2.8
Mussels:
    fresh, raw, in shell, 1 lb. 3.2
    fresh, raw, meat only, 4 oz. 2.5
    canned, drained, meat only, 4 oz. 3.7
Mustard, prepared, 1 tsp., except as noted:
    (Heinz Pourable) 2
    (Kraft)   0
    (Mr. Mustard) 8

---

* *Prepared according to package directions*

Mustard, continued
> (Nalley) 6
> brown *(Heinz)* 4
> Chinese *(Chun King)*, 4.5-oz. jar 8.0
> Dijon *(French's)*, 1 tbsp. 2.0
> Dijon *(Grey Poupon)*, 1 tbsp. 1.0
> with horseradish or onion *(French's)*, 1 tbsp. 1.0
> horseradish *(Kraft)* 0
> horseradish *(Nalley)*, 1 tbsp. 9
> medford, spicy or yellow *(French's)*, 1 tbsp. 1.0
> mild *(Heinz)* 2

Mustard greens:
> fresh, raw, trimmed, 4 oz. 2
> fresh, raw, chopped, 1 cup 1
> boiled, drained, chopped, 1 cup 3
> frozen (all brands), 3.3 oz. 0

Mustard sauce:
> creamy *(French's Dip 'Um)*, 2 tbsp. 3.0
> hot *(French's Dip 'Um)*, 2 tbsp. 1.0
> hot *(Sauceworks)*, 1 tbsp. 2.0

Mustard seed, yellow (all brands), 1 tsp. 1.0

Mustard spinach (tendergreens), fresh:
> raw, 1 lb. 1.3
> boiled, drained, chopped, 1 cup 4

	fat grams
Nathan's:	
hamburger and roll	23.0
hot dog and roll	19.0
French fries, 7-oz. serving	31.0
Nectarine, fresh:	
whole, 1 nectarine, 2½″ diam.	.6
pitted, sliced, 1 cup	.6
New England Brand sausage *(Oscar Mayer)*, .82-oz.	
slice.	1.6
New England loaf *(Usinger's)*, 1 oz.	2.0

New Zealand spinach, fresh:

raw, whole, 1 lb.	.7
raw, chopped, 1 cup	.1
boiled, drained, chopped, 1 cup	.3

Noodle, egg, all varieties (all brands), 2 oz. dry 2.6

Noodle and chicken dinner, frozen *(Swanson),*
10½ oz. 9.0

Noodle, Chinese, canned:

(Chun King), 1 oz.	6.7
chow mein *(La Choy),* ½ cup	8.0
rice *(La Choy),* ½ cup	5.0

Noodle entrée, canned:

and beef *(Hormel* Short Order), 7½ oz.	14.0
and beef, in sauce *(Heinz),* 7½ oz.	8.0
and chicken *(Dinty Moore),* 7½ oz.	12.0
and chicken *(Heinz),* 7½ oz.	7.0
with chicken *(Nalley),* 3½ oz.	4.0
with chicken and vegetables *(Nalley),* 3½ oz.	4.0
with franks *(Van Camp's Noodle Weenee),* 1 cup	8.5
and tuna *(Heinz),* 7½ oz.	5.0

Noodle entrée, freeze-dried:

and chicken *(Mountain House),* 1 cup	5.0
with Stroganoff sauce and beef *(Mountain House),* ½ cup	6.0

Noodle entrée, frozen:

and beef *(Banquet Family Entrees),* 8 oz.	18.0
Romanoff *(Stouffer's),* 4 oz.	9.0

Noodle mix*:

all flavors *(Maruchan* Instant Lunch), 1 cup	14.0
Alfredo *(Lipton* Deluxe Noodles and Sauce), ½ cup	11.0
beef flavor *(Lipton* Noodles and Sauce), ½ cup	7.0
butter, butter and herb or cheese flavor *(Lipton* Noodles and Sauce), ½ cup	9.0
chicken flavor or chicken Bombay *(Lipton* Noodles and Sauce), ½ cup	9.0
fettuccine Alfredo *(Betty Crocker* International), ¼ pkg.	11.0
herb tomato *(Lipton* Shells and Sauce), ½ cup	6.0

---

* *Prepared according to package directions*

Noodle mix*, continued

garlic, creamy *(Lipton* Shells and Sauce), 1/2 cup	9.0
Parisienne *(Betty Crocker* International), 1/4 pkg.	9.0
Parmesano *(Lipton* Deluxe Noodles and Sauce), 1/2 cup	11.0
Romanoff *(Betty Crocker* International), 1/4 pkg.	11.0
sour cream and chive *(Lipton* Noodles and Sauce), 1/2 cup	9.0
Stroganoff *(Betty Crocker* International), 1/4 pkg.	11.0
Stroganoff *(Lipton* Deluxe Noodles and Sauce), 1/2 cup.	10.0
Nutmeg, ground (all brands), 1 tsp.	.8
Nuts, see specific listings	
Nuts, mixed, 1 oz.:	
dry-roasted *(Flavor House/Planters)*	14.0
dry-roasted *(Planters* Unsalted)	15.0
oil-roasted *(Planters* Salted or Unsalted)	16.0
oil-roasted *(Planters* Deluxe)	17.0
Nuts, tavern *(Planters),* 1 oz.	15.0

* *Prepared according to package directions*

	fat grams
Ocean perch, fresh:	
Atlantic (redfish), raw, whole, 1 lb.	1.7
Atlantic (redfish), raw, meat only, 4 oz.	1.4
Pacific, raw, whole, 1 lb.	1.8
Pacific, raw, meat only, 4 oz.	1.7
Octopus, raw, 4 oz.	.9
Oil (all brands):	
corn, cottonseed, safflower, sesame, or soybean, 1 cup	218.0
corn, cottonseed, safflower, sesame, or soybean, 1 tbsp.	13.6

Oil, continued
olive or peanut, 1 cup	216.0
olive or peanut, 1 tbsp.	13.5

Okra:
fresh, raw, fully trimmed, 4 oz. or 1 cup slices	.1
fresh, boiled, drained, 8 pods, 3″ × 5/8″ diam.	.1
fresh, boiled, drained, sliced, 1 cup	.3
frozen, whole or cut (all brands), 3.3 oz.	0

Old-fashioned drink mixer *(Holland House)*, 1 fl. oz. — 0

Old-fashioned loaf:
(Armour), 1 oz.	7.0
(Eckrich), 1 slice	6.0
(Eckrich Smorgas Pac, 12 oz.), 1 slice	4.0
(Eckrich Smorgas Pac, 1 lb.), 1 slice	6.0
(Oscar Mayer), 1-oz. slice	4.2

Olive loaf, *(Armour)*, 1-oz. slice — 5.0
(Eckrich), 1 slice	7.0
(Hormel Perma-Fresh), 2 slices	7.0
(Oscar Mayer), 1-oz. slice	4.4
(Usinger's), 1 oz.	5.0

Olives, pickled, canned, drained:
green, 2 oz.	7.2
green, small *(Lindsay)*, 10 olives	3.6
green, large *(Lindsay)*, 10 olives	4.9
green, giant *(Lindsay)*, 10 olives	8.3

ripe:
all sizes, pitted *(S&W)*, 3½ oz.	18.0
Ascolano or Manzanilla, pitted, 2 oz.	7.8
Ascolano, extra large *(Lindsay)*, 10 olives	6.5
Ascolano, mammoth *(Lindsay)*, 10 olives	7.7
Ascolano giant *(Lindsay)*, 10 olives	9.5
Manzanilla, small *(Lindsay)*, 10 olives	4.0
Manzanilla, medium *(Lindsay)*, 10 olives	4.7
Manzanilla, large *(Lindsay)*, 10 olives	5.5
Manzanilla, extra large *(Lindsay)*, 10 olives	6.5
Mission, pitted, 2 oz.	11.4
Mission, small *(Lindsay)*, 10 olives	5.9
Mission, medium *(Lindsay)*, 10 olives	6.9
Mission, large *(Lindsay)*, 10 olives	8.0
Mission, extra large *(Lindsay)*, 10 olives	9.5

Olives, ripe, continued
   Sevillano, pitted, 2 oz. 5.4
   Sevillano, giant *(Lindsay)*, 10 olives 6.5
   Sevillano, jumbo *(Lindsay)*, 10 olives 7.8
   Sevillano, colossal *(Lindsay)*, 10 olives 9.7
   Sevillano, supercolossal *(Lindsay)*, 10 olives . . . 11.6
  salt-cured, Greek style, 2 oz. 20.3
Onion, mature:
  fresh, untrimmed, 1 lb. 1.1
  fresh, raw, chopped, 1 cup 4
  fresh, boiled, drained, chopped, 1 cup 3
  canned, plain or cocktail, small (all brands), 1/2 cup 0
  canned, French fried *(Durkee)*, 1 oz. 15.0
  dry, minced, with green onion *(Lawry's)*, 1 tsp. . .2
  frozen, plain, whole or chopped (all brands), 4 oz. 0
  frozen, small, with cream sauce *(Birds Eye)*, 3 oz. 6.0
  frozen, rings, fried *(Moore's)*, 3 oz. 9.0
  frozen, rings, fried *(Mrs Paul's)*, 2 1/4 oz. 6.0
  frozen, rings, fried *(Ore-Ida)*, 2 oz. 7.0
Onion, young green (scallion), fresh:
  bulb and entire top, trimmed, 1 lb. 6
  bulb and entire top, chopped, 1 cup 1
Onion, Welsh, fresh, raw, trimmed, 4 oz. 5
Onion dip:
  creamy or French *(Kraft* Premium), 1 oz. 4.0
  French or green *(Kraft)*, 2 tbsp. 4.0
  French *(Nalley)*, 1 oz. 10.9
  French *(Thank You)*, 2 tbsp. 7.0
Onion gravy:
  canned *(Heinz* Home Style), 2 oz. 8
  mix *(Durkee)*, 1-oz. pkg. 5
  mix* *(French's)*, 1/4 cup 1.0
Onion powder, (all brands), 1 tsp. . . . . < .1
Onion salt (all brands), 1 tsp. . . . . < .1
Opossum, roasted, meat only, 4 oz. 11.6
Orange, fresh:
  California navels, 1 medium, 2 7/8" diam. 1

---

* Prepared according to package directions

Orange, continued

California navels, sections, without membranes,
1 cup 2
California Valencias, 1 medium, 2⅝″ diam. 4
California Valencias, sections, without membranes,
1 cup 5
Florida, 1 medium, 2¹¹/₁₆″ diam. 3
Florida, sections, without membranes, 1 cup 4
canned, mandarin (all brands), ½ cup . . . . < .3
Orange danish, refrigerated, iced, *(Pillsbury),* 1 danish   7.0
Orange drink, canned, frozen* or mix* (all brands), 6
fl. oz. . . . . < .1
Orange extract *(Virginia Dare),* 1 tsp.   0
Orange juice:
fresh, all varieties, 8 fl. oz. 5
canned or frozen* (all brands), 6 fl. oz. . . . . . . < 1.0
dehydrated, crystals, 1 oz. 5
Orange-grapefruit juice, canned (all brands), 6 fl. oz.   < .1
Orange Julius:
Orange Julius drink, small or regular 1.0
Orange Julius drink, large, 20 fl. oz. 2.0
piñata colada drink, small or regular 1.0
piñata colada drink, large, 20 fl. oz. 2.0
raspberry cream supreme drink, small, 12 fl. oz.   16.0
raspberry cream drink, regular, 16 fl. oz. 23.0
raspberry cream drink, large, 20 fl. oz. 30.0
strawberry *Julius* drink, small, 12 fl. oz. . . . . . . < 1.0
strawberry *Julius* drink, regular, 16 fl. oz. 1.0
strawberry *Julius* drink, large, 20 fl. oz. 1.0
tropical cream supreme drink, small, 12 fl. oz. . . .   18.0
tropical cream supreme drink, regular, 16 fl. oz.   25.0
tropical cream supreme drink, large, 20 fl. oz. . . .   32.0
Orange peel, candied, 1 oz. 1
Orange-pineapple juice, canned (all brands), 6 fl. oz.   < .1
Oregano, ground (all brands), 1 tsp. 2
Oysters:
eastern, fresh, raw, in shell, 1 lb. 8
eastern, fresh, raw, meat only, 8 oz 4.1

---

* *Prepared according to package directions*

Oysters, continued
Pacific/western, fresh, meat only, 8 oz. 5.0
canned, with liquid, 4 oz. 2.5
canned *(Louisiana Brand)*, 4 oz. 4.0
canned, whole *(S&W* Fancy), 2 oz. 4.0

	fat grams
P&P Loaf *(Grillmaster)*, 1 slice	6.5
Pancake, frozen:	
(Aunt Jemima Original), 3 cakes, 4″	3.7
(Pillsbury Microwave), 3 cakes	6.0
blueberry *(Aunt Jemima)*, 3 cakes, 4″	4.0
buttermilk *(Aunt Jemima)*, 3 cakes, 4″	3.7
buttermilk *(Pillsbury* Microwave), 3 cakes	3.0
Pancake batter, frozen:	
plain or blueberry *(Aunt Jemima)*, 3 cakes, 4″ . . .	1.6
buttermilk *(Aunt Jemima)*, 3 cakes, 4″	1.5

Pancake and waffle mix:

(Aunt Jemima Complete), 1/2 cup	3.6
(Aunt Jemima Original), 1/4 cup	.6
(Hungry Jack Extra Lights), 3 cakes,* 4"	7.0
(Hungry Jack Extra Lights Complete), 3 cakes,* 4"	2.0
(Hungry Jack Panshakes), 3 cakes,* 4"	6.0
blueberry *(Hungry Jack)*, 3 cakes,* 4"	7.0
blueberry *(Hungry Jack* Complete), 3 cakes,* 4"	3.0
buttermilk *(Aunt Jemima)*, 1/3 cup	.7
buttermilk *(Aunt Jemima* Complete), 1/2 cup	3.0
buttermilk *(Betty Crocker)*, 3 cakes,* 4"	10.0
buttermilk *(Betty Crocker* Complete), 3 cakes,* 4"	3.0
buttermilk *(Hungry Jack)*, 3 cakes,* 4"	11.0
buttermilk *(Hungry Jack* Complete), 3 cakes,* 4"	1.0
buckwheat *(Aunt Jemima)*, 1/4 cup	.8
whole wheat *(Aunt Jemima)*, 1/3 cup	.5

Pancake breakfast, frozen:

and blueberry sauce *(Swanson)*, 7 oz.	9.0
and sausage *(Swanson)*, 6 oz.	22.0
with strawberries *(Swanson)*, 7 oz.	8.0

Pancake syrup (all brands), 2 tbsp. 0

Pancreas, raw:

beef, fat, 4 oz.	32.9
beef, medium-fat, 4 oz.	28.4
beef, lean, 4 oz.	8.3
calf, 4 oz.	10.0

Papaw, North American type, fresh, peeled and
seeded, 4 oz. 1.0

Papaya nectar, canned, 1 cup 4

Papaya, fresh:

1-lb. papaya, 3 1/2" diam. × 5 1/8"	.4
peeled and seeded, 4 oz. or 1 cup cubes	.2

Paprika, ground (all brands), 1 tsp. 3

Parsley:

fresh, 1 lb.	1.3
fresh, chopped, 1 cup	.2
dried or freeze-dried (all brands), 1 tbsp.	< .1

---

* *Prepared according to package directions*

Parsnips, fresh:
whole, 1 lb.	1.2
boiled, drained, 9″ parsnip or 1 cup slices	.5

Passion fruit (purple granadilla):
raw, whole, 1 average fruit	.1
raw, shelled, 4 oz.	.8

Passion fruit juice, fresh:
purple, 1 cup	.1
yellow, 1 cup	.4

Pasta (spaghetti, vermicelli, etc.), plain:
uncooked, 8-oz. pkg.	2.7
cooked firm, 8–10 minutes, 4 oz.	.6
cooked tender, 14–20 minutes, 4 oz.	.5

Pasta, canned:
(Franco-American UFOs), 7½ oz.	3.0
with meatballs *(Franco-American* UFOs with Meteors), 7½ oz.	9.0

Pasta shells, frozen:
and beef *(The Budget Gourmet),* 1 serving	14.0
and veal with vegetables *(Freezer Queen* Single Serve), 10 oz.	8.0
stuffed with beef and spinach, tomato sauce *(Stouffer's),* 9 oz.	12.0
stuffed with cheese, meat sauce *(Stouffer's),* 9 oz.	16.0
stuffed with chicken, cheese sauce *(Stouffer's),* 9 oz.	24.0

Pastini, dry:
carrot or spinach, 8 oz.	3.6
egg, 8 oz.	9.3

Pastrami:
(Eckrich Calorie Watcher Slender Sliced), 1-oz. slice	2.0
(Oscar Mayer), ¾-oz. slice	.5
smoked *(Carl Buddig),* 1 oz.	2.0

Pâté, canned or in jars:
chicken liver, 1 oz.	3.7
chicken liver, 1 tbsp.	1.7
de foie gras or smoked goose liver, 1 oz.	12.4
de foie gras or smoked goose liver, 1 tbsp.	5.7
liver, 1 oz.	7.9
liver, 1 tbsp.	3.6

Patty shell, frozen *(Pepperidge Farm),* 1 shell 15.0

Pea pods, Chinese, see "Peas, edible podded"

Peach:

fresh, 1 peach, 2½″ diam., 4 per lb.	.1
fresh, pared, sliced, 1 cup	.2
canned, freeze-dried or frozen (all brands), ½ cup	< .1
dehydrated, sulfured, uncooked, 8 oz.	2.3
dehydrated, sulfured, cooked, 8 oz. or 1 cup	1.0
dried, sulfured, uncooked, 8 oz.	1.7
dried, sulfured, uncooked, 10 halves	1.0
dried, cooked, sweetened, 8 oz.	.5

Peach butter *(Smucker's)*, 2 tsp. 0

Peach nectar, canned (all brands), 6 fl. oz. 0

Peach turnover, frozen *(Pepperidge Farm)*, 1 piece 19.0

Peanut:

(Beer Nuts), 1 oz.	14.0
(Flavor House Honey Roasted), 1 oz.	11.0
(Planters Honey Roast), 1 oz.	13.0
(Planters Sweet 'N Crunchy), 1 oz.	8.0
dry-roasted *(Eagle Honey Roast)*, 1 oz.	13.0
dry-roasted *(Flavor House/Frito-Lay's/Planters)*, 1 oz.	14.0
dry-roasted *(Planters* Lite), ⅔ oz.	6.0
dry-roasted *(Planters* Unsalted), 1 oz.	15.0
oil-roasted *(Eagle Honey Roast)*, 1 oz.	13.0
oil-roasted *(Eagle* Salted), 1 oz.	14.0
oil-roasted *(Frito Lay's)*, 1 oz.	15.0
oil-roasted *(Frito-Lay's* Salted in the Shell), 1 oz.	14.0
oil-roasted *(Planters/Planters* Cocktail), 1 oz.	15.0
oil-roasted, redskin *(Planters)*, 1 oz.	15.0
roasted in shell *(Planters)*, 1 oz.	14.0
Spanish *(Planters)*, 1 oz.	15.0
Spanish dry-roasted *(Planters)*, 1 oz.	14.0
Spanish, raw *(Planters)*, 1 oz.	12.0

Peanut butter, 2 tbsp.:

(Smucker's Natural)	16.0
(Smucker's Natural Unsalted)	17.0
creamy or crunchy *(Jif/Peter Pan)*	16.0
creamy or crunchy *(Peter Pan* Sodium & Sugar Free)	17.0
creamy or crunchy *(Skippy)*	17.0

Peanut butter, continued

with grape jam *(Smucker's Goober Grape)*	10.0
Peanut flour, defatted, 1 cup	.3

Pear:

fresh, whole, 1 lb.	1.7
fresh, Bartlett, 1 pear, 2½" diam. × 3½"	.7
candied, 1 oz.	.2
canned (all brands), ½ cup	< .1
dried, sulfured, uncooked, 8 oz.	1.4
dried, sulfured, uncooked, 10 halves	1.1
dried, cooked, sweetened, halves, 1 cup	.8
Pear nectar, canned (all brands), 6 fl. oz.	< .1
Peas, edible podded, frozen, Chinese *(La Choy)*, ½ pkg.	< 1.0

Peas, green, immature:

fresh, raw, shelled, 8 oz.	.9
fresh, boiled, drained, 1 cup	.3
canned or frozen, plain (all brands), ½ cup	< .1
frozen, in butter sauce, early *(LeSueur)*, ½ cup	2.0
frozen, in butter sauce, sweet *(Green Giant)*, ½ cup	1.0
frozen, in cheese sauce *(Birds Eye)*, 5 oz.	5.0
frozen, with cream sauce *(Birds Eye)*, 2.6 oz.	7.0
frozen, in cream sauce *(Green Giant)*, ½ cup	4.0
frozen, with onions and carrots, in butter sauce *(Green Giant)*, ½ cup	3.0
frozen, with pea pods and water chestnuts, in butter sauce *(Green Giant)*, ½ cup	2.0
frozen, and potatoes, in cream sauce *(Birds Eye)*, 2.6 oz.	7.0

Peas, mature seeds, dry:

whole, 8 oz.	2.9
split, without seed coat, 8 oz.	2.3
split, without seed coat, cooked, 8 oz.	.7
Peas and carrots, canned or frozen (all brands), ½ cup	< .1

Pecans:

(Planters), 1 oz.	20.0
dried, shelled, 10 large nuts	6.2
dried, shelled, chopped, 1 cup	80.5
dry-roasted, shelled, 1 oz.	18.4

Pecans, continued
  oil-roasted, shelled, 1 oz. 20.2
  oil-roasted *(Eagle Honey Roast)*, 1 oz. 19.0
Pepper, seasoning:
  black or white (all brands), 1 tsp. 1
  red or cayenne (all brands), 1 tsp. 3
  seasoned *(Lawry's)*, 1 tsp. . . . . < .1
Pepper, banana or cherry *(Vlasic)*, 1 oz. 0
Pepper, chili, green and red:
  raw, whole, 1 lb. 7
  raw, without seeds, chopped, 1/2 cup 2
  canned, with liquid, chopped, 1/2 cup 1
Pepper, green and red, sweet:
  fresh, raw, whole, 1 lb. 1.7
  fresh, raw, 1 pepper, 3¾" long × 3" diam. 3
  fresh, raw, chopped, 1 cup 5
  fresh, boiled, drained, 3¾" pepper 2
  frozen, plain (all brands), 2 oz. . . . . < .1
Pepper, green, stuffed, dinner, frozen:
  (Dinner Classics), 12 oz. 16.0
Pepper, green, stuffed, entrée, frozen:
  with beef *(Stouffer's)*, 7¾ oz. 11.0
Pepper, jalapeño, canned, with liquid, chopped,
  1/2 cup 4
Pepper, pepperoncini, canned *(Vlasic* Greek), 1 oz. . 0
Pepper sauce:
  hot *(Frank's)*, 1/2 tsp. 1.0
  hot *(Tabasco)*, 1/4 tsp. 0
Peppered loaf:
  (Eckrich Calorie Watcher), 1-oz. slice 2.0
  (Oscar Mayer), 1-oz. slice 2.1
  (Usinger's), 1 oz. 5.0
Pepperoni:
  (Hormel), 1 oz. 13.0
  (Hormel Leoni Brand), 1 oz. 12.0
  (Hormel Perma-Fresh), 2 slices 7.0
  (Hormel Rosa/Rosa Grande), 1 oz. 13.0
  chunk *(Hormel)*, 1 oz. 12.0
  sliced or Italian style *(Armour)*, 1 oz. 11.0
  sliced *(Eckrich)*, 2 oz. 24.0

Pepperoni, continued
bits, canned *(Hormel)*, 1 tbsp.	3.0

Perch, fresh, raw:
ocean, see "Ocean perch"
white, whole, 1 lb.	6.5
white, meat only, 4 oz.	4.5
yellow, whole, 1 lb.	1.6
yellow, meat only, 4 oz.	1.0

Perch, frozen:
in batter *(Van de Kamp's)*, 4 oz.	15.0
fillets *(Booth* Light & Tender), 4 oz.	2.0
fillets *(Taste o' Sea)*, 4 oz.	3.0
fillets *(Van de Kamp's* Light & Crispy), 2-oz. piece	10.0
fillets, breaded *(Certi-Fresh* Light & Crunchy), 5 oz.	12.0
fillets, breaded *(Mrs. Paul's)*, 2 fillets	17.0
ocean *(Gorton's Fishmarket Fresh)*, 4 oz.	2.0

Perch dinner, frozen *(Taste o' Sea)*, 9 oz. . . . . — 25.0

Persimmons, fresh:
Japanese or kaki, whole, 1 lb.	.7
Japanese or kaki, 1 average, 2½" diam.	.3
Japanese or kaki, dried, 4 oz.	.7
native, whole, 1 lb.	1.5
native, 1 average fruit	.1

Pheasant, raw:
whole, ready-to-cook, 1 lb.	20.5
meat only, 4 oz.	7.7

Picante sauce, canned or in jars:
(Tostitos), 3⅛ oz.	1.0
(Ortega Salsa), 1 oz.	.1
hot or hot and chunky *(Del Monte)*, ¼ cup	0

Pickerel, chain, raw:
whole, 1 lb.	1.2
meat only, 4 oz.	.6

Pickle, cucumber:
all varieties (all brands), 2 oz.	< .3
relish, all varieties (all brands), 2 oz.	< .3

Pickle loaf:
(Hormel Perma-Fresh), 2 slices	7.0
(Light & Lean), 2 slices	6.0
beef *(Eckrich Smorgas Pac)*, 1 slice	5.0

Pickle and pimento loaf:
(Armour), 1-oz. slice 7.0
(Oscar Mayer), 1-oz. slice 4.4
Picnic loaf *(Oscar Mayer)*, 1-oz. slice 4.4
Pie, frozen, 1 serving:
apple *(Banquet)*, 3¹/₃ oz. 11.0
apple *(Pet-Ritz)*, 4¹/₃ oz. 12.0
banana cream *(Banquet)*, 2¹/₃ oz. 10.0
banana cream *(Pet-Ritz)*, 2¹/₃ oz. 9.0
blackberry or blueberry *(Banquet)*, 3¹/₃ oz. 11.0
blueberry *(Pet-Ritz)*, 4¹/₃ oz. 12.0
cherry *(Banquet)*, 3¹/₃ oz. 11.0
cherry *(Pet-Ritz)*, 4¹/₃ oz. 12.0
chocolate cream *(Banquet)*, 2¹/₃ oz. 10.0
chocolate cream *(Pet-Ritz)*, 2¹/₃ oz. 8.0
coconut cream *(Banquet)*, 2¹/₃ oz. 11.0
coconut cream *(Pet-Ritz)*, 2¹/₃ oz. 8.0
custard, egg *(Pet-Ritz)*, 4 oz. 8.0
lemon cream *(Banquet/Pet-Ritz)*, 2¹/₃ oz. 9.0
mince meat *(Banquet)*, 3¹/₃ oz. 11.0
mince meat *(Pet-Ritz)*, 4 oz. 9.0
peach *(Banquet)*, 3¹/₃ oz. 11.0
peach *(Pet-Ritz)*, 4¹/₃ oz. 12.0
pumpkin *(Banquet)*, 3¹/₃ oz. 8.0
pumpkin *(Pet-Ritz)*, 4¹/₃ oz. 9.0
strawberry cream *(Banquet/Pet-Ritz)*, 2¹/₃ oz. . . . 9.0
Pie, mix,* chocolate mint *(Royal No Bake)*, ¹/₈ pie 15.0
Pie, snack, 1 pie:
apple *(Drake's)* 10.0
apple *(Hostess)* 20.0
apple *(Tastykake)* 14.2
apple, French *(Tastykake)* 11.4
berry or blueberry *(Hostess)* 20.0
blueberry *(Tastykake)* 11.4
cherry *(Hostess)* 20.0
cherry *(Tastykake)* 9.5
coconut creme *(Tastykake)* 32.1
lemon *(Hostess)* 22.0

---

* *Prepared according to package directions*

Pie, snack, continued
lemon *(Tastykake)*	14.6
peach *(Hostess)*	20.0
peach *(Tastykake)*	13.1
pineapple *(Tastykake)*	12.1
pumpkin *(Tastykake)*	11.5
strawberry *(Hostess)*	14.0
(Tastykake Tasty Klair)	16.6

Pie crust mix:
(Flako), 1 oz.	3.4
(General Mills), 1/16 packet	8.0
(Pillsbury), 1/6 of 2 crust pie*	17.0

Pie crust shell, frozen or refrigerated:
(Pet-Ritz), .8 oz. or 1/6 pie	7.0
(Pillsbury All Ready), 1/8 of pie	15.0
deep dish *(Pet-Ritz)*, 1 oz. or 1/6 pie	12.0

Pie crust stick:
(General Mills), 1/8 stick	8.0
(Pillsbury), 1/6 of 2 crust pie	17.0

Pie filling, canned:
all fruits, except banana and lemon *(Comstock/ Thank You)*, 3.5 oz.	0
banana *(Comstock)*, 3.5 oz. or 1/6 pie	2.0
chocolate *(Comstock)*, 3.5 oz. or 1/6 pie	3.0
coconut *(Comstock)*, 3.5 oz. or 1/6 pie	3.0
lemon *(Comstock)*, 3.5 oz. or 1/6 pie	1.0
mincemeat *(Comstock)*, 3.5 oz. or 1/6 pie	1.0
mincemeat, condensed *(None Such)*, 1/3 cup	2.0
mincemeat, with brandy *(S&W* Old Fashioned), 3.5 oz.	2.0
mincemeat, with brandy and rum *(None Such)*, 1/3 cup	2.0

Pie filling, mix, see "Pudding and pie fillings"

Pierogis, frozen:
(Golden), 1 piece	4.0
potato and cheese *(Mrs. Paul's)*, 3 pieces	7.0

Pigeon peas:
raw, shelled, 1/2 cup	1.3

---

* *Prepared according to package directions*

Pigeon peas, continued
  boiled, drained, ½ cup 1.1
Pig's feet, pickled, 4 oz. 16.8
Pignolia nuts, see "Pine nuts"
Pike, fresh, raw:
  blue, whole, 1 lb. 1.8
  blue, meat only, 4 oz. 1.0
  northern, whole, 1 lb. 1.3
  northern, meat only, 4 oz. 1.2
  walleye, whole, 1 lb. 3.1
  walleye, meat only, 4 oz. 1.4
Pili nuts, dried:
  shelled, 4 oz. 90.4
  shelled, 1 cup 95.5
Pimentos, canned or in jars (all brands), 1 oz. . . . . . . < .1
Pineapple:
  fresh, trimmed, 4 oz. 5
  fresh, diced, 1 cup 7
  fresh, sliced, 1 slice, 3½" diam. × ¾" 4
  candied, 1 oz. .1
  canned or frozen (all brands), ½ cup . . . . < .5
Pineapple juice, canned or frozen* (all brands), 6 fl.
  oz. . . . . < .2
Pineapple-grapefruit juice drink, canned or frozen*
  (all brands), 6 fl. oz. 1
Pineapple-orange juice, frozen* (all brands), 6 fl. oz. < .1
Pine nuts, dried:
  pignolias, shelled, 4 oz. 57.6
  pignolias, shelled, 1 tbsp. 5.1
  piñons, in shell, 1 lb. 157.6
  piñons, shelled, 4 oz. 69.3
  piñons, shelled, 10 nuts 6
Pistachio nuts:
  dried, in shell, 1 lb. 109.7
  dried, shelled, 1 cup 61.9
  dry-roasted, in shell, 1 lb. 124.5
  dry-roasted, shelled, 1 cup 67.6
  red or white *(Planters),* 1 oz. 15.0

---

* Prepared according to package directions

Pitanga (Surinam cherry):

raw, whole, 2 average	.1
raw, 1 cup	.7

Pizza, frozen:

Canadian bacon *(Celeste)*, 7¾-oz. pie	26.0
Canadian bacon *(Celeste)*, ¼ of 19-oz. pie	16.9
Canadian bacon *(Tombstone)*, ⅛ of 22-oz. pie	4.0
Canadian bacon *(Totino's My Classic)*, ¼ pie	12.0
Canadian bacon *(Totino's* Party Pizza), ⅓ pie	9.0
(Celeste Deluxe), 8¼-oz. pie	31.8
(Celeste Deluxe), ¼ of 22¼-oz. pie	22.1
(Celeste Suprema), 9-oz. pie	39.3
(Celeste Suprema), ¼ of 23-oz. pie	24.1
cheese *(Celeste)*, 6½-oz. pie	24.5
cheese *(Celeste)*, ¼ of 17¾-oz. pie	16.6
cheese *(Tombstone)*, ⅛ of 20-oz. pie	5.0
cheese *(Totino's Extra!)*, ¼ pie	12.0
cheese *(Totino's Fox Deluxe)*, ⅓ pie	4.0
cheese *(Totino's* Heat 'n Eat), 4.1 oz.	11.0
cheese *(Totino's* Microwave), 3.9 oz.	9.0
cheese *(Totino's My Classic* Deluxe), ¼ pie	15.0
cheese *(Totino's* Party Pizza), ⅓ pie	10.0
cheese *(Totino's* Single Serve Microwave), 7.1-oz. pie	21.0
cheese and hamburger *(Tombstone)*, ⅛ of 22-oz. pie	6.0
cheese and sausage *(Tombstone)*, ⅛ of 22-oz. pie	6.0
combination *(Tombstone)*, ⅛ of 22.5-oz. pie	7.0
combination *(Totino's* Heat 'n Eat), 4.8 oz.	21.0
combination *(Totino's My Classic* Deluxe), ¼ pie	25.0
combination *(Totino's* Single Serve Microwave), 9-oz. pie	39.0
hamburger *(Totino's Fox Deluxe)*, ⅓ pie	7.0
hamburger or nacho *(Totino's* Party Pizza), ⅓ pie	14.0
Mexican style *(Totino's* Party Pizza), ⅓ pie	15.0
pepperoni *(Celeste)*, 6¾-oz. pie	29.6
pepperoni *(Celeste)*, ¼ of 19-oz. pie	21.3
pepperoni *(Totino's Extra!)*, ¼ pie	12.0
pepperoni or sausage *(Totino's Fox Deluxe)*, ⅓ pie	7.0
pepperoni *(Totino's* Heat 'n Eat), 4.6 oz.	18.0
pepperoni *(Totino's* Microwave), 4.2 oz.	15.0

Pizza, frozen, continued

pepperoni *(Totino's My Classic* Deluxe), 1/4 pie . . .	20.0
pepperoni *Totino's* Party Pizza), 1/3 pie	12.0
pepperoni *(Totino's* Single Serve Microwave), 81/2-oz. pie	31.0
sausage *(Celeste)*, 71/2-oz. pie	31.7
sausage *(Celeste)*, 1/4 of 20-oz. pie	21.7
sausage *(Totino's Extra!)*, 1/4 pie	16.0
sausage *(Totino's* Heat 'n Eat), 4.8 oz.	20.0
sausage *(Totino's* Microwave), 4.2 oz.	15.0
sausage *(Totino's My Classic* Deluxe), 1/4 pie	24.0
sausage *(Totino's* Party Pizza), 1/3 pie	14.0
sausage *(Totino's* Single Serve Microwave), 83/4-oz. pie	37.0
sausage and mushroom *(Celeste)*, 81/2-oz. pie	32.3
sausage and mushroom *(Celeste)*, 1/4 of 221/2-oz. pie	22.4
sausage and pepperoni *(Totino's Extra!)*, 1/4 pie	16.0
sausage and pepperoni *(Totino's Fox Deluxe)*, 1/3 pie	7.0
sausage and pepperoni *(Totino's* Microwave), 4.2 oz.	15.0
sausage and pepperoni *(Totino's* Party Pizza), 1/3 pie	13.0
(Tombstone Special Deluxe), 1/8 of 24-oz. pie	6.0

Pizza, mix*:

thick crust *(Contadina* Pizzeria), 1/4 pie	3.8
thin crust *(Contadina* Pizzeria), 1/4 pie	3.0

Pizza, French bread, frozen:

cheese *(Stouffer's)*, 5.2 oz.	13.0
deluxe *(Stouffer's)*, 6.2 oz.	21.0
hamburger or pepperoni *(Stouffer's)*, 6.1 oz.	18.0
sausage *(Stouffer's)*, 6 oz.	20.0
sausage and mushroom *(Stouffer's)*, 61/4 oz.	17.0

Pizza sauce, chunky *(Ragú Pizza Quick)*, 3 tbsp. . . . 2.0

Plantain (baking banana) fresh:

whole, 1 banana, 9.7 oz.	.7
peeled, 4 oz.	.4
cooked, sliced, 1 cup	.3

Plum:

fresh, whole, 1 lb.	2.6

---

* *Prepared according to package directions*

Plum, continued
fresh, pitted, sliced, 1 cup	1.0
fresh, Japanese or hybrid, 1 plum, 2⅛" diam.	.4
canned (all brands), ½ cup	< .1

Poi, 1 cup 3

Poke shoots (pokeberry):
raw, 1 lb.	1.8
raw, 1 cup.	.6
boiled, drained, 1 cup	.7

Polish sausage, see "Kielbasa"

Pollack, fresh:
raw, drawn, 1 lb.	1.8
raw, fillets, 1 lb.	4.1

Pollack, frozen:
sticks *(Taste o' Sea,* 8 and 14 oz.), 4 oz.	12.0
sticks *(Taste o' Sea,* 24 oz.), 3.4 oz.	11.0

Polynesian style dinner, frozen *(Swanson)*, 12 oz. . . . 8.0

Pomegranate, fresh:
whole, 1 lb.	.8
1 average, 3⅜" diam. × 3¾"	.5

Pompano, fresh:
raw, whole, 1 lb.	24.1
raw, meat only, 4 oz.	10.8

Popcorn, popped:
(Bachman), 1 oz.	11.0
(Orville Redenbacher's Gourmet), 4 cups	1.0
(Pop Secret Natural Flavor), 4 cups	13.0
butter flavor *(Pop Secret)*, 4 cups	14.0
butter flavor *(Wise)*, ½ oz.	4.0
caramel, see "Candy"	
cheese *(Bachman/Wise)*, 1 oz.	12.0
with oil, salt *(Orville Redenbacher's Gourmet)*,	
4 cups	8.0
white or yellow *(Jolly Time)*, 4 cups	1.0
microwave *(Orville Redenbacher's Gourmet)*, 4 cups	8.0
microwave *(Pillsbury* Original), 4 cups	15.0
microwave *(Pops-Rite)*, 4 cups	7.0
microwave, natural flavor *(Jolly Time)*, 4 cups . . .	14.0
microwave, salt free *(Orville Redenbacher's*	
Gourmet), 4 cups	9.0

Popcorn, continued
microwave, salt free *(Pillsbury)*, 4 cups	8.0
microwave, butter flavored *(Orville Redenbacher's Gourmet)*, 4 cups	7.0
microwave, butter flavored *(Pillsbury)*, 4 cups . . .	14.0
microwave, with butter *(Jolly Time)*, 4 cups	14.0
microwave, with cheese *(Pops-Rite)*, 4 cups	10.0
Popover mix *(Flako)*, 1.7 oz.	1.2
Poppy seeds (all brands), 1 tsp.	1.3
Porgy, fresh:	
raw, whole, 1 lb.	6.3
raw, meat only, 4 oz.	3.9
Pork, fresh (see also "Ham"), retail cuts, meat only:	
Boston blade (shoulder), lean with fat:	
braised, 3 oz. (5.6 oz. raw with bone)	24.4
broiled, 3 oz. (4.9 oz. raw with bone)	24.2
roasted, 3 oz. (4.9 oz. raw with bone)	21.5
Boston blade (shoulder), lean (fat trimmed):	
braised, 3 oz. (6.9 oz. raw with bone and fat) . . .	15.0
broiled, 3 oz. (6.9 oz. raw with bone and fat) . . .	15.7
roasted, 3 oz. (5.7 oz. raw with bone and fat) . . .	14.3
center loin, lean with fat:	
braised, 3 oz. (6 oz. raw with bone)	21.6
broiled, 3 oz. (5.2 oz. raw with bone)	18.8
pan-fried, 3 oz. (5.1 oz. raw with bone)	25.9
roasted, 3 oz. (5.1 oz. raw with bone)	18.5
center loin, lean (fat trimmed):	
braised, 3 oz. (7.4 oz. raw with bone and fat) . . .	11.7
broiled, 3 oz. (6.3 oz. raw with bone and fat) . . .	8.9
pan-fried, 3 oz. (6.7 oz. raw with bone and fat) . . .	13.5
roasted, 3 oz. (6 oz. raw with bone and fat) . . .	11.1
center rib, lean and fat:	
braised, 3 oz. (6.8 oz. raw with bone)	23.1
broiled, 3 oz. (5.9 oz. raw with bone)	22.4
pan-fried, 3 oz. (5.1 oz. raw with bone)	28.0
roasted, 3 oz. (5.7 oz. raw with bone)	20.1
center rib, lean (fat trimmed):	
braised, 3 oz. (8.6 oz. raw with bone and fat) . . .	12.3
broiled, 3 oz. (7.2 oz. raw with bone and fat) . . .	12.7
pan-fried, 3 oz. (7.3 oz. raw with bone and fat) . . .	13.0

Pork, fresh, center rib, continued

roasted, 3 oz. (6.8 oz. raw with bone and fat)	11.7
loin, blade, lean with fat:	
braised, 3 oz. (6.8 oz. raw with bone)	29.0
broiled, 3 oz. (5.9 oz. raw with bone)	28.8
pan-fried, 3 oz. (5.1 oz. raw with bone)	31.4
roasted, 3 oz. (5.1 oz. raw with bone)	25.9
loin, blade, lean (fat trimmed):	
braised, 3 oz. (9.1 oz. with bone and fat)	17.5
broiled, 3 oz. (7.6 oz. raw with bone and fat)	18.3
pan-fried, 3 oz. (7.3 oz. raw with bone and fat)	16.9
roasted, 3 oz. (6.4 oz. raw with bone and fat)	13.7
loin, whole, lean with fat:	
braised, 3 oz. (6.4 oz. raw with bone)	23.7
broiled, 3 oz. (5.5 oz. raw with bone)	23.2
roasted, 3 oz. (5.5 oz. raw with bone)	20.7
loin, whole, lean (fat trimmed):	
braised, 3 oz. (8.2 oz. raw with bone and fat)	12.4
broiled, 3 oz. (6.9 oz. raw with bone and fat)	13.0
roasted, 3 oz. (6.6 oz. raw with bone and fat)	11.8
picnic (shoulder), lean with fat:	
braised, 3 oz. (6.8 oz. with bone and skin)	21.7
braised, 1 cup	35.7
roasted, 3 oz. (5.5 oz. with bone and skin)	22.2
roasted, 1 cup	36.5
picnic (shoulder), lean (fat trimmed):	
braised, 3 oz. (8.6 oz. raw with bone, skin and fat)	10.4
braised, 1 cup	17.1
roasted, 3 oz. (7.1 oz. raw with bone, skin and fat)	10.7
roasted, 1 cup	17.7
shoulder, roasted:	
lean with fat, 3 oz. (5.1 oz. raw with bone and skin)	21.8
lean with fat, 1 cup	36.0
lean (fat trimmed), 3 oz. (6.2 oz. raw with bone, skin, and fat)	12.7
lean (fat trimmed), 1 cup	21.0

Pork, fresh, continued
  sirloin, lean with fat:
    braised, 3 oz. (6.3 oz. raw with bone) 21.9
    broiled, 3 oz. (5.4 oz. raw with bone) 21.5
    roasted, 3 oz. (5.4 oz. raw with bone) 17.4
  sirloin, lean (fat trimmed):
    braised, 3 oz. (7.9 oz. raw with bone and fat) 11.1
    broiled, 3 oz. (6.7 oz. raw with bone and fat) 11.5
    roasted, 3 oz. (6.1 oz. raw with bone and fat) 11.2
  sparerib, lean with fat:
    braised, 6.3 oz. (1 lb. raw with bone) 53.6
    braised, 3 oz. (7.7 oz. raw with bone) 25.8
  tenderloin, lean:
    roasted, 12.6 oz. (1 lb. raw) 17.2
    roasted, 3 oz. (from 3.8 oz. raw) 4.1
  top loin, lean with fat:
    braised, 3 oz. (6.4 oz. raw with bone) 24.8
    broiled, 3 oz. (5.5 oz. raw with bone) 24.3
    pan-fried, 3 oz. (5.2 oz. raw with bone) 28.2
    roasted, 3 oz. (5.4 oz. raw with bone) 21.4
  top loin, lean (fat trimmed):
    braised, 3 oz. (8.4 oz. raw with bone and fat) 12.3
    broiled, 3 oz. (7.1 oz. raw with bone and fat) 12.7
    pan-fried, 3 oz. (7.4 oz. raw with bone and fat) 13.0
    roasted, 3 oz. (6.7 oz. raw with bone and fat) 11.7
Pork, cured, see "Ham"
Pork, smoked *(Eckrich* Calorie Watcher Slender
  Sliced), 1 oz. 3.0
Pork dinner, frozen:
  loin *(Swanson),* 11¼ oz. 11.0
  sweet and sour *(Dinner Classics),* 12 oz. 18.0
Pork entrées, canned:
  chow mein, drained *(Chun King* Stir-Fry), 6 oz. 3.8
  chow mein *(La Choy* Bi-Pack), ¾ cup 4.0
Pork entrée, frozen:
  gravy and breaded patties *(Freezer Queen),* 10.67
    oz. 25.0
  roast, and Chinese vegetables *(Benihana),* 1 serving 5.0
  roast, lo mein *(Benihana),* 1 serving 17.0
  sweet and sour *(Chun King* Boil-in-Bag), 10 oz. 6.5

Pork entrée, continued

sweet and sour *(La Choy)*, ⅔ cup	3.0
sweet and sour, with rice *(Van de Kamp's* Chinese Classics), 11 oz.	15.0

Pork gravy:

canned *(Franco-American)*, 2 oz.	3.0
canned *(Heinz* Home Style), 2 oz.	1.7
mix *(Durkee)*, 1-oz. pkg.	.5
mix *(Durkee Roastin' Bag)*, 1.5-oz. pkg.	1.0
mix* *(French's* Gravy for Pork), ¼ cup	1.0

Pork luncheon meat, canned *(Hormel)*, 3 oz.	21.0
Pork rind snack *(Baken-Ets)*, 1 oz.	9.0
Pork tongue, cured, canned *(Hormel)*, 3 oz.	13.0

Pot roast, Yankee, dinner, frozen:

(Dinner Classics), 11 oz.	12.0
(Le Menu), 11 oz.	15.0

Pot roast gravy mix:

(Durkee Roastin' Bag), 1.5-oz. pkg.	1.0
onion *(Durkee Roastin' Bag)*, 1.5-oz. pkg.	.1

Potato, fresh:

raw, with skin, 1 lb.	.3
raw, peeled, diced, 1 cup	.2
baked in skin, 1 potato, 4¾" long, 2⅓" diam. . . .	.2
baked, 1 skin, 4¾" × 2⅓"	.1
boiled in skin, peeled, 1 round, 2½" diam.	.1

Potato, canned:

plain (all brands), 1 cup	< .5
au gratin, with bacon *(Hormel* Short Order), 7½ oz.	14.0
scalloped, and ham *(Hormel* Short Order), 7½ oz.	16.0
scalloped, and pepperoni *(Hormel* Short Order), 7½ oz.	15.0
sliced, and beef *(Hormel* Short Order), 7½ oz. . . .	12.0

Potato, frozen:

plain (all brands), 3 oz.	< .1
au gratin *(Stouffer's)*, 3.8 oz.	6.0
fried or frying:	
(Ore-Ida Crispers!), 3 oz.	16.0

---

* *Prepared according to package directions*

Potato, frozen, fried or frying, continued

(Ore-Ida Crispy Crowns), 3 oz.	9.0
(Ore-Ida Country Style/Golden Fries), 3 oz.	5.0
(Ore-Ida Homestyle Wedges), 3 oz.	3.0
with cheese (Ore-Ida Cheddar Browns), 3 oz.	2.0
cottage fries (Ore-Ida), 3 oz.	5.0
crinkle cut (Ore-Ida Golden Crinkles), 3 oz.	4.0
crinkle cut (Ore-Ida Lites), 3 oz.	2.0
crinkle cut (Ore-Ida Pixie Crinkles), 3 oz.	6.0
French fries (Ore-Ida Lites), 3 oz.	3.0
hash brown or O'Brien (Ore-Ida Southern Style), 3 oz.	0
microwave, crinkle cut (Ore-Ida), 3.5-oz. pkg.	8.0
microwave, French fries (Simplot Micromagic), 3 oz.	12.1
microwave, puffs (Ore-Ida Tater Tots), 4-oz. pkg.	8.0
with onion (Ore-Ida Crispy Crowns), 3 oz.	10.0
patties (Ore-Ida Golden Patties), 2.5 oz.	9.0
puffs, all varieties (Ore-Ida Tater Tots), 3 oz.	7.0
natural fries (Ore-Ida Lites), 3 oz.	3.0
shoestring (Ore-Ida), 3 oz.	7.0
shoestring (Ore-Ida Lites), 3 oz.	4.0
steak fries (Ore-Ida Lites), 3 oz.	2.0
thins (Ore-Ida Homestyle), 3 oz.	6.0
scalloped (Stouffer's), 4 oz.	6.0

Potato, mix*:

(Betty Crocker Potato Buds), 1/2 cup	6.0
au gratin (Betty Crocker/French's), 1/2 cup	6.0
cheddar with onion, twice baked (Betty Crocker), 1/2 cup	12.0
cheese, hickory smoke (Betty Crocker), 1/2 cup	6.0
chicken 'n herb (Betty Crocker), 1/2 cup	4.0
creamed, oven, pan or parsley (Betty Crocker), 1/2 cup	8.0
hash brown, with onion (Betty Crocker), 1/2 cup	6.0
Italian style, creamy, with Parmesan (French's), 1/2 cup	4.0
julienne (Betty Crocker), 1/2 cup	6.0

* Prepared according to package directions, with butter, milk, salt

Potato, mix*, continued

mashed *(French's Idaho)*, ½ cup	6.0
mashed *(French's Idaho/Hungry Jack* Flakes), ½ cup	7.0
scalloped *(Betty Crocker)*, ½ cup	6.0
scalloped, cheese or with onion *(French's)*, ½ cup	5.0
sour cream 'n chive *(Betty Crocker)*, ½ cup	11.0
sour cream and chives *(French's)*, ½ cup	6.0
Stroganoff, creamy *(French's)*, ½ cup	4.0

Potato, stuffed, frozen:

baked, with cheese flavor topping *(Green Giant)*, 5 oz.	6.0
baked, with sour cream and chives *(Green Giant)*, 5 oz.	10.0
seafood *(Wakefield)*, 3 oz.	2.0

Potato chips, 1 oz., except as noted:

(Bachman)	10.0
(Eagle/Eagle Crispy Cut/Lattice Cut)	10.0
(Eagle Hawaiian/Russet)	8.0
(Lay's), 1⅛ oz.	11.0
(O'Grady's)	9.0
(Pringles Light)	8.0
(Pringles Regular)	13.0
(Ruffles)	10.0
au gratin cheese flavor *(O'Grady's)*	10.0
barbecue flavor or hot *(Bachman)*	9.0
barbecue flavor *(Lay's/Ruffles)*	10.0
cheese flavor *(Pringles Cheez-Ums)*	12.0
hearty seasoning *(O'Grady's)*	8.0
salt and vinegar flavor *(Lay's)*	9.0
sour cream and onion flavor *(Bachman)*	9.0
sour cream and onion flavor *(Lay's)*, 1⅛ oz.	11.0
sour cream and onion flavor *(Pringles)*	12.0
sour cream and onion flavor *(Ruffles)*	9.0
vinegar *(Bachman)*	9.0

Potato flour, 1 cup . . . . | 1.4 |

---

* *Prepared according to package directions, with butter, milk, salt*

Potato pancakes:
frozen *(Golden)*, 1 piece 2.0
frozen *(Mother's Latka)*, 2 pieces 5.6
mix,* dinner *(French's)*, 1/2 cup 1.0

Potato salad:
(Knudsen), 1/2 cup 9.0
canned, German *(Joan of Arc)*, 1/2 cup 2.0
canned, German *(Nalley)*, 3 1/2 oz. 6.0
canned, home style *(Joan of Arc)*, 1/2 cup 9.0

Potato starch *(Manischewitz)*, 1 cup 0

Potato sticks, canned *(O&C)*, 1 1/2 oz. 15.0

Preserves, see "Jams and preserves"

Pretzels, 1 oz., except as noted:
(A & Eagle) 2.0
(Mister Salty Juniors), 29 or 1 oz. 1.0
(Mister Salty Mini), 16 or 1 oz. 1.0
(Planters) 1.0
all varieties, plain *(Bachman)* 2.0
all varieties, plain *(Rold Gold)* 1.0
Dutch or rods *(Mister Salty)*, 2 or 1 oz. 1.0
logs *(Mister Salty)*, 9 or 1 oz. 1.0
nuggets *(Mister Salty)*, 21 or 1 oz. 1.0
sticks *(Mister Salty)*, 90 or 1 oz. 1.0
sticks *(Mister Salty Veri-Thin)*, 45 or 1 oz. 1.0
twists *(Mister Salty)*, 5 or 1 oz. 2.0
butter-flavored, all varieties *(Mister Salty)* 1.0
butter- or cheese-flavored *(Bachman)* 2.0

Prickly pear:
raw, whole, 1 lb. 1.7
peeled and seeded, 4 oz. 6

Prosciutto *(Hormel)*, 1 oz. 7.0

Prune:
canned, with pits, 1 cup 5
dehydrated (low moisture), uncooked, 8 oz. 1.7
dehydrated (low moisture), cooked, with liquid,
  1 cup 7
dried, uncooked, with pits, 8 oz. 1.0
dried, cooked, with pits, 1 cup 5

_____
* *Prepared according to package directions*

Prune juice, canned (all brands), 6 fl. oz. . . . . < .1
Pudding, ready-to-serve, canned, dairy, or frozen:
  banana *(Del Monte* Pudding Cup), 5 oz. 5.0
  banana *(Hunt's Snack Pack),* 5 oz. 11.0
  butterscotch *(Del Monte* Pudding Cup), 5 oz. 5.0
  butterscotch *(Hunt's Snack Pack),* 5 oz. 9.0
  butterscotch *(Rich's),* 3 oz. 5.9
  butterscotch *(Swiss Miss),* 4 oz. 6.0
  chocolate *(Del Monte* Pudding Cup), 5 oz. 6.0
  chocolate *(Hunt's Snack Pack),* 5 oz. 9.0
  chocolate *(Rich's),* 3 oz. 7.1
  chocolate *(Swiss Miss),* 4 oz. 6.0
  chocolate, with fudge topping *(Swiss Miss),* 4 oz. 7.0
  chocolate, German or marshmallow *(Hunt's Snack
    Pack),* 5 oz. 9.0
  chocolate fudge *(Del Monte* Pudding Cup), 5 oz. 6.0
  chocolate fudge *(Hunt's Snack Pack),* 5 oz. 10.0
  chocolate fudge *(Swiss Miss),* 4 oz. 6.0
  lemon *(Hunt's Snack Pack),* 5 oz. 4.0
  rice *(Comstock),* 1/2 cup 3.0
  rice *(Hunt's Snack Pack),* 5 oz. 12.0
  tapioca *(Del Monte* Pudding Cup), 5 oz. 4.0
  tapioca *(Hunt's Snack Pack),* 5 oz. 6.0
  tapioca *(Swiss Miss),* 4 oz. 4.0
  vanilla *(Del Monte* Pudding Cup), 5 oz. 5.0
  vanilla *(Hunt's Snack Pack),* 5 oz. 9.0
  vanilla *(Rich's),* 3 oz. 5.9
  vanilla *(Swiss Miss),* 4 oz. 6.0
  vanilla, with fudge topping *(Swiss Miss),* 4 oz. . . . 7.0
Pudding and pie filling, mix,* 1/2 cup, except as
  noted:
  banana cream *(Jell-O* Instant) 4.0
  banana cream *(Royal/Royal* Instant) 4.0
  butter almond, toasted *(Royal* Instant) 4.0
  butter pecan *(Jell-O* Instant) 5.0
  butterscotch *(Jell-O/Jell-O* Instant) 4.0
  butterscotch *(Royal)* 4.0
  butterscotch *(Royal* Instant) 5.0

---

* *Prepared according to package directions, with whole milk*

Pudding and pie filling, mix, continued

chocolate *(Jell-O/Jell-O* Instant*/Royal/Royal* Instant)	4.0
chocolate, chocolate chip *(Royal* Instant)	4.0
chocolate, dark *(Royal/Royal* Dark 'N Sweet)	4.0
chocolate, fudge or milk chocolate *(Jell-O)*	4.0
chocolate, fudge or milk chocolate *(Jell-O* Instant)	5.0
chocolate mousse pie *(Jell-O)*, 1/8 pie	12.0
coconut *(Royal* Tembleque*/Royal* Instant Toasted)	4.0
coconut cream *(Jell-O* Instant)	7.0
custard *(Royal)*	5.0
custard, egg *(Jell-O* Golden)	5.0
flan, with caramel sauce *(Royal)*	5.0
lemon *(Jello-O* Instant)	4.0
lemon *(Royal)*	3.0
lemon *(Royal* Instant)	5.0
lime, key *(Royal)*	3.0
pineapple cream *(Jell-O* Instant)	4.0
pistachio *(Jell-O* Instant)	5.0
pistachio *(Royal* Instant)	4.0
rennet, all flavors *(Junket)*	4.0
rice pudding *(Jell-O Americana)*	4.0
tapioca, chocolate *(Jell-O Americana)*	5.0
tapioca, vanilla *(Jell-O Americana)*	4.0
tapioca, vanilla *(Royal)*	1.0
vanilla *(Jell-O/Jell-O* French*/Jell-O* Instant)	4.0
vanilla *(Royal)*	4.0
vanilla *(Royal* Instant)	5.0
Pudding bars, frozen, 1 bar:	
all flavors *(Bullwinkle* Pudding Stix), 2 1/2 fl. oz.	2.0
all flavors *(Good Humor* Pudding Stix)	2.0
all flavors, uncoated *(Jell-O* Pudding Pops)	2.0
chocolate or vanilla, chocolate coated *(Jell-O* Pudding Pops)	8.0
Pummelo, fresh:	
whole, 1 lb. or 1 cup sections	.1
1 pummelo, 5 1/2" diam.	.2

* Prepared according to package directions, with whole milk

Pumpkin, fresh:
    raw, pulp only, cubed, 1 cup 1
    boiled, drained, mashed, 1 cup 2
    canned, plain (all brands), 1/2 cup   0
Pumpkin flowers:
    raw, trimmed, 1 cup . . . .   < .1
    boiled, drained, 1 cup 1
Pumpkin pie spice, 1 tsp. 2
Pumpkin seed kernels, dry:
    whole, weighed in hull, 4 oz. 39.2
    hulled, 4 oz. 53.0
Purslane, fresh:
    raw, whole, with stems, 1 lb. 3
    boiled, drained, 1 cup 2

	fat grams
Quail, raw:	
whole, ready-to-cook, 1 lb.	27.8
meat and skin only, 4 oz.	7.9
giblets, 2 oz.	3.5
Quiche:	
bacon and onion *(Pour-A-Quiche)*, 4⅓ oz.	18.0
ham *(Pour-A-Quiche)*, 4⅓ oz.	17.0
spinach and onion *(Pour-A-Quiche)*, 4⅓ oz.	16.0
three cheese *(Pour-A-Quiche)*, 4⅓ oz.	18.0
Quince, fresh:	
whole, 1 lb.	.3
whole, 1 quince, 5.3 oz.	.1
peeled and seeded, 4 oz.	.1

	fat grams
Rabbit:	
domestic, raw, whole, ready-to-cook, 1 lb.	29.0
domestic, stewed, meat only, 4 oz.	11.5
wild, raw, whole, ready-to-cook, 1 lb.	18.0
Raccoon, roasted, meat only, 4 oz.	16.4
Radish:	
raw, whole, 10 medium, 3/4"–1" diam.	.2
raw, sliced, 1 cup	.6
Radish, Oriental:	
raw, 1 radish, 7" × 2 1/4" diam.	.3

Radish, Oriental, continued

raw, pared, sliced, 1 cup	.1
boiled, drained, sliced, 1 cup	.4
dried, 4 oz.	.8

Radish, white icicle, raw, 5.4-oz. radish or 1/2 cup

slices	.1

Radish seeds, sprouted:

raw, 1 lb.	11.5
raw, 1 cup	1.0

Raisins:

seeded, 8 oz.	1.2
seeded, 1 cup packed	.9
seedless, 8 oz.	1.0
seedless, 1 cup packed	.8
with nuts *(Carnation)*, .9-oz. pouch	7.0

Ranch house dip *(Nalley)*, 1 oz. 13.0

Raspberry:

fresh, trimmed, 1 pint	1.7
fresh, trimmed, 1 cup	.7
canned or frozen (all brands), 1 cup	< .5

Raspberry danish *(Hostess)*, 1 piece 10.0

Raspberry drink or juice, canned or mix* (all

brands), 6 fl. oz.	0

Raspberry turnover, frozen *(Pepperidge Farm)*, 1 piece 18.0

Ratatouille, frozen *(Stouffer's)*, 5 oz. 4.0

Ravioli, canned:

beef *(Franco-American)*, 7 1/2 oz.	5.0
beef *(Franco-American* RavioliOs), 7 1/2 oz.	7.0
beef *(Nalley)*, 3 1/2 oz.	2.0
cheese, round *(Buitoni)*, 4 oz.	8.0
cheese, square *(Buitoni)*, 4 oz.	4.0
chicken *(Nalley)*, 3 1/2 oz.	3.0
meat, square *(Buitoni)*, 4 oz.	5.0

Red snapper, see "Snapper, red and gray"

Red horse, silver:

raw, drawn, 1 lb.	4.8
raw, meat only, 4 oz.	2.6

Redfish, see "Ocean perch, Atlantic"

---

* *Prepared according to package directions*

Reindeer, raw, lean meat only, 4 oz. 4.3
Relish, see "Pickle, cucumber"
Rennet *(Junket)*, 1 tablet 0
Rhubarb:
  fresh, raw, well trimmed, 1 lb. 9
  fresh, raw, diced, 1 cup 2
  frozen, sweetened, cooked with added sugar, 1 cup .1
Rice:
  brown *(Mahatma/River)*, 1 oz. dry 0
  brown, cooked* *(Uncle Ben's)*, 2/3 cup 3.6
  brown, cooked** *(Uncle Ben's)*, 2/3 cup 1.5
  white *(Carolina/Mahatma/River/Water Maid)*,
    1 oz. dry 0
  white, cooked** *(Minute Rice)*, 2/3 cup 0
  white, cooked* *(Uncle Ben's Converted)*, 2/3 cup 2.3
  white, cooked** *(Uncle Ben's Converted)*, 2/3 cup .2
  white *(Comet/Adolphus)*, 1 oz. 0
  white, instant *(Carolina/Mahatma)*, 1 oz. dry . . . 0
  white, parboiled *(Comet* Extra Fluffy), 1/2 cup . . . 0
Rice, canned:
  fried *(La Choy)*, 3/4 cup 1.0
  Spanish *(Heinz)*, 7¼ oz. 5.0
  Spanish *(Van Camp's)*, 1 cup 2.7
Rice, frozen:
  apple pecan *(Stouffer's)*, 2.9 oz. 4.0
  Chinese fried *(Birds Eye)*, 3.6 oz. 0
  Chinese fried, with meat *(La Choy)*, 3/4 cup 2.0
  Chinese fried, with pork *(Chun King* Boil-in-Bag),
    10 oz. 7.4
  French style *(Birds Eye)*, 3.6 oz. 0
  Italian style *(Birds Eye)*, 3.6 oz. 1.0
  Italian blend and spinach in cheese sauce *(Green
    Giant Rice Originals)*, 1/2 cup 7.0
  jubilee *(Green Giant Rice Originals)*, 1/2 cup 6.0
  long grain white and wild *(Green Giant Rice
    Originals)*, 1/2 cup 2.0
  medley *(Green Giant Rice Originals)*, 1/2 cup 3.0

---

* *Prepared according to package directions, with butter and salt*

** *Prepared according to package directions, without butter and salt*

Rice, frozen, continued
medley *(Stouffer's)*, 3 oz. 2.0
pilaf *(Green Giant Rice Originals)*, ½ cup 2.0
Spanish style *(Birds Eye)*, 3.6 oz. 1.0
and broccoli, in flavored cheese sauce *(Green Giant Rice Originals)*, ½ cup 4.0
with herb and butter sauce *(Green Giant Rice Originals)*, ½ cup 5.0
with peas and mushrooms *(Birds Eye)*, 2.3 oz. . . . 0

Rice, mix*:
beef or chicken flavor *(Lipton Rice and Sauce)*, ½ cup 4.0
drumstick *(Minute)*, ½ cup 4.0
fried *(Minute)*, ½ cup 5.0
herb and butter *(Lipton Rice and Sauce)*, ½ cup 5.0
long grain and wild *(Minute)*, ½ cup 4.0
mushroom *(Lipton Rice and Sauce)*, ½ cup 3.0
rib roast *(Minute)*, ½ cup 4.0
rice and peas or rice medley *(Lipton Rice and Sauce Combinations)*, ½ cup 3.0
Spanish *(Lipton Rice and Sauce)*, ½ cup 3.0

Rice, mix, dry form:
all varieties *(Comet)*, 1 oz. 0
chicken or beef flavored *(Make-It-Easy)*, 1.3 oz. 1.0
pilaf, nutted *(Casbah)*, 1 oz. 2.0
pilaf, regular or Spanish *(Casbah)*, 1 oz. 0

Rice cake:
(Chico-San), 1 cake 0

Rice and chicken, freeze-dried:
(Mountain House), 1 cup 13.0

Rice seasoning mix:
beef flavor and onion *(French's Spice Your Rice)*, 1 pkg. 0
buttery herb *(French's Spice Your Rice)*, 1 pkg. . . . 1.0
cheese and chives *(French's Spice Your Rice)*, 1 pkg. 0
chicken and herb *(French's Spice Your Rice)*, 1 pkg. 1.0
chicken Parmesan *(French's Spice Your Rice)*, 1 pkg. 1.0

* *Prepared according to package directions*

Rice seasoning mix, continued

fried *(Durkee)*, 1-oz. pkg.	1.1
Rice, wild, raw, 8 oz.	1.6
Rice bran, 4 oz.	17.9
Rice polish, 4 oz.	14.5
Rockfish, fillets, raw, meat only, 1 lb.	8.2

Roe (see also "Caviar"):

raw, carp, cod, haddock, herring, pike or shad, 4 oz.	2.6
canned, with liquid, cod, haddock and herring, 4 oz.	3.2

Roll, 1 roll:

brown and serve *(Wonder* Half and Half/Home Bake)	2.0
brown and serve, with buttermilk *(Wonder)*	2.0
brown and serve, club *(Pepperidge Farm)*	1.0
brown and serve, gem style *(Wonder)*	2.0
butter crescent *(Pepperidge Farm)*	6.0
dinner *(Home Pride)*	2.0
dinner *(Wonder)*	1.0
French style *(Pepperidge Farm)*	1.0
hamburger or hot dog *(Pepperidge Farm)*	3.0
hamburger or hot dog *(Wonder)*	1.0
hoagie *(Wonder)*	7.0
Parkerhouse or party *(Pepperidge Farm)*	1.0
sandwich, onion-poppy seed or sesame *(Pepperidge Farm)*	3.0
sourdough French *(Pepperidge Farm)*	1.0
Roll mix,* hot *(Pillsbury)*, 1 roll	2.0

Roll, refrigerated, 1 roll:

(Pillsbury Butterflake)	4.0
cinnamon, iced *(Hungry Jack Butter Tastin')*	7.0
cinnamon, iced *(Pillsbury)*	4.5
cinnamon, iced *(Pillsbury Best* Quick)	9.0
crescent *(Pillsbury)*	5.5

Roll dough, frozen:

(Rich's Homestyle), 2 rolls	2.4
French or honey-wheat *(Bridgford)*, 1½-oz. roll	1.0

---

* *Prepared according to package directions*

Roll dough, continued
Parkerhouse *(Bridgford)*, 1-oz. roll 2.0
white *(Bridgford)*, 1-oz. roll 1.0
Rose apples:
raw, whole, 1 lb. 9
raw, trimmed and seeded, 4 oz. 3
Roselle, fresh:
raw, whole, 1 lb. 1.8
raw, 1 cup 4
Rosemary, dried (all brands), 1 tsp. 2
Roy Rogers:
breakfast, 1 serving:
crescent roll, 2.5-oz. roll 17.7
crescent sandwich, 4.5 oz. 27.3
crescent sandwich, with bacon, 4.75 oz. 29.7
crescent sandwich, with ham, 5.9 oz. 41.7
crescent sandwich, with sausage, 5.8 oz. 29.4
egg and biscuit platter, 5.9 oz. 26.5
egg and biscuit platter, with bacon, 6.2 oz. 29.6
egg and biscuit platter, with ham, 7.15 oz. 28.6
egg and biscuit platter, with sausage, 7.25 oz.   40.9
pancake platter, 5.9 oz. 15.2
pancake platter, with bacon, 6.2 oz. 18.3
pancake platter, with ham, 7.15 oz. 17.3
pancake platter, with sausage, 7.25 oz. 29.6
chicken, fried:
breast, 5.15-oz. piece 23.7
breast and wing, 7-oz. serving 36.5
leg (drumstick), 1.9-oz. piece 8.0
thigh, 3.5-oz. piece 19.5
thigh and leg, 5.4-oz. serving 27.5
wing, 1.87-oz. piece 12.8
sandwiches, 1 serving:
bacon cheeseburger, 6.4 oz. 39.2
bar burger, 7.43 oz. 39.4
cheeseburger, 6.2 oz. 37.3
hamburger, 5.1 oz. 28.3
roast beef, 5.5 oz. 10.2
roast beef, large, 6.5 oz. 11.9
roast beef with cheese, 6.5 oz. 19.2

Roy Rogers, sandwiches, continued

roast beef with cheese, large, 7.5 oz.	20.9

hot top potatoes:

plain, 8 oz.	.2
with oleo, 8.4 oz.	7.3
with sour cream and chives, 10.6 oz.	20.9
with bacon 'n cheese, 8.8 oz.	21.7
with broccoli 'n cheese, 11.1 oz.	18.1
with taco beef 'n cheese, 12.8 oz.	21.8

side dishes, 1 serving:

biscuit, 2.25 oz.	12.1
cole slaw, 3.5 oz.	6.9
French fries, 3 oz.	13.5
French fries, large, 4 oz.	18.4
macaroni, 3.5 oz.	10.7
potato salad, 3.5 oz.	6.1

salad dressings:

bacon 'n tomato, 2 tbsp.	12.0
blue cheese, 2 tbsp.	16.0
Italian lo-cal, 2 tbsp.	6.0
ranch or Thousand Island, 2 tbsp.	14.0

desserts and shakes, 1 serving:

brownie, 2.3 oz.	11.4
danish, apple, 2.53 oz.	11.6
danish, cherry, 2.53 oz.	14.4
danish, cheese, 2.53 oz.	12.2
shake, chocolate or strawberry, 1 shake	10.2
shake, vanilla, 1 shake	10.7
strawberry shortcake, 7.3 oz.	19.2
sundae, caramel, 5.2 oz.	8.5
sundae, hot fudge, 5.4 oz.	12.5
sundae, strawberry, 5 oz.	7.1

beverages:

hot chocolate, 6 fl. oz.	2.0
orange juice, 10 fl. oz.	.3
milk, 8 fl. oz.	8.2

Rutabaga (yellow turnip):

fresh, raw, trimmed, 4 oz.	.2
fresh, raw or boiled, cubed, 1 cup	.3
frozen (all brands), 4 oz.	0

	fat grams
Sablefish:	
raw, whole, 1 lb.	28.4
raw, meat only, 4 oz.	16.9
Safflower seed kernels, dry, 1 oz.	16.9
Safflower seed meal, partially defatted, 4 oz.	9.3
Saffron (all brands), 1 tsp.	< .1
Sage, ground (all brands), 1 tsp.	.1
Salad dressing, bottled, 1 tbsp.:	
(Bama)	4.0
(Miracle Whip)	7.0

Salad dressing, bottled, continued

(Mrs. Filbert's)	6.0
bacon and buttermilk *(Kraft)*	8.0
bacon and tomato *(Kraft)*	7.0
bacon and tomato or creamy bacon *(Kraft* Reduced Calorie)	2.0
blue cheese *(Roka Brand/Kraft* Chunky)	6.0
blue cheese *(Roka Brand* Reduced Calorie)	1.0
blue cheese, chunky *(Kraft* Reduced Calorie)	2.0
blue cheese, chunky *(Wish-Bone)*	8.0
blue cheese, chunky *(Wish-Bone* Lite)	4.0
blue cheese and bacon *(Philadelphia Brand)*	7.0
buttermilk *(Wish-Bone* Lite)	5.0
buttermilk, creamy *(Kraft* Reduced Calorie)	3.0
buttermilk, regular or with chives, creamy *(Kraft)*	8.0
Caesar *(Bernstein* Extra Rich)	5.1
Caesar *(Wish-Bone)*	8.0
Caesar, golden *(Kraft)*	7.0
cheddar and bacon *(Wish-Bone)*	7.0
coleslaw *(Kraft)*	6.0
cucumber, creamy *(Kraft)*	8.0
cucumber, creamy *(Kraft* Reduced Calorie)	3.0
cucumber, creamy *(Wish-Bone)*	8.0
cucumber, creamy *(Wish-Bone* Lite)	4.0
cucumber, dill *(Hain Naturals)*	8.0
French *(Catalina/Kraft)*	6.0
French *(Catalina* Reduced Calorie)	0
French *(Kraft* Reduced Calorie)	2.0
French *(Nalley)*	5.3
French *(Wish-Bone* Deluxe)	5.0
French *(Wish-Bone* Lite French Style)	2.0
French, garlic, herbal or sweet 'n spicy *(Wish-Bone)*	6.0
French, sweet 'n spicy *(Wish-Bone* Lite)	2.0
French, vinaigrette *(Bernstein)*	5.4
garlic, creamy *(Wish-Bone)*	8.0
garlic and chives *(Philadelphia Brand)*	7.0
garlic and oil *(Hain Naturals)*	14.0
garlic and sour cream *(Hain Naturals)*	7.0
Italian *(Bernstein* Low Calorie)	< 1.0
Italian *(Bernstein* Restaurant Recipe)	7.1

Salad dressing, bottled, continued

Italian *(Kraft Reduced Calorie)*	0
Italian *(Kraft Zesty)*	8.0
Italian *(Presto/Wish-Bone)*	7.0
Italian *(Wish-Bone Lite)*	3.0
Italian *(Wish-Bone Robusto)*	8.0
Italian, with cheese *(Bernstein)*	3.3
Italian, with cheese and garlic *(Bernstein)*	5.0
Italian, creamy *(Kraft Reduced Calorie)*	2.0
Italian, creamy *(Wish-Bone)*	6.0
Italian, creamy *(Wish-Bone Lite)*	3.0
Italian, creamy, with sour cream *(Kraft)*	6.0
Italian, herb *(Philadelphia Brand)*	7.0
Italian, herbal *(Wish-Bone)*	7.0
Italian, marinade *(Bernstein)*	5.6
Italian, oil free *(Kraft)*	0
mayonnaise, see "Mayonnaise"	
oil and vinegar *(Kraft)*	7.0
onion 'n chive *(Wish-Bone)*	3.0
onion and chive, creamy *(Kraft)*	7.0
Roquefort *(Bernstein)*	6.6
Russian *(Kraft)*	5.0
Russian *(Kraft Reduced Calorie)*	1.0
Russian *(Wish-Bone)*	2.0
Russian *(Wish-Bone Lite)*	0
Russian, tangy *(Hain Naturals)*	5.0
sour cream and bacon *(Wish-Bone)*	7.0
Thousand Island *(Bernstein)*	6.2
Thousand Island *(Hain Naturals)*	5.0
Thousand Island *(Kraft)*	5.0
Thousand Island *(Kraft Reduced Calorie)*	2.0
Thousand Island *(Nalley)*	5.6
Thousand Island *(Wish-Bone/Wish-Bone Southern Recipe)*	6.0
Thousand Island *(Wish-Bone Lite)*	3.0
Thousand Island, and bacon *(Kraft)*	6.0
Thousand Island, with bacon *(Wish-Bone Southern Recipe)*	6.0
vinaigrette *(Bernstein Low Calorie)*	< 1.0

Salad dressing, mix,* 1 tbsp.:

all varieties, except blue cheese *(Hain* Natural No Oil)	0
blue cheese *(Hain* Natural No Oil)	1.0
Italian or herb *(Good Seasons)*	9.0
Italian *(Good Seasons* Lite)	3.0
Italian *(Good Seasons* Low Calorie)	< .1

Salad sprinkles *(Lawry's),* 1 tsp. — .4

Salami:

(Hormel Party), 1 oz.	8.0
hard *(Eckrich),* 1-oz. slice	12.0
hard *(Hormel),* 1 oz.	10.0
hard *(Hormel* National Brand), 1 oz.	11.0
hard *(Hormel* Perma-Fresh), 2 slices	7.0
hard *(Hormel* Sliced), 1-oz. slice	10.0
hard *(Oscar Mayer),* 1/3-oz. slice	2.9
hard or Genoa *(Armour),* 1 oz.	10.0
cooked *(Armour),* 1 oz.	7.0
cooked, club *(Eckrich),* 1 oz.	6.0
beef *(Hormel* Perma-Fresh), 2 slices	5.0
beef *(Usinger's),* 1 oz.	9.0
beer *(Eckrich),* 1 slice	6.0
beer *(Oscar Mayer),* .82-oz. slice	4.5
beer *(Usinger's* Beerwurst), 1 oz.	7.0
beer, beef *(Oscar Mayer),* .82-oz. slice	4.4
cotto *(Eckrich),* 1 slice	5.0
cotto *(Grillmaster),* 1 slice	6.6
cotto *(Hormel* Chub), 1 oz.	9.0
cotto *(Hormel* Perma-Fresh), 2 slices	7.0
cotto *(Light & Lean),* 2 slices	6.0
cotto *(Oscar Mayer),* .82-oz. slice	4.4
cotto, beef *(Eckrich),* 2 slices	8.0
cotto, beef *(Oscar Mayer),* .82-oz. slice	3.4
Genoa *(Hormel),* 1 oz.	10.0
Genoa *(Hormel DiLusso),* 1 oz.	8.0
Genoa *(Hormel* Gran Valore/San Remo Brand), 1 oz.	10.0
Genoa *(Oscar Mayer),* 1/3-oz. slice	3.0

---

* *Prepared according to package directions*

Salami, continued
- piccolo *(Hormel* stick), 1 oz. 11.0
- soft *(Usinger's),* 1 oz. 9.0

Salisbury steak dinner, frozen:
- *(Banquet American Favorites),* 11 oz. 26.0
- *(Banquet Extra Helpings),* 19 oz. 65.0
- *(Classic Lite),* 10 oz. 13.0
- *(Dinner Classics),* 11 oz. 26.0
- *(Lean Cuisine),* 9½ oz. 13.0
- *(Swanson),* 11 oz. 22.0
- *(Swanson Hungry-Man),* 16½ oz. 40.0

Salisbury steak entrée, frozen:
- *(Banquet Cookin' Bag),* 5 oz. 20.0
- *(Swanson),* 5½ oz. 21.0
- *(Swanson Main Course),* 10 oz. 21.0
- *(Swanson Hungry-Man),* 11¾ oz. 38.0
- char-broiled, with vegetables *(Freezer Queen Single Serve),* 10 oz. 25.0
- with creole sauce *(Dining Lite),* 9.5 oz. 9.3
- gravy and *(Banquet Family Entrees),* 32 oz. 76.0
- gravy and *(Freezer Queen,* 2 lb.), 10.67 oz. 27.0
- gravy and *(Freezer Queen* Cook-in-Pouch), 5 oz. .. 12.0
- gravy and *(Morton Lite),* 8 oz. 12.0
- with onion gravy *(Stouffer's),* 6 oz. 14.0

Salmon, fresh:
- Atlantic, raw, whole 1 lb. 39.5
- Atlantic, raw, meat only, 4 oz. 15.2
- Chinook (king), raw, steak, 1 lb. 62.3
- Chinook (king), raw, meat only, 4 oz. 17.7
- pink (humpback), raw, steak, 1 lb. 14.8
- pink (humpback), raw, meat only, 4 oz. 4.2
- broiled or baked, meat only, 4 oz. 8.4

Salmon, canned:
- blueback *(Gill Netters Best),* 3.5 oz. 9.0
- chum *(Humpty-Dumpty),* 3.5 oz. 5.0
- pink *(Del Monte),* ½ cup 7.0
- pink, Alaska *(Double "Q"),* 3.5 oz. 6.0
- red *(Del Monte),* ½ cup 9.0
- red sockeye *(Deming's/Peter Pan),* 3.5 oz. 9.0
- red sockeye, blueback *(S&W* Fancy), ½ cup 10.0

Salmon, frozen, steaks *(Wakefield),* 3 oz. 4.0
Salmon, smoked, 4 oz. 10.6
Salsa (see also "Chili sauce" and "Picante sauce"):
  (Del Monte Roja), 1/4 cup   0
  (Ortega Ranchera), 1 oz. 1
  hot, medium or mild *(Ortega),* 1 oz. 1
Salsify, fresh:
  raw, trimmed, 8 oz. 5
  raw, sliced, 1 cup 3
  boiled, drained, sliced, 1 cup 2
Salt:
  1 cup   0
  seasoned *(Lawry's),* 1 tsp. . . . .   < .1
Salt pork, raw, 1 oz. 22.8
Sand dab:
  raw, whole, 1 lb. 1.2
  raw, meat only, 4 oz. 9
Sandwich spread (see also individual listings):
  (Best Foods/Hellman's), 1 tbsp. 5.0
  (Kraft), 1 tbsp. 5.0
  (Oscar Mayer), 1 oz. 4.9
Sapodilla, fresh:
  1 fruit, 3″ diam × 2½″ 1.9
  pulp only, 1 cup 2.7
Sapotes (marmalade plums), fresh:
  1 fruit, 11.2-oz. 1.4
  peeled and seeded, 4 oz. 7
Sardines, fresh, Pacific, raw, meat only, 4 oz. 9.8
Sardines, canned:
  in oil, Norwegian Brisling *(King David Brand),* 3¾
    oz. 23.0
  in oil, Norwegian Brisling *(S&W),* 1.5 oz. 10.0
  in oil, Norwegian Brisling *(Queen Helga Brand),*
    3¾ oz. 26.0
  in oil, *(Granadaisa Brand),* 3¾ oz. 19.0
  in tomato sauce *(Empress* Fancy), 3¾ oz. 18.0
  in tomato sauce *(Del Monte),* 1/2 cup 12.0
  in tomato sauce *(Granadaisa Brand),* 3¾ oz. 13.0
  in mustard sauce *(Empress* Fancy), 3¾ oz. 18.0
  in water *(Empress* Fancy), 3¾ oz. 13.0

Sauces, see specific listings
Sauerkraut, canned or in jars (all brands), 1/2 cup . . . < .2
Sauerkraut juice, canned *(S&W)*, 5 fl. oz. 0
Sauger, fresh:
  raw, whole, 1 lb. 1.3
  raw, meat only, 4 oz. 9
Sausage (see also specific listings):
  beef *(Jones Dairy Farm)*, 1-oz. roll 10.9
  breakfast links or roll *(Jones Dairy Farm* Light), 1
    oz. 5.5
  brown and serve *(Jones Dairy Farm)*, 1-oz. link . . . 12.9
  brown and serve, beef *(Swift* Original), 2 links . . . 15.0
  brown and serve, beef, smoked *(Jones Dairy Farm)*,
    1-oz. link 10.6
  brown and serve, breakfast links *(Jones Dairy Farm*
    Light), 1-oz. link 5.5
  brown and serve, cooked *(Hormel)*, 1 link 6.5
  brown and serve, pork *(Swift* Original), 2 links . . . 18.0
  brown and serve, pork *(Swift* Country Recipe), 2
    links 19.0
  brown and serve, pork *(Swift* Original), 2 patties . . 18.0
  brown and serve, pork and bacon *(Jones Dairy
    Farm)*, 1-oz. link 10.0
  brown and serve, uncooked *(Hormel)*, 1 link 8.5
  dried, see "Sausage sticks"
  hot *(Grillmaster* Red Hots), 1 link 15.1
  hot or mild patties *(Hormel)*, 1 patty 13.0
  Italian, hot or mild *(Hillshire Farms)*, 3 1/2 oz. . . . 29.0
  Italian, pork *(Jones Dairy Farm)*, 1-oz. link 8.4
  pork, cooked *(Eckrich* Link), 2 links 20.0
  pork, cooked *(Eckrich* Patty), 1 patty 26.0
  pork, cooked *(Hormel* Little Sizzlers), 2 links 9.0
  pork, cooked *(Hormel* Midget Links), 2 links 13.0
  pork, cooked *(Oscar Mayer* Little Friers), 3/4-oz.
    link 7.0
  pork, hot, fresh, roll, cooked *(Eckrich)*, 2 oz. 26.0
  pork, uncooked *(Jones Dairy Farm)*, 1-oz. link . . . 13.2
  pork, uncooked *(Jones Dairy Farm)*, 1-oz. patty . . 9.4
  pork, roll, regular or hot *(Jones Dairy Farm)*, 1 oz. 9.4
  smoked *(Eckrich)*, 2-oz. link 17.0

Sausage, continued

smoked *(Eckrich* Skinless), 1 link	15.0
smoked *(Eckrich* Skinless), 1-oz. link	7.0
smoked *(Eckrich Smok-Y-Links* Skinless), 2 links	13.0
smoked *(Hillshire Farms* Endless or Links), 3½ oz.	30.0
smoked *(Hormel),* 3 oz.	27.0
smoked *(Hormel* Smokies), 2 links	14.0
smoked *(Oscar Mayer* Little Smokies), ⅓-oz. link	2.5
smoked *(Oscar Mayer* Smokie Links), 1.5-oz. link	11.2
smoked, beef *(Eckrich),* 2-oz. link	17.0
smoked, beef *(Eckrich Smok-Y-Links),* 2 links . . .	12.0
smoked, beef *(Hillshire Farms),* 3½ oz.	29.5
smoked, beef *(Oscar Mayer* Smokies), 1.5-oz. link	10.9
smoked, beef *(Usinger's),* 1 oz.	8.0
smoked, with cheese *(Eckrich),* 1 link	20.0
smoked, with cheese *(Hormel* Smokie Cheezers), 2 links	15.0
smoked, cheese *(Eckrich),* 2 oz.	15.0
smoked, cheese *(Oscar Mayer* Smokies), 1.5-oz. link	11.2
smoked, cocktail *(Kahn's* Cocktail Smokies), 1 link	2.5
smoked, ham *(Eckrich Smok-Y-Links),* 2 links . . .	13.0
smoked, hickory *(Usinger's* Hickory Twig), 3-oz. link	30.0
smoked, hot *(Eckrich),* 1 link	21.0
smoked, maple-flavored *(Eckrich Smok-Y-Links),* 2 links	13.0
Vienna, canned *(Hormel),* 4 links	18.0

Sausage sticks:

beef *(Tombstone),* 1-oz. stick	13.0
beef *(Tombstone* Snappy), 1-oz. stick	12.0
beef roll *(Hormel* Lumberjack), 1 oz.	9.0
hot *(Frito Lay's),* 1 oz.	7.0
jerky *(Laura Schudder's* Natural), 1 oz.	1.0
jerky *(Laura Schudder's* Tender), 1 oz.	2.0
jerky, beef *(Frito-Lay's),* .23 oz.	1.0
jerky, beef *(Laura Schudder's),* ¼ oz.	1.0
smoked *(Laura Schudder's* Snack), .54 oz.	7.0
smoked, beef *(Frito-Lay's),* ½ oz.	7.0
Savory, ground (all brands), 1 tsp.	.1

Scallop, fresh, bay and sea:

raw, meat only, 4 oz. 2

steamed, meat only, 4 oz. 1.6

Scallop, frozen:

in batter *(Taste o' Sea Batter Dipt)*, 3½ oz. 7.0

breaded, French fried *(Mrs. Paul's)*, 3½ oz. 7.0

French fried *(Taste o' Sea Crispy Light)*, 4 oz. . . . 9.0

Scallop dinner, frozen:

(Taste o' Sea), 8 oz. 22.0

Oriental *(Lean Cuisine)*, 11 oz. 3.0

Scallop entrée, frozen, Mediterranean *(Mrs. Paul's

Light)*, 11 oz. 5.0

Scallop and shrimp entrée, frozen, Mariner

***(Stouffer's)*, 10¼ oz.** 18.0

Schinkenwurst *(Usinger's)*, 1 oz. 8.0

Scrapple *(Jones Dairy Farm)*, 1 oz. 3.9

Scrod dinner, frozen, in batter *(Taste o' Sea Batter

Dipt)*, 8¾ oz. 28.0

Scrod entrée, frozen, baked, stuffed *(Gorton's* Light

Recipe)*, 1 pkg. 15.0

Sea bass, fresh, white, raw, meat only, 4 oz. 6

Sea bass entrée, frozen, in lemon butter *(Certi-Fresh)*,

9 oz. 14.0

Seafood, see specific listings

Seafood dinner, frozen:

(Taste o' Sea Platter), 9 oz. 25.0

natural herbs *(Classic Lite)*, 11½ oz. 6.0

Newburg *(Dinner Classics)*, 10½ oz. 10.0

Seafood entrée, frozen:

breaded *(Mrs. Paul's Combination Platter)*, 9 oz. 25.0

Newburg *(Mrs. Paul's Light)*, 8½ oz. 13.0

Seasoned coating mix, for barbecue chicken or pork

***(Shake 'n Bake)*, ¼ pouch** 2.0

Seasoning, see specific listings

Seasoning, salt-free *(Lawry's)*, 1 tsp. . . . . < .1

Seaweed:

agar, raw, 4 oz. . . . . < .1

agar, dried, 4 oz. 3

Irish moss, raw, 4 oz. 2

kelp, raw, 4 oz. 6

Seaweed, continued

laver, raw, 4 oz.	.3
spirulina, raw, 4 oz.	.5
spirulina, dried, 4 oz.	8.8
wakame, raw, 4 oz.	.7
Sesame butter, raw *(Hain)*, 2 tbsp.	15.0

Sesame flour:

high-fat, 4 oz.	42.2
partially defatted, 4 oz.	13.5
lowfat, 4 oz.	2.0

Sesame paste (see also "Tahini"):

1 oz.	14.5
1 tbsp.	8.1

Sesame seeds, dry:

whole, 4 oz.	55.7
(all brands), 1 tbsp.	4.4

Sesame snacks:

(Flavor Tree Party Mix), 1 oz.	11.0
(Flavor Tree Sesame Crunch), 1 oz.	10.0
bars *(Sahadi* Sesame Crunch), 3/4 oz.	7.0
chips or sticks *(Flavor Tree)*, 1 oz.	10.0
nut mix, dry roasted *(Planters)*, 1 oz.	12.0
sticks, with bran *(Flavor Tree)*, 1 oz.	11.0
Sesbania flower, fresh, raw, 1 cup flowers	< .1

Shad, fresh:

raw, whole, 1 lb.	21.8
raw, meat only, 4 oz.	11.3
Shad, gizzard, raw, meat only, 4 oz.	15.9

Shad roe, see "Roe"

Shallot, raw, peeled, 1 oz. or 1 tbsp. chopped	< .1

Sheepshead, fresh:

Atlantic, raw, whole, 1 lb.	3.9
Atlantic, raw, meat only, 4 oz.	3.2

Sherbet, 1/2 cup:

all fruit flavors *(Dole* Fruit Sorbet)	< .1
chocolate coconut *(Shamitoff's* Sorbet)	16.0
lemon or orange *(Borden)*	1.0
lemon, raspberry, or strawberry *(Shamitoff's* Sorbet)	0
Sherbet bar, chocolate fudge *(Eskimo)*, 3 fl. oz.	0

Shortening:
soybean, cottonseed, palm, vegetable, or lard, 1 cup 205.0
soybean, cottonseed, palm, vegetable, or lard, 1
tbsp. 12.8
regular or butter flavor *(Crisco)*, 1 tbsp. 12.0

Shrimp, fresh:
raw, whole, in shell, 1 lb. 2.5
raw, shelled and cleaned, 4 oz. 9

Shrimp, canned, cooked:
(Louisiana Brand), 2 oz. 1.0
(Sau-Sea), 2½ oz. 1.0
medium, whole, deveined *(S&W)*, 1 oz. 1.0

Shrimp, frozen:
in batter *(SeaPak Shrimp 'n Batter)*, 4 oz. 13.0
in batter *(Taste o' Sea Batter Dipt)*, 3 oz. 9.0
breaded *(Mrs. Paul's)*, 3 oz. 10.0
French fried *(Taste o' Sea Crispy Light)*, 4 oz. . . . 12.0

Shrimp cocktail, in jars *(Sau-Sea)*, 4 oz. 1.0

Shrimp dinner, frozen:
(Taste o' Sea), 7 oz. 18.0
baby, in sherried cream sauce *(Classic Lite)*, 10½
oz. 8.0
chow mein *(La Choy)*, 12 oz. 1.0

Shrimp entrée, canned:
chow mein, drained *(Chun King Stir-Fry)*, 7.14 oz. 2.1
chow mein *(La Choy)*, ¾ cup 1.0
chow mein *(La Choy Bi-Pack)*, ¾ cup* 3.0

Shrimp entrée, frozen:
baked, stuffed *(Gorton's Light Recipe)*, 1 pkg. . . . 15.0
chow mein *(La Choy)*, ⅔ cup 1.0
Creole *(Light & Elegant)*, 10 oz. 2.0
Creole, with rice *(Dining Lite)*, 10 oz. 1.9
and lobster sauce *(Benihana)*, 1 serving 6.0
Oriental *(Gorton's Light Recipe)*, 1 pkg. 2.0
Oriental *(Mrs. Paul's Light)*, 11 oz. 2.0
and pasta *(Gorton's Light Recipe)*, 1 pkg. 19.0
Primavera *(Mrs. Paul's Light)*, 11 oz. 9.0
Scampi *(Gorton's Light Recipe)*, 1 pkg. 24.0

* *Prepared according to package directions*

Shrimp entrée, frozen, continued

and vegetables *(Benihana)*, 1 serving	5.0
Shrimp paste, canned, 1 oz.	2.7
Side dish, mix (see also "Noodles," "Rice," etc.):	
chicken, meatless *(Hain* 3 Grain), ½ cup*	1.0
chicken, meatless *(Hain* 3 Grain), ½ cup**	3.0
herb *(Hain* 3 Grain), ½ cup*	1.0
herb *(Hain* 3 Grain), ½ cup**	2.0
Italian *(Hain* 3 Grain), ½ cup*	2.0
Italian *(Hain* 3 Grain), ½ cup**	4.0
Spanish *(Hain* 3 Grain), ½ cup*	2.0
Spanish *(Hain* 3 Grain), ½ cup**	4.0
Skate (Raja fish), raw, meat only, 4 oz.	.8
Sloppy joe, canned *(Nalley)*, 3½ oz.	10.0
Sloppy joe seasoning mix:	
(Durkee), 1.5-oz. pkg.	.2
(French's), ⅛ pkg.	0
(Hunt's Manwich), .3-oz. pkg.	< 1.0
(Hunt's Manwich), 4.5 oz.***	11.0
Italian *(Durkee)*, 1-oz. pkg.	5.0
Smelt, Atlantic, jack or bay:	
raw, whole, 1 lb.	5.2
raw, meat only, 4 oz.	2.4
Snails, raw, meat only, 4 oz.	1.6
Snapper, red and gray:	
raw, whole, 1 lb.	2.1
raw, meat only, 4 oz.	1.0
Soft drinks, all varieties (all brands) 12 fl. oz.	0
Sole, fresh:	
raw, whole, 1 lb.	1.2
raw, fillets, 4 oz.	.9
Sole, frozen:	
(Gorton's Fishmarket Fresh), 4 oz.	1.0
in batter *(Van de Kamp's)*, 4 oz.	15.0
breaded *(Van de Kamp's)*, 5 oz.	15.0
fillets *(Booth* Light & Tender), 4 oz.	1.0

---

* *Prepared according to package directions, without meat*

** *Prepared according to package directions, with meat*

*** *Prepared according to package directions*

Sole, frozen, continued

fillets *(Taste o' Sea)*, 4 oz.	1.0
fillets, breaded *(Certi-Fresh* Light & Crunchy), 5 oz.	17.0
fillets, breaded *(Mrs. Paul's)*, 1 fillet	13.0
fillets, with lemon butter sauce *(Gorton's* Light Recipe), 1 pkg.	13.0
New England style *(Booth* Light & Tender), 3 oz.	6.0

Sole dinner, frozen:

(Taste o' Sea), 8 oz.	25.0
in wine sauce *(Taste o' Sea* Gourmet), 12 oz.	12.0

Sole entrée, frozen:

in butter sauce *(Certi-Fresh)*, 9 oz.	15.0
crab stuffing in lemon sauce *(Wakefield)*, 8 oz. . . .	5.0
Florentine, mornay sauce *(Wakefield)*, 8 oz.	13.0

Sorghum grain, 4 oz.	3.7

Soup, canned, ready-to-serve:

bean *(Grandma Brown's)*, 8 oz.	3.4
bean and ham *(Campbell's* Chunky), 9⅝ oz. . . .	8.0
bean and ham *(Progresso)*, 9½ oz.	1.0
beef *(Campbell's* Chunky), 9½ oz.	4.0
beef *(Progresso)*, 9½ oz.	4.0
beef broth *(Swanson)*, 7¼ oz.	1.0
beef minestrone *(Progresso)*, 9½ oz.	4.0
beef Stroganoff style *(Campbell's* Chunky), 10¾ oz.	15.0
beef vegetable *(Progresso)*, 9½ oz.	2.0
borscht *(Mother's* Old Fashioned/Unsalted), 8-oz. cup	.2
borscht, with beets *(Manischewitz)*, 8 fl. oz.	0
chickarina, with tiny meatballs *(Progresso)*, 9½ oz.	6.0
chicken *(Campbell's* Chunky), 9½ oz.	4.0
chicken *(Progresso* Home Style), 9½ or 10½ oz.	2.0
chicken broth *(Hain Naturals)*, 8¾ fl. oz.	3.0
chicken broth *(Swanson)*, 7¼ oz.	2.0
chicken minestrone *(Progresso)*, 9½ oz.	6.0
chicken noodle *(Hain Naturals)*, 9½ oz.	3.0
chicken noodle *(Hain Naturals* No Salt Added), 9½ oz.	5.0
chicken noodle *(Progresso)*, 9½ or 10½ oz.	4.0
chicken noodle, with mushrooms *(Campbell's* Chunky), 9½ oz.	6.0

Soup, canned, ready-to-serve, continued

chicken rice *(Campbell's* Chunky), 9½ oz.	4.0
chicken rice, with vegetables *(Progresso)*, 9½ oz.	3.0
chicken vegetable *(Hain Naturals)*, 9½ oz.	3.0
chili beef *(Campbell's* Chunky), 9¾ oz.	6.0
clam chowder, Manhattan *(Campbell's* Chunky), 9½ oz.	4.0
clam chowder, Manhattan *(Progresso)*, 9½ oz. . . .	3.0
clam chowder, New England *(Campbell's* Chunky), 9½ oz.	15.0
clam chowder, New England *(Hain Naturals)*, 9½ oz.	5.0
escarole in chicken broth *(Progresso)*, 9½ oz.	3.0
fisherman chowder *(Campbell's* Chunky), 9½ oz.	13.0
Goetta *(Stegner's)*, 4 oz.	10.0
ham and butterbean *(Campbell's* Chunky), 10¾ oz.	10.0
lentil *(Hain Naturals)*, 9½ oz.	5.0
lentil *(Progresso)*, 9½ or 10½ oz.	2.0
macaroni and beef *(Progresso)*, 9½ oz.	3.0
minestrone *(Campbell's* Chunky), 9½ oz.	5.0
minestrone *(Hain Naturals)*, 9½ oz.	4.0
minestrone *(Hain Naturals* No Salt Added), 9½ oz.	5.0
minestrone *(Progresso)*, 9½ oz.	3.0
mushroom *(Hain Naturals)*, 9½ oz.	5.0
mushroom *(Hain Naturals* No Salt Added), 9½ oz.	3.0
onion, French *(Progresso)*, 9½ oz.	9.0
pea *(Progresso)*, 9½ oz.	2.0
pea, split *(Hain Naturals)*, 9½ oz.	2.0
pea, split *(Grandma Brown's)*, 8 oz.	3.0
pea, split, with ham *(Campbell's* Chunky), 9½ oz.	5.0
pea, split, with ham *(Progresso)*, 9½ oz.	3.0
sirloin burger *(Campbell's* Chunky), 9½ oz.	8.0
steak and potato *(Campbell's* Chunky), 9½ oz. . . .	4.0
steak and potato *(Campbell's* Chunky), 10¾ oz. . .	5.0
tomato *(Hain Naturals)*, 9½ oz.	5.0
tomato *(Hain Naturals* No Salt Added), 9½ oz.	6.0
tomato, with macaroni shells *(Progresso)*, 10½ oz.	2.0
tomato, vegetables and macaroni *(Progresso)*, 9½ oz.	2.0
tortellini *(Progresso)*, 9½ oz.	2.0

Soup, canned, ready-to-serve, continued

turkey rice *(Hain Naturals)*, 9½ oz.	2.0
turkey rice *(Hain Naturals No Salt Added)*, 9½ oz.	4.0
turkey vegetable *(Campbell's Chunky)*, 9⅜ oz.	6.0
turtle, mock *(Stegner's)*, 7½ oz.	8.0
vegetable *(Campbell's Chunky)*, 9½ or 10¾ oz.	4.0
vegetable beef *(Campbell's Chunky)*, 9½ oz.	4.0
vegetable, Italian *(Hain Naturals Vege-Pasta)*, 9½ oz.	5.0
vegetable, Mediterranean *(Campbell's Chunky)*, 9½ oz.	5.0
vegetable, vegetarian *(Hain Naturals)*, 9½ oz.	6.0
vegetable, vegetarian *(Hain Naturals No Salt Added)*, 9½ oz.	5.0

Soup, canned, condensed*:

asparagus, cream of *(Campbell's)*, 8 oz.	4.0
bean, with bacon *(Campbell's)*, 8 oz.	5.0
bean, black *(Campbell's)*, 8 oz.	2.0
beef *(Campbell's)*, 8 oz.	2.0
beef broth, bouillon or consommé *(Campbell's)*, 8 oz.	0
beef noodle *(Campbell's/Campbell's Homestyle)*, 8 oz.	3.0
beefy mushroom *(Campbell's)*, 8 oz.	3.0
celery, cream of *(Campbell's)*, 8 oz.	7.0
celery, cream of *(Rokeach)*, 10 oz.	4.0
celery, cream of *(Rokeach)*, 10 oz.**	9.0
cheddar cheese *(Campbell's)*, 8 oz.	8.0
chicken, cream of *(Campbell's)*, 8 oz.	7.0
chicken alphabet *(Campbell's)*, 8 oz.	3.0
chicken and dumplings *(Campbell's)*, 8 oz.	3.0
chicken broth, plain or with noodles *(Campbell's)*, 8 oz.	2.0
chicken broth and rice *(Campbell's)*, 8 oz.	1.0
chicken gumbo *(Campbell's)*, 8 oz.	2.0
chicken mushroom, creamy *(Campbell's)*, 8 oz.	8.0
chicken noodle *(Campbell's)*, 8 oz.	2.0

* *Prepared with equal amounts of soup and water, except as noted*

** *Prepared with equal amounts soup and whole milk*

Soup, canned, condensed*, continued

chicken noodle *(Campbell's* Homestyle), 8 oz. . . .	3.0
chicken noodle *(Campbell's* NoodleOs), 8 oz.	2.0
chicken with rice *(Campbell's),* 8 oz.	2.0
chicken vegetable *(Campbell's),* 8 oz.	3.0
chili beef *(Campbell's),* 8 oz.	5.0
clam chowder, Manhattan *(Campbell's),* 8 oz. . . .	2.0
clam chowder, Manhattan *(Snow's),* 7½ oz.	2.0
clam chowder, New England *(Campbell's),* 8 oz.	3.0
clam chowder, New England *(Campbell's),* 8 oz.**	7.0
clam chowder, New England *(Snow's),* 7½ oz.**	6.0
corn or fish chowder *(Snow's),* 7½ oz.**	6.0
gazpacho *(Campbell's),* 8 oz.	0
meatball alphabet *(Campbell's),* 8 oz.	4.0
minestrone *(Campbell's),* 8 oz.	2.0
mushroom, cream of *(Campbell's),* 8 oz.	7.0
mushroom, cream of *(Rokeach),* 10 oz.	10.0
mushroom, cream of *(Rokeach),* 10 oz.**	15.0
mushroom, golden *(Campbell's),* 8 oz.	3.0
noodle, curly, with chicken *(Campbell's),* 8 oz. . . .	3.0
noodles and ground beef *(Campbell's),* 8 oz.	4.0
onion, cream of *(Campbell's),* 8 oz.	5.0
onion, French *(Campbell's),* 8 oz.	2.0
oyster stew *(Campbell's),* 8 oz.	5.0
oyster stew *(Campbell's),* 8 oz.**	9.0
pea, green *(Campbell's),* 8 oz.	3.0
pea, split, with ham and bacon *(Campbell's),* 8 oz.	4.0
pepper pot *(Campbell's),* 8 oz.	4.0
potato, cream of *(Campbell's),* 8 oz.	3.0
Scotch broth *(Campbell's),* 8 oz.	3.0
seafood chowder *(Snow's),* 7½ oz.**	6.0
shrimp, cream of *(Campbell's),* 8 oz.	6.0
shrimp, cream of *(Campbell's),* 8 oz.**	10.0
tomato *(Campbell's),* 8 oz.	2.0
tomato *(Campbell's),* 8 oz.**	6.0
tomato *(Rokeach),* 10 oz.	1.0
tomato *(Rokeach),* 10 oz.**	6.0

* *Prepared with equal amounts of soup and water, except as noted*
** *Prepared with equal amounts soup and whole milk*

Soup, canned, condensed*, continued
tomato, cream of *(Campbell's* Homestyle), 8 oz.   3.0
tomato, cream of *(Campbell's* Homestyle), 8 oz.**   7.0
tomato bisque *(Campbell's)*, 8 oz. 3.0
tomato rice *(Campbell's)*, 8 oz. 2.0
tomato rice *(Rokeach)*, 10 oz. 5.0
turkey noodle *(Campbell's)*, 8 oz. 2.0
turkey vegetable *(Campbell's)*, 8 oz. 3.0
vegetable *(Campbell's/Campbell's* Homestyle), 8 oz.   2.0
vegetable, vegetarian *(Campbell's)*, 8 oz. 2.0
vegetable, vegetarian *(Rokeach)*, 10 oz. 3.0
vegetable beef *(Campbell's)*, 8 oz. 2.0
won ton *(Campbell's)*, 8 oz. 1.0

Soup, frozen, ready-to-serve:
bean and barley or northern bean *(Tabatchnick)*, 8
oz. 2.0
bean and ham *(Myers/Supper Bell)*, 3½ oz. 1.0
broccoli, cream of *(Myers/Supper Bell)*, 3½ oz.   4.0
cabbage *(Tabatchnick)*, 8 oz. 2.0
chicken corn or noodle *(Myers/Supper Bell)*, 3½
oz. 1.0
chicken noodle or with kreplach *(Tabatchnick)*, 8
oz. 2.0
clam chowder *(Myers/Supper Bell)*, 3½ oz. 2.0
chowder, Manhattan *(Tabatchnick)*, 8 oz. 1.5
clam chowder, New England *(Stouffer's)*, 8 oz. . . .   11.0
chowder, New England *(Tabatchnick)*, 8 oz. 1.0
lentil, minestrone, or mushroom barley
(Tabatchnick), 8 oz. 2.0
mushroom, cream of *(Myers/Supper Bell)*, 3½ oz.   4.0
pea *(Tabatchnick)*, 8 oz. 2.0
pea, split, with ham *(Myers/Supper Bell)*, 3½ oz.   1.0
pea, split, with ham *(Stouffer's)*, 8 oz. 3.0
potato *(Tabatchnick)*, 8 oz. 1.0
potato, cream of *(Myers/Supper Bell)*, 3½ oz. . . .   2.0
seafood bisque *(Myers/Supper Bell)*, 3½ oz. 3.0
seafood chowder *(Tabatchnick* Salt Free), 8 oz.   2.0

---

* *Prepared with equal amounts of soup and water, except as noted*
** *Prepared with equal amounts soup and whole milk*

Soup, frozen, ready-to-serve, continued

spinach, cream of *(Stouffer's)*, 8 oz.	14.0
vegetable *(Tabatchnick)*, 8 oz.	1.0
vegetable *(Myers/Supper Bell)*, 3½ oz.	2.0
won ton *(Tabatchnick)*, 8 oz.	2.0
won ton, chicken *(La Choy)*, ½ pkg.	1.0
Soup greens *(Durkee)*, 2.5-oz. jar	3.0
Sour cream and onion sticks *(Flavor Tree)*, 1 oz.	10.0
Sour drink mix* *(Bar-Tender's)*, 3½ fl. oz. with whiskey	0
Soursop, fresh:	
1 soursop, 32.9 oz.	1.9
pulp only, 1 cup	.7
Soybean, green:	
raw, in pods, 1 lb.	16.4
raw, shelled, 1 cup	17.4
boiled, drained, 1 cup	11.5
canned, drained, 8 oz.	11.3
Soybean, fermented:	
natto, 4 oz.	8.4
miso, with cereal, 4 oz.	5.2
Soybean curd (tofu), 4 oz.	4.8
Soybean kernels, roasted and toasted, 1 oz.	6.8
Soybean "milk":	
fluid, 4 oz.	1.7
powder, 4 oz.	23.0
dry *(Worthington Soyamel* fortified), 1 oz.	7.0
Soybean protein, 4 oz.	.1
Soybean proteinate, 4 oz.	.1
Soybean seeds, mature, dry:	
uncooked, 8 oz.	40.1
cooked, 8 oz.	12.9
Soy sauce:	
(Chun King), 1 tbsp.	1.0
(Kikkoman), 1 tbsp.	< .1
Spaghetti, see "Pasta"	
Spaghetti, canned:	
and beef *(Hormel* Short Order), 7½ oz.	14.0

---

* *Prepared according to package directions*

Spaghetti, canned, continued

in meat sauce *(Franco-American)*, 7½ oz.	8.0
in tomato sauce, with cheese *(Franco-American)*, 7⅜ oz.	2.0
in tomato sauce, with cheese *(Heinz)*, 7¾ oz.	2.0
in tomato and cheese sauce *(Franco-American SpaghettiOs)*, 7½ oz.	2.0
in tomato sauce, with meat *(Heinz)*, 7½ oz.	6.0
with franks *(Van Camp's Skettee Weenee)*, 1 cup	7.4
with franks, in tomato sauce *(Franco-American SpaghettiOs)*, 7⅜ oz.	7.0
with meat *(Nalley)*, 3½ oz.	5.0
with meatballs *(Hormel* Short Order), 7½ oz.	8.0
with meatballs *(Nalley)*, 3½ oz.	4.0
with meatballs, tomato sauce *(Franco-American)*, 7⅜ oz.	8.0
with meatballs, tomato sauce *(Franco-American SpaghettiOs)*, 7⅜ oz.	8.0
with sausage, Italian *(Hormel* Short Order), 7½ oz.	9.0

Spaghetti, freeze-dried, with meat sauce *(Mountain House)*, 1 cup ... 5.0

Spaghetti dinner, frozen:

(Morton), 11.5 oz.	11.4
with beef and mushroom sauce *(Lean Cuisine)*, 11½ oz.	7.0
with meatballs *(Dinner Classics)*, 11 oz.	24.0
with meatballs *(Swanson)*, 12½ oz.	15.0

Spaghetti dinner, mix*:

American or Italian style *(Kraft)*, 1 cup	8.0
with meat sauce *(Kraft)*, 1 cup	14.0

Spaghetti entrée, frozen:

with beef and mushrooms *(Dining Lite)*, 11 oz.	8.3
casserole *(Morton)*, 8 oz.	5.1
with meat sauce *(Light & Elegant)*, 10¼ oz.	8.0
with meat sauce *(Morton* Lite), 8 oz.	4.0
with meat sauce *(Stouffer's)*, 14 oz.	15.0
with meat sauce, casserole *(Banquet)*, 8 oz.	8.0
with meatballs *(Stouffer's)*, 12⅝ oz.	13.0

---

* *Prepared according to package directions*

Spaghetti entrée, continued

and sauce, with ground veal and mushrooms *(The Budget Gourmet)*, 1 serving	14.0
in tomato sauce, with breaded veal *(Swanson)*, 8¼ oz.	12.0

Spaghetti sauce, canned or in jars:

(Prego), 4 oz.	6.0
(Ragú), 4 oz.	3.0
(Ragú Homestyle), 4 oz.	2.0
ground beef sirloin, with onions *(Prego* Plus), 4 oz.	7.0
Italian sausage and green peppers *(Prego* Plus), 4 oz.	9.0
marinara *(Aunt Millie's)*, ½ cup	4.0
marinara *(Ragú)*, 4 oz.	4.0
meat flavored *(Aunt Millie's)*, ½ cup	3.0
meat flavored *(Prego)*, 4 oz.	6.0
meat flavored *(Ragú* Extra Thick & Zesty), 4 oz.	4.0
meatless or mushroom *(Aunt Millie's)*, ½ cup . . .	3.0
mushrooms and chunk tomatoes *(Prego* Plus), 4 oz.	5.0
with mushrooms *(Prego)*, 4 oz.	5.0
with mushrooms *(Ragú)*, 4 oz.	4.0
with mushrooms *(Ragú* Homestyle), 4 oz.	2.0
with mushrooms and green pepper *(Enrico's)*, 4 oz.	1.0
pepper and mushroom *(Aunt Millie's)*, ½ cup . . .	4.0
pepper and onion or sausage *(Aunt Millie's)*, ½ cup	3.0
sausage *(Aunt Millie's)*, ½ cup	3.0
veal and sliced mushrooms *(Prego* Plus), 4 oz. . . .	5.0

Spaghetti sauce, mix:

(Durkee), 1.5-oz. pkg.	.4
(Spatini), 1 fl. oz.*	0
with mushrooms *(Durkee)*, 1.1-oz. pkg.	.1
with tomato paste *(Durkee* Extra Thick & Rich), 1.3-oz. pkg.	.7

Spanish mackerel:

raw, whole, 1 lb.	28.8
raw, meat only, 4 oz.	11.8

Sparerib sauce mix *(Durkee Roastin' Bag)*, 1.9-oz. pkg. . . . . | 2.0

---

* *Prepared according to package directions*

Spinach:
fresh, raw, trimmed, 10-oz. pkg. 7
fresh, raw, chopped, 1 cup 2
fresh, boiled, drained, leaves, 1 cup 5
canned or frozen, plain (all brands), 1 cup . . . . .   < .2
frozen, creamed *(Birds Eye)*, 3 oz. 3.0
frozen, creamed *(Green Giant)*, 1/2 cup 3.0
frozen, creamed *(Stouffer's)*, 41/2 oz. 15.0
frozen, cut leaf, in butter sauce *(Green Giant)*, 1/2
  cup 2.0
Spinach crepes, frozen, with cheddar cheese sauce
  (Stouffer's), 91/2 oz. 27.0
Spinach soufflé, frozen *(Stouffer's)*, 4 oz. 9.0
Spleen, fresh:
raw, beef or calf, 4 oz. 3.4
raw, hog, 4 oz. 2.9
braised, hog, 3 oz. (4.6 oz. raw spleen) 2.7
raw, lamb, 4 oz.   4.4
Sports drink *(Max)*, 6 fl. oz.   0
Spot, fresh, raw, fillets, 4 oz. 18.0
Squab (pigeon), raw:
whole, dressed, ready-to-cook, 1 lb. 70.7
meat only, 4 oz. 8.5
breast meat only, 1 breast, 3.6 oz. 4.6
Squash:
summer, fresh:
  crookneck and straightneck, raw, trimmed, 8 oz.   .5
  crookneck and straightneck, raw, sliced, 1 cup   .3
  crookneck and straightneck, boiled, sliced, 1 cup   .6
  scallop, raw, trimmed, 8 oz. 5
  scallop, raw or boiled, sliced, 1 cup 3
  scallop, boiled, drained, mashed, 1 cup 4
  zucchini, raw, trimmed, 8 oz. 3
  zucchini, raw, sliced, 1 cup 2
  zucchini, boiled, drained, sliced, 1 cup 1
winter, fresh:
  acorn, raw, 1 squash, 41/3" × 4" diam. 4
  acorn, baked, 8 oz. or 1 cup cubed 3
  acorn, boiled, mashed, 1 cup 2
  butternut, raw, peeled and seeded, 8 oz. 2

Squash, winter, continued

butternut, raw, cubed, 1 cup	.1
butternut, baked, 8 oz. or 1 cup cubed	.2
hubbard, raw, peeled and seeded, 8 oz.	1.1
hubbard, raw, cubed, 1 cup	.6
hubbard, baked, cubed, 1 cup	1.3
spaghetti, raw, peeled and seeded, 8 oz.	1.3
spaghetti, raw, cubed, 1 cup	.6
spaghetti, baked or boiled and drained, 1 cup	.4
canned, crookneck, drained, 1 cup	.2
frozen, all varieties, plain (all brands), 3.3 oz.	< .1
frozen, prepared *(Southland)*, 3.6 oz.	2.0
Squash seed kernels, dry, 4 oz.	53.0
Squid, raw, meat only, 4 oz.	1.0
Steak, see "Beef" and "Salisbury steak"	
Steak sauce, bottled (all brands), 1 tbsp.	< .3
Stomach, pork, raw, 4 oz.	10.0
Strawberry:	
fresh, whole, fully trimmed, 1 lb.	1.7
fresh, whole, 1 cup	.6
canned, freeze-dried or frozen (all brands), ½ cup	< .3
Strawberry drink or juice, canned or mix* (all brands), 6 fl. oz.	< .1
Stroganoff sauce mix *(Durkee)*, 1.2-oz. pkg.	.7
Stuffing, all varieties *(Pepperidge Farm)*, 1 oz.	1.0
Stuffing, frozen:	
chicken *(Green Giant Stuffing Originals)*, ½ cup	7.0
cornbread *(Green Giant Stuffing Originals)*, ½ cup	6.0
mushroom *(Green Giant Stuffing Originals)*, ½ cup	7.0
wild rice *(Green Giant Stuffing Originals)*, ½ cup	7.0
Stuffing, mix*:	
(Bell's Premium Blend), ½ cup	6.0
(Bell's Ready Mix), ½ cup	13.0
beef, chicken, pork, or turkey flavor *(Stove Top)*, ½ cup	9.0
chicken flavor *(Bell's)*, ½ cup	8.0
chicken or pork flavor *(Betty Crocker)*, ⅙ pkg.	9.0
cornbread *(Stove Top)*, ½ cup	9.0

---

* *Prepared according to package directions*

Stuffing, mix*, continued
cornbread or herb *(Betty Crocker)*, ⅙ pkg.	9.0
New England or San Francisco *(Stove Top)*, ½ cup	9.0
with rice *(Stove Top)*, ½ cup	8.0

Sturgeon:
fresh, raw, meat only, 4 oz.	2.2
fresh, steamed, meat only, 4 oz.	6.5
fresh, roe, see "Caviar"	
smoked, 4 oz.	2.0

Succotash (corn and lima beans):
fresh, boiled, drained, ½ cup	.8
canned or frozen (all brands), 1 cup	< 1.0

Sucker carp:
raw, whole, 1 lb.	5.7
raw, meat only, 4 oz.	3.6

Sucker, white and mullet:
raw, whole, 1 lb.	3.5
raw, meat only, 4 oz.	2.0
Suet (beef kidney fat), raw, 1 oz.	26.6
Sugar, all varieties, 1 cup	0

Sugar apple (sweetsop), fresh:
1 apple, 2⅞" diam. × ¾"	.5
pulp only, 1 cup	.7
Sugar substitute (all brands), 1 tbsp.	0
Sukiyaki, canned *(Chun King* Stir-Fry), 6 oz.	16.7
Sukiyaki dinner mix *(La Choy)*, ⅕ pkg.	0
Sukiyaki entrée, canned *(La Choy* Bi-Pack), ¾ cup*	1.0

Summer sausage:
(Eckrich), 1 slice	7.0
(Hormel Perma-Fresh), 2 slices	11.0
(Hormel Tangy), 1 oz.	7.0
(Hormel Thuringer), 1 oz.	9.0
(Light & Lean), 2 slices	8.0
(Oscar Mayer), .82-oz. slice	6.5
(Usinger's Thueringer/Thueringer Blood), 1 oz.	9.0
beef *(Hormel)*, 1 oz.	9.0
beef *(Oscar Mayer)*, .82-oz. slice	6.3
beef *(Usinger's)*, 1 oz.	8.0

* *Prepared according to package directions*

Summer sausage, continued

cheese *(Armour)*, 1 oz.	8.0
smoked *(Eckrich Smoky Tang)*, 1 oz.	7.0
soft *(Usinger's)*, 1 oz.	8.0
turkey *(Louis Rich)*, 1-oz. slice	3.5
Sunflower butter, raw, *(Hain)*, 2 tbsp.	15.0
Sunflower nuts:	
dry-roasted *(Planters)*, 1 oz.	14.0
dry-roasted *(Planters* Unsalted), 1 oz.	15.0
oil-roasted *(Planters)*, 1 oz.	15.0
Sunflower seeds:	
dry, hulled, 4 oz.	53.6
(Frito-Lay's), 1 oz.	16.0
(Frito-Lay's Kernels), 1 oz.	17.0
(Planters), 1 oz.	14.0
dry-roasted *(Flavor House)*, 1 oz.	15.0
Sunflower seed butter, salted or unsalted, 1 tbsp.	7.6
Sunflower seed flour, partially defatted, 1 cup	1.3
Swamp cabbage:	
raw, trimmed, 1 lb.	.9
boiled, drained, chopped, 1 cup	.2
Sweet and sour dinner mix *(La Choy)*, 1/4 pkg.	0
Sweet and sour drink mixer (all brands), 1 fl. oz.	0
Sweet and sour sauce:	
(Chun King), 1.8 oz.	.1
(Contadina), 4 oz.	3.0
(French's Dip 'Um/Sauceworks), 2 tbsp.	0
(Kikkoman), 1 tbsp.	< .1
mix *(Durkee)*, 2-oz. pkg.	5.7
Sweetbreads:	
beef (yearling), raw, 1 lb.	72.6
beef (yearling), braised, 4 oz.	26.3
calf, raw, 1 lb.	9.1
calf, braised, 4 oz.	3.6
lamb, raw, 1 lb.	17.2
lamb, braised, 4 oz.	6.9
Sweet potato (see also "Yams"):	
fresh, raw, 1 potato, 5″ × 2″ diam.	.4
fresh, raw, cubed, 1 cup	.4
fresh, baked in skin, 1 potato, 5″ × 2″ diam.	.1

Sweet potato, continued
fresh, baked in skin, mashed, 1 cup	.2
fresh, boiled, pared, mashed, 1 cup	1.0
candied, 4 oz.	3.7
canned, yams, plain or in syrup (all brands), 1 cup	< 1.0
dehydrated, flakes, dry form, 4 oz.	.7

Sweet potato leaves, fresh:
raw, whole, 1 lb.	1.3
raw, chopped, 1 cup	.1
steamed, 1 cup	.2

Swiss steak gravy, mix:
(Durkee), 1-oz. pkg.	.2
(Durkee Roastin' Bag), 1.5-oz. pkg.	.9

Swordfish:
fresh, raw, meat only, 1 lb.	18.1
canned, with liquid, 8 oz.	6.8
frozen, steaks *(Wakefield)*, 6 oz.	7.0

Swordfish dinner, frozen, in lemon sauce *(Taste o' Sea Gourmet)*, 12 oz. 15.0

Syrup, see specific listings

	fat grams
Tabouly mix *(Casbah)*, 1 oz. dry	1.0
Taco, frozen:	
beef *(Patio)*, 2 tacos or 4 oz.	9.0
beef, snack *(Patio)*, 4 tacos or 2 oz.	5.0
Taco dinner, frozen, beef, chili 'n beans *(Patio)*, 11 oz.	32.0
Taco dip *(Hain* Taco Dip & Sauce), 1/4 cup	0
Taco sauce, canned or in jars:	
hot or mild *(Del Monte)*, 1/4 cup	0
hot, hot salsa, mild, or western *(Ortega)*, 1 oz.	.1
mild salsa *(Ortega)*, 1 oz.	0

Taco seasoning mix:

(Durkee), 1.1-oz. pkg.	1.0
(French's), 1/6 pkg.	0
mild *(Ortega),* 1 oz.	1.0
Taco starter *(Del Monte),* 8 oz.	1.0

Tahini:

raw, stone ground kernels, 1 tbsp.	7.2
unroasted kernels, 1 tbsp.	7.9
roasted or toasted kernels, 1 tbsp.	8.1
in jars *(Sahadi),* 2 tbsp.	17.0
mix *(Casbah),* 1 oz. dry	5.0

Tamale, canned:

(Van Camp's), 1 cup	16.2
(Wolf), 7 1/2 oz.	24.5
beef *(Hormel),* 2 tamales	10.0
beef *(Hormel* Hot 'N Spicy), 2 tamales	10.0
beef *(Hormel* Short Order), 7 1/2 oz.	19.0
beef *(Nalley),* 3 1/2 oz.	6.0
chicken *(Nalley),* 3 1/2 oz.	4.0

Tamale, frozen:

beef *(Hormel),* 1 tamale	7.0
and beef chili gravy *(Patio),* 5.3 oz.	16.0
Tamale pie, canned *(Nalley),* 3 1/2 oz.	8.0

Tamarind, fresh:

1 fruit, 3" × 1"	< .1
pulp only, 1 cup	.7

Tangerine (Dancy variety), fresh:

1 tangerine, 2 3/8" diam.	.2
sections, without membranes, 1 cup	.4

Tangerine juice:

fresh, 1 cup	.5
canned or frozen* (all brands), 6 fl. oz.	< .4

Taquito entrée, frozen, shredded beef with guacamole
(Van de Kamp's Mexican Classic), 8 oz. 25.0

Taro, raw or cooked, sliced, 1 cup	.2
Taro chips, 1/2 cup	3.1

Taro leaves:

raw, whole, 1 lb.	2.0

---

* Prepared according to package directions

Taro leaves, continued
steamed, 1 cup 6
Taro shoots:
raw, 1 shoot, 15½" long × 1⅛" 1
raw or cooked, sliced, 1 cup 1
Taro, Tahitian:
raw, sliced, 1 cup 1.2
cooked, sliced, 1 cup 9
Tarragon, ground (all brands), 1 tsp. 1
Tartar sauce:
(Best Foods/Hellmann's), 1 tbsp. 8.0
(Kraft/Sauceworks), 1 tbsp. 8.0
(Nalley), 1 tbsp. 10.2
Tautog (blackfish):
raw, whole, 1 lb. 1.8
raw, meat only, 4 oz. 1.2
Tea, all varieties, regular or herbal (all brands), 1 cup . 0
Teawurst *(Usinger's),* 1 oz. 11.0
Teriyaki sauce:
(Kikkoman), 1 tbsp. . . . . < .1
(Kikkoman Baste and Glaze), 1 tsp. . . . . < .1
(La Choy Marinade & Sauce), 1 oz. 0
Terrapin (diamondback), fresh:
raw, in shell, 1 lb. 3.3
raw, meat only, 4 oz. 4.0
Thuringer cervelat:
(Hormel Old Smokehouse), 1 oz. 8.0
(Hormel Old Smokehouse, 11 oz. club), 1 oz. 9.0
(Hormel Old Smokehouse Sliced), 1 oz.-slice 9.0
Thyme, ground (all brands), 1 tsp. 1
Tilefish, fresh:
raw, whole, 1 lb. 1.2
raw, meat only, 4 oz. 6
Tofu, see "Soybean curd"
Tofu entrées, frozen:
cannelloni Florentine, with sauce *(Legume),* 11 oz. . 7.0
enchilada, Mexican, with sauce *(Legume),* 11 oz. . . 9.0
lasagna, with sauce *(Legume* Classic), 8 oz. 8.0
lasagna, vegetable, with sauce *(Legume),* 12 oz. . . 8.0
manicotti, with sauce *(Legume* Classic), 8 oz. . . . 11.0

Tofu entrées, continued
    pepper steak, whole wheat noodles *(Legume)*, 10½
      oz. 3.0
    sesame ginger stir-fry, with sauce and brown rice
      (Legume), 11½ oz. 10.0
    shells, stuffed, Provencale, with sauce *(Legume)*, 11
      oz. 12.0
    sweet and sour, whole wheat noodles *(Legume)*,
      11½ oz. 3.0
Tom Collins drink mixer (all brands), 1 fl. oz. 0
Tomato:
    fresh, green, whole, 1 lb. 8
    fresh, ripe, whole, 1 lb. 9
    fresh, ripe or green, 1 tomato, 2⅗″ diam. 3
    fresh, chopped, 1 cup 4
    canned, all styles (all brands), ½ cup . . . . < .1
Tomato, pickled *(Claussen* Kosher), 1-oz. piece . . . . < .1
Tomato juice, canned (all brands), 6 fl. oz. 0
Tomato paste, canned (all brands), 2 oz. . . . . < .3
Tomato sauce, canned:
    (Del Monte), 1 cup 1.0
    (Hunt's/S&W/Stokely's Finest), ½ cup 0
    Italian style *(Hunt's)*, 4 oz. 2.0
    with onion *(Del Monte)*, 1 cup 1.0
Tomcod, Atlantic:
    raw, whole, 1 lb. .7
    meat only, 4 oz. .5
Tongue:
    beef, medium-fat, braised, 4 oz. 18.9
    calf, braised, 4 oz. 6.8
    hog, braised, 4 oz. 21.1
    lamb, braised, 4 oz. 20.6
    sheep, braised, 4 oz. 28.7
    pickled, 4 oz. 23.0
    potted or deviled, 4 oz. 26.1
Toppings, dessert:
    all flavors *(Smucker's Magic Shell)*, 2 tbsp. 15.0
    all fruit flavors *(Kraft)*, 1 tbsp. 0
    all fruit flavors *(Smucker's)*, 2 tbsp. 0
    butterscotch *(Kraft)*, 1 tbsp. 1.0

Toppings, dessert, continued

butterscotch *(Smucker's)*, 2 tbsp.	1.0
caramel or chocolate *(Kraft)*, 1 tbsp.	0
caramel *(Smucker's)*, 2 tbsp.	1.0
caramel, hot *(Smucker's)*, 2 tbsp.	4.0
chocolate, syrup *(Smucker's)*, 2 tbsp.	0
chocolate fudge *(Hershey's)*, 1 oz. or 2 tbsp.	4.0
chocolate fudge *(Smucker's)*, 2 tbsp.	1.0
chocolate fudge, hot *(Kraft)*, 1 tbsp.	3.0
chocolate fudge, hot *(Smucker's)*, 2 tbsp.	4.0
chocolate fudge, Swiss milk *(Smucker's)*, 2 tbsp.	1.0
marshmallow creme *(Kraft)*, 1 oz.	0
nut *(Planters)*, 1 oz.	16.0
peanut butter caramel *(Smucker's)*, 2 tbsp.	2.0
pecans, in syrup *(Smucker's)*, 2 tbsp.	1.0
walnut *(Kraft)*, 1 tbsp.	5.0
walnuts, in syrup *(Smucker's)*, 2 tbsp.	1.0
Tortilla, frozen *(Patio)*, 2 tortillas or 1.5 oz.	1.0
Tortilla chips, see "Corn chips, puffs, and similar snacks"	
Tostada entrée, frozen, beef, supreme *(Van de Kamp's Mexican Classic)*, 8½ oz.	30.0
Towel gourd, see "Gourd, dishcloth"	
Tree fern, cooked, chopped, ½ cup	.1
Tripe, beef:	
fresh, 4 oz.	2.3
pickled, 4 oz.	1.5
Trout, brook:	
raw, whole, 1 lb.	4.7
raw, meat only, 4 oz.	2.4
Trout, rainbow:	
fresh, raw, meat with skin, 4 oz.	12.9
canned, 4 oz.	15.2
Tuna, fresh:	
bluefin, raw, meat only, 4 oz.	4.6
yellowfin, raw, meat only, 4 oz.	3.4
Tuna, canned:	
in oil, chunk light *(Bumble Bee)*, 2 oz.	14.0
in oil, chunk light *(S&W* Fancy), 2 oz.	10.0
in oil, solid or chunk light *(Star-Kist)*, 2 oz.	13.0

Tuna, canned, continued
  in oil, solid white *(Bumble Bee)*, 2 oz. 10.0
  in oil, solid white *(S&W Fancy)*, 2 oz. 12.0
  in oil, solid or chunk white *(Star-Kist)*, 2 oz. 10.0
  in water, chunk light *(Bumble Bee)*, 2 oz. 2.0
  in water, chunk light *(S&W Fancy)*, 2 oz. 1.0
  in water, chunk light *(Star-Kist low sodium)*, 2 oz. 1.0
  in water, solid light or chunk light *(Star-Kist)*, 2 oz. < 1.0
  in water, solid white *(Bumble Bee)*, 2 oz. 8.0
  in water, solid white, imported albacore *(Star-Kist)*,
    2 oz. 1.0
  in water, solid white, local albacore *(Star-Kist)*, 2
    oz. 5.0
Tuna entrée, mix*:
  au gratin *(Tuna Helper)*, 1/5 pkg. 13.0
  cold salad *(Tuna Helper)*, 1/5 pkg. 30.0
  noodle, cheese sauce *(Tuna Helper)*, 1/5 pkg. 8.0
  noodle, creamy *(Tuna Helper)*, 1/5 pkg. 12.0
  tetrazzini *(Tuna Helper)*, 1/5 pkg. 11.0
Tuna noodle casserole, frozen *(Stouffer's)*, 5¾ oz. 8.0
Tuna pie, frozen *(Banquet)*, 8 oz. 27.0
Tuna salad sandwich spread *(The Spreadables)*, 1.9 oz. 7.0
Turbot, frozen, fillets *(Taste o' Sea)*, 4 oz. 0
Turf and surf dinner, frozen *(Classic Lite)*, 10 oz. . . . 7.0
Turkey, fresh:
  fryer-roaster, roasted:
    meat and skin, 8.1 oz. (from 1 lb. raw ready-to-
      cook) 13.1
    meat and skin, 4 oz. 6.5
    meat only, 1 cup 3.7
    breast, with skin, ½ breast, 12.1 oz. 11.0
    breast, meat only, ½ breast, 10.8 oz. 2.3
    leg, with skin, 1 leg, 8.6 oz. 13.3
    leg, meat only, 1 leg, 7.9 oz. 8.5
    wing, with skin, 1 wing, 3.2 oz. 8.9
    wing, meat only, 1 wing, 2.1 oz. 2.1
    skin only, 1 oz. 6.6

* *Prepared according to package directions*

Turkey, continued
young hen, roasted:
meat and skin, 8.6 oz. (from 1 lb. raw ready-to-
cook) 26.4
meat and skin, 4 oz. 12.3
meat only, 1 cup 7.7
breast, with skin, 1/2 breast, 24.2 oz. 53.9
leg, with skin, 1 leg, 15.8 oz. 47.1
wing, with skin, 1 wing, 6.1 oz. 23.4
skin only, 1 oz. 12.6
young tom, roasted:
meat and skin, 8.4 oz. (from 1 lb. raw ready-to-
cook) 21.6
meat and skin, 4 oz. 10.3
meat only, 1 cup 6.6
breast, with skin, 1/2 breast, 46.9 oz. 98.3
leg, with skin, 1 leg, 28.4 oz. 77.5
wing, with skin, 1 wing, 8.4 oz. 27.3
skin only, 1 oz. 10.6
Turkey, frozen:
breast *(Weaver* Gourmet), 3 oz. 4.1
breast, roll *(Weaver)*, 3 oz. 1.0
butter or broth baste *(Armour Star)*, 4 oz. 10.0
cured, breast *(Armour)*, 4 oz. 2.0
roasted, white meat only *(Beatrice Butterball)*, 3 1/2
oz. 4.0
roasted, dark meat only *(Beatrice Butterball)*, 3 1/2
oz. 10.0
roasted, white and dark meat and skin:
10–12-lb. hen *(Beatrice Butterball)*, 3 1/2 oz. . . . 9.0
14–16-lb. tom *(Beatrice Butterball)*, 3 1/2 oz. . . . 10.0
roasted, skin only:
10–12-lb. hen *(Beatrice Butterball)*, 3 1/2 oz. . . . 37.0
14–16-lb. tom *(Beatrice Butterball)*, 3 1/2 oz. . . . 38.0
white meat, with gravy *(Armour Star)*, 3.7 oz. . . . 6.0
white and dark meat, with gravy *(Armour Star)*, 3.7
oz. 8.0
Turkey, boneless, cooked:
breast *(Louis Rich)*, 1 oz. 1.9
breast, oven roasted *(Louis Rich)*, 1 oz. 1.1

Turkey, boneless, continued
breast, with skin *(Boar's Head)*, 1 oz. 1.0
breast, skinless *(Boar's Head)*, 1 oz. 4
breast, slices *(Louis Rich)*, 1 slice 9
breast, tenderloin *(Louis Rich)*, 1 oz. 5
breast, barbecued *(Louis Rich)*, 1 oz. 1.3
butter added *(Golden Star)*, 4 oz. 8.6
ground *(Louis Rich)*, 1 oz. 3.5
smoked *(Carl Buddig)*, 1 oz. 2.5
smoked *(Louis Rich)*, 1-oz. slice 1.1
smoked, breast *(Hormel* Perma-Fresh), 2 slices . . . 2.0
smoked, breast *(Louis Rich)*, 1 oz. 1.1
smoked, breast *(Oscar Mayer)*, 3/4-oz. slice 3
smoked, breast, chunk *(Louis Rich)*, 1 oz. 1.0
smoked, breast, sliced *(Louis Rich)*, .7-oz. slice 3
smoked, with barbecue or spice sauce *(Armour*
   Star), 4 oz. 5.0
white meat, with gravy *(Armour Star)*, 4 oz. 4.0
white meat, roll *(Avondale)*, 3 oz. 7.0
white meat, roll *(Gold Band/Magic Slice)*, 3 oz. 5.0
white and dark meat, with gravy *(Armour Star)*, 4
   oz. 5.0
white and dark meat, roll *(Avondale)*, 3 oz. 7.0
white and dark meat, roll *(Gold Band)*, 3 oz. 6.0
white and dark meat, roll *(Magic Slice)*, 3 oz. . . . 5.0
with dressing and gravy *(Armour Star)*, 4 oz. 8.0
Turkey, canned, chunk *(Hormel)*, 6 3/4 oz. 10.0
Turkey bologna:
   (Armour), 4 oz. 16.0
   (Louis Rich), 1-oz. slice 4.6
Turkey dinner, frozen:
   (Banquet American Favorites), 11 oz. 9.0
   (Banquet Extra Helpings), 19 oz. 23.0
   (Morton), 11 oz. 4.9
   (Swanson), 11 1/2 oz. 10.0
   (Swanson Hungry-Man), 18 1/2 oz. 18.0
   Dijon *(Lean Cuisine)*, 9 1/2 oz. 11.0
   Parmesan *(Classic Lite)*, 11 oz. 8.0
   sliced breast, with mushrooms *(Le Menu)*, 11 1/4 oz. 24.0
   tetrazzini *(Morton Lite)*, 11 oz. 4.0

Turkey entrée, freeze-dried, tetrazzini *(Mountain House)*, 1 cup 8.0
Turkey entrée, frozen:
 (Swanson), 8¾ oz. 10.0
 (Swanson Hungry-Man), 13¼ oz. 14.0
 à la king, with rice *(The Budget Gourmet)*, 1
  serving 18.0
 casserole *(Stouffer's)*, 9¾ oz. 19.0
 with gravy *(Swanson* Main Course), 9¼ oz. 10.0
 sliced *(Light & Elegant)*, 8 oz. 5.0
 sliced, gravy and *(Freezer Queen*, 2 lb.), 10.67 oz. 11.0
 sliced, gravy and *(Banquet Cookin' Bag)*, 5 oz. . . . 8.0
 sliced, gravy and *(Banquet Family Entrees)*, 8 oz. 22.0
 sliced, gravy and *(Freezer Queen* Cook-in-Pouch), 5
  oz. 3.0
 sliced, gravy and *(Freezer Queen*, 2 lb.), 8 oz. 16.0
 sliced, gravy and *(Freezer Queen* Single Serve), 10
  oz. 5.0
 sliced, gravy and *(Morton Lite)*, 8 oz. 4.0
 tetrazzini *(Freezer Queen* Single Serve), 9 oz. 8.0
 tetrazzini *(Stouffer's)*, 6 oz. 14.0
Turkey frankfurter:
 (Armour Star), 2-oz. link 8.0
 (Louis Rich), 1 link 8.5
 cheese *(Louis Rich)*, 1 link 8.6
Turkey ham:
 (Armour), 4 oz. 4.0
 (Louis Rich), 1 oz. 1.2
 (Louis Rich Water Added), 1 oz. 1.4
 (Weaver), 3 oz. 6.4
 chopped *(Louis Rich)*, 1 oz. 2.3
 smoked *(Carl Buddig)*, 1 oz. 1.7
Turkey gravy:
 canned *(Franco-American)*, 2 oz. 2.0
 canned *(Heinz* Home Style), 2 oz. 2.0
 mix *(Durkee)*, 1-oz. pkg. 1
 mix *(French's* Gravy for Turkey), ¼ cup 1.0
Turkey meat loaf *(Armour)*, 3 oz. 8.0
Turkey patties:
 (Land o' Lakes), 2¼ oz. 11.0

Turkey patties, continued
　　frozen *(Tyson Chick'N Quick)*, 3 oz. . . . . 　14.0
Turkey pie, frozen:
　　(Banquet), 8 oz. 　32.0
　　(Stouffer's), 10 oz. . . . . 　35.0
　　(Swanson), 8 oz. . . . . 　24.0
　　(Swanson Chunky), 10 oz. . . . . 　31.0
　　(Swanson Hungry-Man), 16 oz. . . . . 　41.0
Turkey salad sandwich spread *(The Spreadables)*, 1.9
　　oz. . . . . 　8.0
Turkey salami:
　　(Louis Rich), 1-oz. slice . . . . 　3.7
　　cotto *(Armour)*, 4 oz. . . . . 　11.0
　　cotto *(Louis Rich)*, 1-oz. slice . . . . 　3.7
Turkey sausage:
　　breakfast *(Louis Rich)*, 1 oz. . . . . 　3.9
　　smoked *(Louis Rich)*, 1 oz. . . . . 　3.8
Turkey sticks *(Land o' Lakes)*, 2 sticks or 2 oz. . . . 　10.0
Turmeric, ground (all brands), 1 tsp. . . . . 　.2
Turnip:
　　fresh, raw, whole, untrimmed, 1 lb. . . . . 　.4
　　fresh, raw or boiled, cubed, 1 cup . . . . 　.1
　　fresh, boiled, drained, mashed, 1 cup . . . . 　.2
　　frozen, mashed *(Southland)*, 3.6 oz. . . . . 　6.0
Turnip greens:
　　fresh, raw, trimmed, 1 lb. . . . . 　1.4
　　fresh, raw, chopped, 1 cup . . . . 　.2
　　fresh, boiled, drained, chopped, 1 cup . . . . 　.3
　　canned or frozen (all brands), 1/2 cup . . . . 　< .2
Turtle, green:
　　raw, in shell, 1 lb. . . . . 　.5
　　raw, meat only, 4 oz. . . . . 　.6
　　canned, 4 oz. . . . . 　.8

	fat grams
Vanilla extract, pure *(Virginia Dare)*, 1 tsp.	0
Veal, fresh, retail cuts, meat only:	
chuck cuts and boneless for stew, lean with fat, stewed, 4 oz.	14.5
loin cuts, lean with fat, broiled, 4 oz.	15.2
plate (breast), lean with fat, stewed, 4 oz.	24.0
rib roast, lean with fat, roasted, 4 oz.	19.2
round with rump (roasts and leg cutlets), lean with fat, broiled, 4 oz.	12.9
Veal, frozen:	
steaks *(Hormel)*, 4 oz.	4.0

Veal, continued
steaks, breaded *(Hormel)*, 4 oz. 13.0
Veal dinner, frozen:
Parmigiana *(Banquet International Favorites)*, 11 oz. 21.0
Parmigiana *(Banquet Extra Helpings)*, 20 oz. 57.0
Parmigiana *(Dinner Classics)*, 10¾ oz. 20.0
Parmigiana *(Morton)*, 12 oz. 8.2
Parmigiana *(Morton)*, 20 oz. 15.3
Parmigiana *(Morton Lite)*, 11 oz. 7.0
Parmigiana *(Swanson)*, 12¾ oz. 21.0
Parmigiana *(Swanson Hungry-Man)*, 20 oz. 28.0
pepper steak *(Classic Lite)*, 11 oz. 8.0
Veal entrée, frozen:
Parmigiana *(Banquet International Favorites*
Cookin' Bag)*, 5 oz. 17.0
Parmigiana *(Banquet Family Entrees)*, 6.4 oz. 18.0
Parmigiana *(Freezer Queen Cook-in-Pouch)*, 5 oz. 15.0
Parmigiana *(Freezer Queen, 2 lb.)*, 8 oz. 23.0
Veal loaf *(Usinger's)*, 1 oz. 6.0
Vegetable juice, canned (all brands), 6 fl. oz. 0
Vegetable seasoning *(Lawry's Natural Choice for*
Vegetables), 1 tsp. .2
Vegetables, see specific listings
Vegetables, mixed:
canned or frozen, plain (all brands), 1 cup . . . . . < 1.0
frozen, in sauce:
(LeSueur Valley Combination), ½ cup 2.0
American style *(Green Giant Valley*
Combination), ½ cup 2.0
in butter sauce *(Green Giant)*, ½ cup 2.0
Chinese style *(Birds Eye)*, 3 oz. 5.0
Far Eastern style *(Birds Eye)*, 3.3 oz. 5.0
Italian style *(Birds Eye)*, 3.3 oz. 7.0
Italian style *(Green Giant Valley Combination)*,
½ cup 2.0
Japanese style *(Birds Eye)*, 3.3 oz. 6.0
Japanese style *(Green Giant Valley Combination)*,
½ cup 1.0
Mexican style *(Green Giant Valley Combination)*,
½ cup 5.0

Vegetables, mixed, frozen, in sauce, continued

Mexicana style *(Birds Eye)*, 3.3 oz.	6.0
New England style *(Birds Eye)*, 3.3 oz.	7.0
with onion sauce *(Birds Eye)*, 2.6 oz.	5.0
San Francisco style *(Birds Eye)*, 3.3 oz.	5.0

Vegetable entrée:

canned, chow mein *(La Choy Bi-Pack)*, 3/4 cup*	2.0
canned, stew *(Dinty Moore)*, 8 oz.	8.0
freeze-dried, stew, with beef *(Mountain House)*, 1 cup	7.0

Vegetable sticks, frozen:

breaded, fried *(Chill Ripe)*, 4 oz.	9.2
breaded, fried *(Farm Rich)*, 4 oz.	10.0

Vegetarian foods, canned and dry:

"beef" bits *(Loma Linda)*, 4 pieces	3.0
"beef" roast *(Loma Linda)*, 2 oz.	11.0
"beef" slices *(Worthington)*, 2 oz.	6.0
"beef" steak *(Worthington Prime Stakes)*, 1 piece	12.0
"beef" steak *(Worthington Vegetable Steaks)*, 2.5-oz. piece	2.0
burgers and burger granules:	
(Loma Linda Burger-Like), 4 oz.	.2
(Loma Linda Burger-Mix), 1 oz.	.7
(Loma Linda Patty Mix), 1/4 cup	1.0
(Loma Linda Redi-Burger), 1/2" slice	0
(Loma Linda Vege-Burger), 1/2 cup	1.0
(Loma Linda Vege-Burger, Granules), 1/2 cup	1.7
(Loma Linda Vege-Burger, No Salt Added), 1/2 cup	2.0
(Loma Linda Vita-Burger, Chunks or Granules), 3 tbsp.	< 1.0
(Loma Linda Vita-Burger), 1/4 cup	< 1.0
(Worthington Granburger), 6 tbsp.	1.0
(Worthington Vegetarian Burger), 1/2 cup	3.0
(Worthington Vegetarian Burger No Salt Added), 1/2 cup	3.0
"chicken," diced *(Worthington)*, 1/4 cup	6.0
"chicken," fried *(Loma Linda)*, 2-oz. piece	14.0

---

* *Prepared according to package directions*

Vegetarian foods, canned and dry, continued

"chicken," fried *(Worthington Fri Chik)*, 2 pieces	12.0
"chicken," fried, with gravy *(Loma Linda)*, 2 pieces	10.0
"chicken," sliced *(Worthington)*, 2 slices	6.0
"chicken" supreme *(Loma Linda)*, 1/4 cup dry . . .	< 1.0
chili *(Worthington)*, 2/3 cup	11.0
chops *(Worthington Choplets)*, 2 slices	2.0
cold cuts:	
(Loma Linda Nuteena), 1/2" slice	12.0
(Loma Linda Proteena), 1/2" slice	5.0
(Loma Linda Vegelona), 1/2" slice	1.0
(Worthington Numete), 1/2" slice	11.0
(Worthington Protose), 1/2" slice	9.0
cutlets *(Worthington)*, 1.5-oz. slice	2.0
"fish" *(Loma Linda Ocean Platter)*, 1/4 cup	< 1.0
franks *(Loma Linda Big Franks)*, 1 frank	5.0
franks *(Loma Linda Sizzle Franks)*, 2 franks	13.0
fries *(Loma Linda Wheat Fries)*, 2.5 oz.	.9
links *(Loma Linda Linketts)*, 2 links	8.0
links *(Loma Linda Little Links)*, 2 links	5.0
links *(Worthington Saucettes)*, 2 links	11.0
links *(Worthington Super Links)*, 1 link	7.0
links *(Worthington Vege-Links)*, 2 links	7.0
(Loma Linda Dinner Cuts), 3.5 oz.	1.0
(Loma Linda Savorex), 1 tsp.	1.0
(Loma Linda Tasty Cuts), 2 cuts	1.0
(Loma Linda Tender Cuts), 3.6 oz.	1.2
"meat" balls *(Worthington)*, 3 pieces	6.0
"meat" balls, gravy *(Loma Linda Tender Rounds)*, 6 pieces	4.0
"meat" loaf *(Loma Linda)*, 1 oz.	.8
"meat" loaf *(Loma Linda Savory Dinner Loaf)*, 1/4 cup dry	< 1.0
nut meat *(Loma Linda)*, 2.5 oz.	10.0
sandwich spread *(Loma Linda)*, 3 tbsp.	4.0
"scallops" *(Loma Linda Vege-Scallops)*, 6 pieces	1.0
"scallops" *(Worthington Skallops)*, 1/2 cup	1.0
stew *(Loma Linda Stew Pac)*, 2 oz.	2.0
stew *(Worthington Country Stew)*, 9.5 oz.	12.0
Stroganoff *(Worthington)*, 6.7 oz.	7.0

Vegetarian foods, canned and dry, continued

Swiss "steak," with gravy *(Loma Linda)*, 1 steak	8.0
"turkey" *(Worthington 209)*, 2 slices	9.0

Vegetarian foods, frozen:

"bacon" *(Morningstar Farms)*, 3 pieces	6.0
"bacon" *(Worthington Stripples)*, 4 pieces	10.0
"beef," corned, sliced *(Worthington)*, 4 slices . . .	7.0
"beef," smoked, sliced *(Worthington)*, 6 slices . . .	4.0
"beef" pot pie *(Worthington)*, 8 oz.	24.0
"bologna" *(Loma Linda)*, 2 oz. or 2 slices	9.0
"bologna" *(Worthington Bolono)*, 2 slices	3.0
burger *(Loma Linda Sizzle Burger)*, 1 burger	11.0
"chicken" *(Loma Linda)*, 2 oz. or 2 slices	13.0
"chicken" *(Worthington Chic-Ketts)*, 1/2 cup	8.0
"chicken" *(Worthington Chik-Stiks)*, 1 piece	8.0
"chicken," diced *(Worthington)*, 1/2 cup	11.0
"chicken," sliced *(Worthington)*, 2 slices	7.0
"chicken" nuggets *(Loma Linda Chik-Nuggets)*, 5 pieces	13.0
"chicken" patties *(Loma Linda Chik-Patties)*, 1 patty	13.0
"chicken" pot pie *(Worthington)*, 8 oz.	22.0
corn dog *(Loma Linda)*, 1 piece	10.0
egg roll *(Worthington)*, 1 roll	7.0
"eggs" *(Morningstar Farms Scramblers)*, 1/4 cup . .	3.0
fillets *(Worthington)*, 2 pieces	9.0
"fish" *(Loma Linda Ocean Fillet)*, 1 fillet	8.0
franks *(Worthington Dixie Dogs)*, 1 piece	7.0
grillers *(Morningstar Farms)*, 1 piece	12.0
"ham," sliced *(Worthington Wham)*, 3 slices	6.0
links *(Morningstar Farms Breakfast)*, 3 links	12.0
links *(Worthington Leanies)*, 1 link	9.0
links *(Worthington Prosage)*, 3 links	14.0
"meat" balls, Swedish *(Loma Linda)*, 8 pieces . . .	8.0
patties *(Morningstar Farms Breakfast)*, 2 patties . .	11.0
patties *(Worthington FriPats)*, 1 piece	12.0
patties *(Worthington Prosage)*, 2 patties	15.0
roast *(Worthington Dinner Roast)*, 2 oz.	8.0
roll *(Worthington Prosage)*, 2³/₈" slices	14.0
"salami" *(Loma Linda)*, 2 oz. or 2 slices	7.0

Vegetarian foods, frozen, continued
"salami" *(Worthington)*, 2 slices 4.0
"steak" *(Loma Linda Griddle Steaks)*, 1 steak . . . 13.0
"steak" *(Worthington Stakelets)*, 1 piece 7.0
"tuna" *(Worthington Tuno Roll)*, 2 oz. 5.0
"turkey" *(Loma Linda)*, 2 oz. or 2 slices 12.0
"turkey," smoked, sliced *(Worthington)*, 4 slices 11.0
Venison, raw, lean meat only, 4 oz. 4.5
Vine spinach, raw, 4 oz. 3
Vinegar, all varieties (all brands), 2 tbsp. or 1 fl. oz. 0

	fat grams
Waffles:	
mix, see "Pancake and waffle mix"	
frozen, regular or nutri-grain *(Eggo)*, 1 waffle	5.0
frozen *(Roman Meal)*, 2 waffles or 3 oz.	14.0
frozen, bran *(Eggo)*, 1 waffle	8.0
frozen, with imitation blueberries or strawberries *(Eggo)*, 1 waffle	5.0
Walnuts:	
black, dried, shelled, 4 oz.	64.2
black, dried, shelled, chopped, 1 cup	70.7

Walnuts, continued
  (Planters), 1 oz. 17.0
  English or Persian, in shell, 1 lb. 126.3
  English or Persian, shelled, 1 oz. or 14 halves . . . 17.6
  English or Persian, shelled, halves, 1 cup 61.9
  English or Persian *(Planters)*, 1 oz. 20.0
Water chestnuts, Chinese:
  fresh, whole, 1 lb. 4
  fresh, 4 chestnuts, 1¼"–2" diam. . . . . < .1
  fresh, peeled, 4 oz. or 1 cup sliced 1
  canned, whole or sliced, drained *(Chun King)*, 8.5
  oz. 5
Watercress, fresh:
  whole, with stems, 1 lb. 4
  chopped, 1 cup . . . . < .1
Watermelon, fresh:
  1 wedge, 10" diam., 1" thick 2.1
  diced, 1 cup 7
Watermelon seed kernels, dried:
  shelled, 4 oz. 53.8
  shelled, 1 cup 51.2
Wax gourd (Chinese preserving melon):
  raw, cubed, 1 cup 3
  boiled, drained, cubed, 1 cup 4
Weakfish, fresh:
  raw, whole, 1 lb. 12.2
  raw, meat only, 4 oz. 6.4
Welsh rarebit:
  frozen *(Stouffer's)*, 5 oz. 30.0
  sauce, canned *(Snow's)*, ½ cup 11.0
Wendy's:
  breakfast, 1 serving:
    bacon, 2 strips 10.0
    breakfast sandwich, 4.6 oz. 19.0
    danish, 3 oz. 18.0
    eggs, scrambled, 3.25 oz. 12.0
    French toast, 2 slices 19.0
    home fries, 3.7 oz. 22.0
    omelet, ham and cheese, 4 oz. 17.0
    omelet, ham, cheese & mushroom, 4.2 oz. 21.0

Wendy's, breakfast, continued

omelet, ham, cheese, onion, green pepper, 4.6 oz.	19.0
omelet, mushroom, onion, green pepper, 4 oz.	15.0
sausage, 1 patty	18.0
toast with margarine, 2 slices	9.0
chili, 8 oz.	8.0
sandwiches, without condiments, 1 serving:	
bacon cheeseburger, white bun, 5.25 oz.	28.0
chicken, wheat bun, 4.6 oz.	10.0
hamburger, single, wheat bun, 4.25 oz.	17.0
hamburger, single, white bun, 4.2 oz.	18.0
hamburger, double, white bun, 7 oz.	34.0
hamburger, *Kids' Meal*, 2.7 oz.	8.0
condiments:	
American cheese, .6-oz. slice	6.0
bacon, 3½ slices	8.0
catsup, lettuce, pickle, tomato, mustard, onion	< 1.0
mayonnaise, 1 tbsp.	11.0
baked potato, hot stuffed, 1 serving:	
plain, 8.8 oz.	2.0
bacon and cheese, 12.5 oz.	30.0
broccoli and cheese, 13 oz.	25.0
cheese, 12.5 oz.	34.0
chicken à la king, 12.8 oz.	6.0
chili and cheese, 14.2 oz.	20.0
sour cream and chives, 11 oz.	24.0
Stroganoff and sour cream, 14.5 oz.	21.0
salads and side dishes:	
French fries, regular, 3.5 oz.	14.0
pick-up window side salad, 18.2 oz.	6.0
taco salad, 12.75 oz.	18.0
dessert, dairy, frosty, 12 fl. oz.	14.0
Western style dinner, frozen:	
(Banquet American Favorites), 11 oz.	29.0
(Morton), 11.1 oz.	14.7
(Morton Lite), 11 oz.	12.0
(Swanson), 12¼ oz.	19.0
(Swanson Hungry-Man), 17½ oz.	34.0
Whale, raw, meat only, 4 oz.	8.5
Wheat, parboiled, see "Bulgur"	

Wheat, whole-grain:

durum, 4 oz.	2.8
hard red spring, 4 oz.	2.5
hard red winter, 4 oz.	2.0
soft winter or white, 4 oz.	2.3

Wheat bran:

crude, commercially milled, 4 oz.	5.2
toasted *(Kretschmer)*, 1 oz.	1.0
unprocessed *(Quaker)*, 2 tbsp.	.2

Wheat germ:

crude, commercially milled, 4 oz.	12.4
(Kretschmer), ¼ cup	3.0
honey *(Kretschmer)*, ¼ cup	2.0
Wheat nuts *(Flavor Tree)*, 1 oz.	18.0
Wheat pilaf mix *(Casbah)*, 1 oz. dry	0

Whey:

dry, 4 oz.	1.2
fluid, 8 oz.	.7
Whiskey, all varieties (all brands)	0
Whiskey sour drink mixer (all brands), 1 fl. oz.	0

White Castle:

sandwiches, 1 serving:

bun only, .89 oz.	.9
cheese only, .31 oz.	1.6
cheeseburger, 2.29 oz.	11.2
chicken, 2.25 oz.	7.5
fish, without tartar sauce, 2.09 oz.	5.0
hamburger, 2.06 oz.	7.9
sausage, 1.72 oz.	12.3
sausage and egg, 3.39 oz.	22.0

side dishes:

French fries, 3.42 oz.	14.7
onion chips, 3.29 oz.	16.6
onion rings, 2.12 oz.	13.4
White sauce mix *(Durkee)*, 1-oz. pkg.	11.0

Whitefish, lake:

raw, whole, 1 lb.	17.5
raw, meat only, 4 oz.	9.3
smoked, 4 oz.	8.3
Whiting, frozen, fillets *(Taste o' Sea)*, 4 oz.	0

Wieners, see "Frankfurters and wieners"

Wine, table or dessert, all varieties (all brands)   0

Winged bean:

  raw, whole, 1 lb.   3.9

  raw or boiled, sliced, 1 cup 4

Winged bean leaves, raw, 4 oz. 1.2

Winged bean tuber, raw, 4 oz. 1.0

Worcestershire sauce (all brands), 1 tbsp. . . . .   < .1

Wreckfish, fresh, raw, meat only, 4 oz. 4.4

	fat grams
Yachtwurst *(Usinger's)*, 1 oz.	6.0
Yams:	
fresh, raw, whole, with skin, 1 lb.	.7
fresh, cooked, drained, cubed, 1 cup	.2
canned, see "Sweet potato"	
frozen, and apples *(Stouffer's)*, 5 oz.	3.0
frozen, candied, and apples *(Mrs. Paul's)*, 4 oz.	< 1.0
Yam bean, tuber, fresh:	
raw, pared, 4 oz. or 1 cup sliced	.2
boiled, drained, 4 oz.	.1

Yardlong bean:
raw, whole, 1 lb. 1.7
raw, sliced, 1 cup 4
boiled, drained, sliced, 1 cup 1
Yeast, baker's:
active dry, 1 oz. 5
active dry or rapid rise *(Fleischmann's)*, 1 packet 0
compressed, 1 oz. 1
compressed *(Fleischmann's)*, 1 cube 0
Yeast, brewer's, debittered, 1 oz. 3
Yellowtail, raw, meat only, 4 oz. 6.1
Yogurt:
plain:
(Columbo) 8 oz. 7.0
(Columbo Natural Lite), 8 oz. 0
(Crowley Whole Milk), 8 oz. 8.0
(Crowley Lowfat), 8 oz. 2.0
(Dannon Lowfat), 8 oz. 4.0
(Knudsen), 8 oz. 9.0
(Knudsen Lowfat), 8 oz. 5.0
(Lite-line Lowfat Swiss Style), 8 oz. 4.0
(Yoplait), 6 oz. 5.0
all flavors *(Crowley* Swiss or Sundae Style), 8 oz. 2.0
all flavors *(Dannon* Hearty Nuts & Raisins), 8 oz. 3.0
all flavors *(Dannon* Mini-Pack), 4.4 oz. 2.0
all flavors *(Dannon* Lowfat), 8 oz. 3.0
all flavors, except granola *(Columbo)*, 8 oz. 7.0
all fruit flavors *(Dannon Supreme)*, 6 oz. 2.0
all fruit flavors *(New Country/New Country*
Supreme), 6 oz. 2.0
all fruit flavors *(Yoplait/Yoplait* Custard Style), 6
oz. 4.0
all fruit flavors *(Yoplait* Fruit-on-the-Bottom), 6 oz. 2.0
granola *(Columbo* Breakfast Yogurt), 8 oz. 6.0
Yogurt, frozen:
all flavors *(Danny-Yo)*, 3½ oz. 1.0
blueberry, raspberry, or strawberry *(Danny)*, 1 cup 2.0
chocolate *(Danny)*, 1 cup 3.0
piña colada *(Danny)*, 1 cup 4.0
vanilla *(Danny)*, 1 cup 2.0

Yogurt bars, frozen:

boysenberry, carob-coated *(Danny)*, 2½-fl.-oz. bar	8.0
chocolate or piña colada *(Danny)*, 2½-fl.-oz. bar	1.0
chocolate or vanilla, chocolate-coated *(Danny)*, 2½-fl.-oz. bar	8.0
raspberry or strawberry, chocolate-coated *(Danny)*, 2½-fl.-oz. bar	7.0
vanilla *(Danny)*, 2½-fl.-oz. bar	1.0

	fat grams
Ziti dinner, Italian style, frozen, *(Morton* Lite), 11 oz.	6.0
Zucchini:	
fresh, see "Squash, summer"	
canned in tomato sauce *(Del Monte),* ½ cup	0
canned, Italian style, in sauce *(S&W),* ½ cup . . .	1.0
frozen, plain (all brands), 3.3 oz.	< .1
frozen, sticks, in batter *(Mrs. Paul's),* 3 oz.	9.0